RESILIENCE

Resilience has become a central concept in government policy understandings over the last decade. In our complex, global and interconnected world, resilience appears to be the policy 'buzzword' of choice, alleged to be the solution to a wide and ever-growing range of policy issues. This book analyses the key aspects of resilience-thinking and highlights how resilience impacts upon traditional conceptions of governance.

This concise and accessible book investigates how resilience-thinking adds new insights into how politics (both domestically and internationally) is understood to work and how problems are perceived and addressed; from educational training in schools to global ethics and from responses to shock events and natural disasters to long-term international policies to promote peace and development. This book also raises searching questions about how resilience-thinking influences the types of knowledge and understanding we value and challenges traditional conceptions of social and political processes.

It sets forward a new and clear conceptualisation of resilience, of use to students, academics and policy-makers, emphasising the links between the rise of resilience and awareness of the complex nature of problems and policy-making.

David Chandler is Professor of International Relations and Director of the Centre for the Study of Democracy, Department of Politics and International Relations, University of Westminster. He is the founding editor of the journal *Resilience: International Policies, Practices and Discourses*. His recent books include: *Hollow Hegemony: Rethinking Global Politics, Power and Resistance* (Pluto, 2009); *International Statebuilding: The Rise of Post-Liberal Governance* (Routledge, Critical Issues in Global Politics, 2010); and *Freedom vs Necessity in International Relations: Human-Centred Approaches to Security and Development* (Zed, 2013).

Critical Issues In Global Politics

This series engages with the most significant issues in contemporary global politics. Each text is written by a leading scholar and provides a short, accessible and stimulating overview of the issue for advanced undergraduates and graduate students of international relations and global politics. As well as providing a survey of the field, the books also contain original and groundbreaking thinking which will drive forward debates on these key issues.

RESILIENCE

The governance of complexity

David Chandler

Routledge
Taylor & Francis Group

LONDON AND NEW YORK

First published 2014
by Routledge
2 Park Square, Milton Park, Abingdon, Oxon OX14 4RN

and by Routledge
711 Third Avenue, New York, NY 10017

Routledge is an imprint of the Taylor & Francis Group, an informa business

© 2014 David Chandler

British Library Cataloguing in Publication Data
A catalogue record for this book is available from the British Library

Library of Congress Cataloging in Publication Data
Chandler, David, 1962-
Resilience : the governance of complexity / David Chandler.
pages cm. — (Critical issues in global politics)
Includes bibliographical references and index.
1. Crisis management in government. 2. Political science—Philosophy.
3. International relations—Philosophy. 4. Complexity (Philosophy)
5. Organizational resilience—Political aspects. I. Title.
JF1525.C74C43 2014
327.101—dc23   2013046623

ISBN: 978-0-415-74139-2 (hbk)
ISBN: 978-0-415-74140-8 (pbk)
ISBN: 978-1-315-77381-0 (ebk)

Typeset in 10/12 Bembo
by codeMantra

CONTENTS

ACKNOWLEDGEMENTS

This book would not have been possible without having opportunities to work through these themes with colleagues over the past few years at numerous conferences and workshops. A few colleagues whom I would especially like to thank for their input over this time are Claudia Aradau, Gideon Baker, Morgan Brigg, Peter Finkenbusch, Jonathan Joseph, Kai Koddenbrock, Michelle Ledda, Pol Pedreny, Jonathan Pugh, Julian Reid, Jessica Schmidt, Giorgio Shani and Paulina Tambakaki. I am also grateful for the German Ministry of Education's financial support for a Senior Visiting Fellowship at the Centre for Global Cooperation Research, Käte Hamburger Kolleg, University of Duisburg-Essen, Germany, for the academic year 2012–13.

I would particularly like to thank the organisers of a number of seminars and conferences that were important for the development of these ideas: the seminar 'Emotional Well-being in Education: Implications for Policy, Pedagogy and Purposes', Nottingham University, 19 November 2009; the Postcolonial Studies Research Network symposium on 'Vulnerability', University of Otago, Dunedin, New Zealand, 26–28 November 2010; the workshop 'Resilient Futures: The Politics of Preventive Security' at the University of Warwick, 27 June 2011; the Open University CCIG Forum, 'Resisting (In)Security, Securing Resistance', London, 12 July 2011; the Global Development Working Group workshop 'The Afterlives of Neoliberalism: Development, Postdevelopment and International Relations' at the ISA annual convention, San Diego, 31 March 2012; 'Materialism and World Politics', the *Millennium* journal conference, at the London School of Economics, 20–21 October 2012; the 'Practices of Resilience and the Changing Logics of Security and Protection' workshop at the University of Copenhagen, 13

December 2012; the Leibniz Institute for Regional Development and Structural Planning (IRS) international conference, 'Constructing Resilience', Berlin, 17–18 January 2013; the conference roundtable 'Assemblages and IR Theory: Linking the Spaces of IR' at the ISA annual convention, San Francisco, 4 April 2013; the Raumwissenschaftliches Kolloquium on 'Vulnerability and Resilience', organized by the Leibniz Association, Dusseldorf, 16 May 2013; the workshop 'Rethinking Governance in a World of Complexity' at the Centre for Global Cooperation Research, University of Duisburg-Essen, 27–28 June 2013; the COST workshop 'Resilience, Security and Law After Liberalism' at King's College, London, 4–5 July 2013; the 'Resilience: International Policies, Practices and Discourses' section at the EISA Pan-European Conference on International Relations, Warsaw, 18–21 September 2013; and the BISA International Political Economy Group workshop, 'Financial Resilience in the Wake of the Crisis', University of Warwick, 15 November 2013.

Some of the chapters draw from public presentations and recently published or forthcoming articles. Chapter 1 draws upon the paper 'Democracy, Visibility and Resistance', 3rd Käte Hamburger Lecture, University of Duisburg-Essen, 6 February 2013. In Part I, Chapter 2 develops the paper 'Resistance Is Everywhere! The New Ontology of Resistance', 'Discipline(s), Dissent and Dispossession' workshop, University of Sussex, 9 September 2013 and adapts some material from 'Resilience and the Autotelic Subject: Towards a Critique of the Societalization of Security', *International Political Sociology*, 7:2, (2013), pp.210–26. Chapter 3 draws on some of the research initially developed for the review article 'From Sour Grapes to Vitalism: The Life Politics of the Left', *Global Change, Peace & Security*, 25:3 (2013), pp.367–70 and the short piece 'The Onto-politics of Assemblage', in Michele Acuto and Simon Curtis (eds) *Reassembling International Theory: Assemblage Thinking and International Relations* (London: Palgrave, 2013).

In Part II, Chapter 4 builds upon the paper 'Resistance without Politics: Rethinking Agency from Below', prepared for the International Association for Peace and Conflict Studies conference 'Epistemology of Peacebuilding: New Frontiers of Peacebuilding', University of Manchester, 13–14 September 2012 and published as 'Peacebuilding and the Politics of Non-Linearity: Rethinking "Hidden" Agency and "Resistance"', *Peacebuilding*, 1:1, (2013), pp.17–32. Chapter 5 adapts material from the paper 'Resilience and the Culture of Lawfulness', for the workshop 'Resilience, Security and Law After Liberalism', King's College, London, 4 July 2013, and forthcoming as 'Resilience and the "Everyday": Beyond the Paradox of "Liberal Peace"', *Review of International Studies*. Chapter 6 draws on the paper prepared for the workshop 'Responsibility and Judgement in a World of Complexity', Institute for Development and Peace (INEF), University Duisburg-Essen, Germany, 4 February 2013, and published as 'Resilience Ethics: Responsibility and the Globally Embedded Subject', *Ethics & Global Politics*, 6:3 (2013), pp.175–94.

In Part III, Chapter 7 builds on the paper 'The Democratization of Evil', prepared for the research workshop 'Evil in International Relations', Peace Research Institute Frankfurt, 11–12 May 2012 and forthcoming as 'Beyond Good and Evil: The Onto-Ethics of Global Complexity', *International Politics*. Chapter 8 draws upon the paper 'Democracy as Distributive Agency: Politics in the Complexity Age', for 'The Promise of Democracy' conference, Department of Politics and International Relations, University of Westminster, London, 3 November 2012 and forthcoming as 'Democracy Unbound? Non-Linear Politics and the Politicisation of Everyday Life', *European Journal of Social Theory*. Chapter 9 adapts the paper 'From Freedom to Necessity: The Governmental Rationality of Post-Humanism', prepared for the *Millennium* journal conference, 'Materialism and World Politics', 20–21 October 2012 and published as 'The World of Attachment? The Post-Humanist Challenge to Freedom and Necessity', *Millennium: Journal of International Studies*, 41:3, (2013), pp.516–34.

If our civilisation survives, which it will do only if it renounces those errors, I believe men will look back on our age as an age of superstition, chiefly connected with the names of Karl Marx and Sigmund Freud. I believe people will discover that the most widely held ideas which dominated the twentieth century, a just distribution, a freeing ourselves from repressions and conventional morals, or permissive education as a way to freedom, and the replacement of the market with a rational arrangement by a body with coercive powers, were all based on superstitions in the strict sense of the word. An age of superstition is a time when people imagine that they know more than they do. In this sense the twentieth century was certainly an outstanding age of superstition, and the cause of this is an overestimation of what science has achieved – not in the field of the comparatively simple phenomena, where it has of course been extraordinarily successful, but in the field of complex phenomena where the application of the techniques which proved so helpful with essentially simple phenomena has proved to be very misleading.

Friedrich Hayek, 'The Three Sources of Human Values', L. T. Hobhouse Memorial Trust Lecture, delivered 17 May 1978, London School of Economics and Political Science.

1

INTRODUCTION

The rise of resilience

Introduction

Resilience has become increasingly central to international and domestic policy-making over the last decade. In fact, it has been argued that resilience is the 'guiding principle' of policy governance and 'one of the key political categories of our time'.[1] Resilience is now the top priority for the sustainable development and international development aid agenda,[2] key to international security concerns, from cyber conflict to the war on terror,[3] and vital for disaster risk reduction,[4] conflict prevention,[5] climate change[6] and social, economic and institutional development.[7] Over the last few years, resilience appears to have become the policy buzzword of choice.[8] This is so much the case that it is not unusual to find commentators querying whether resilience can really be the solution to such a diverse range of governance questions and, if so, how this might work. This book is concerned with precisely these questions of resilience as part of a governance agenda and how resilience-thinking impacts on how politics (both domestically and internationally) is understood to work and how problems are perceived and addressed. In the following chapters, a range of issues and questions will be analysed in terms of resilience frameworks, from educational training in schools to global ethics and from responses to shock events and natural disasters to how resilience has been discussed in the context of international policies to promote peace and development.

I have been interested in the rise of resilience-thinking for some time, and I am lucky enough to be the editor of the first international journal devoted solely to analysing the policies and practices which go under the title of resilience. Yet, I must confess that the diversity of approaches to resilience across a large number of policy and academic fields means that, although resilience seems to be ubiquitous, how the concept operates and the uses to which it is put are not always clear. Even policy practitioners who advocate the need for resilience do not always seem clear on how resilience works or can be developed.[9] As a recent Overseas Development Institute paper argues: 'The concept of resilience is at the centre of current debates in development, climate change adaptation and humanitarian aid. However, it is not clear what resilience is, or how it can or should be promoted during and after crises'.[10] Even though resilience-thinking is emerging across the policy spectrum, its outlines are not clearly demarcated. It does not necessarily help to word-search resilience in policy documents, as it is used in diverse ways and contexts. Nor does it necessarily help to turn to academic and more conceptual works which tend to squeeze resilience into whatever theoretical boxes the researcher works within.[11]

This book is designed to bring some analytical clarity to the rise of resilience-thinking, but it is not a survey of the diverse uses of the concept of resilience in policy-documents, nor is it a conceptual history of the term. Analytical clarity will be sought through engaging with a specific problematic: the rise of resilience-thinking as a response to the problem of governing in a world which appears to be more complex to us. While resilience as a concept has a history that lends it a certain range of meanings, this book is concerned with its meaning as a policy response to policy problems as they are increasingly perceived today. In this sense, the book is a 'history of the present'; it seeks to engage analytically with what resilience appears to be doing today and how the rise of resilience-thinking enables us to reflect upon shifts in the understanding of governance. To put it another way: if resilience is the answer, suggested by policy interventions in every area, from education to the environment to conflict-resolution and poverty-reduction, what does this tell us about the questions we are asking of the world and how we understand ourselves in relation to this world?

I do not wish to suggest that all policy-understandings start from the perspective of resilience as a governing response. Rather, I merely want to emphasize that this framing is becoming increasingly dominant in both international and domestic policy-making, as previous approaches appear to become less and less viable today. In order to develop this conceptual analysis of resilience-thinking, the study of resilience will not be narrowly confined to a set of empirical policy practices, developed to work on resilience (as a set of capacities) in the face of crisis or threats. This book is not a handbook for policy-makers,[12] and, more importantly, resilience-thinking operates at a much broader level of political thinking about governance than that covered in policy documents. The key aspects that define resilience approaches to policy-making are methodological assumptions about the nature of the world, the complex problem of governance, and the policy processes suitable to governing this complexity. It is thus quite possible to chart a rise in resilience-thinking as a governing rationality without mentioning the word 'resilience' and, equally, to see the word 'resilience' crop up many times in a policy paper without this being evidence that a clear conceptualisation of resilience forms the basis of understanding.

Teaching resilience

Complex economic, social, political and environmental problems no longer seem amenable to old-fashioned or top-down, state-based, interventions of government operating at a macro-level. It seems that some of the most intractable problems of government are being re-thought in a more people-centred or 'bottom-up' way. A recent example, which caught my eye when I was preparing the manuscript for this book, was a call for resilience to be taught in all UK schools (from an All-Party group of Members of the House of Commons and House of Lords, supported by children's charities and the Open University).[13] The call for mainstreaming resilience in the school curriculum was a response to the recognition of the problems of social mobility: the reproduction of entrenched patterns of economic and social deprivation, which is a particular problem for the UK when international standards are considered.[14] Interestingly, the All-Party's focus was not upon how young people could achieve success but upon how they could change their approach to failure.

As we will see in the course of this book, changing our approach to failure is a central tenet of resilience-thinking. Using failure productively – that is, seeing failing as an opportunity for growth rather than as a final judgement – in this case, was understood to be essential for social mobility, especially for children from more deprived backgrounds who need to be able to 'deal with life's problems without being knocked off course'.[15] As the head of the All-Party group argued, schools in the UK were unintentionally undermining UK social and economic development by focusing on success rather than on failure:

> Whatever your GCSE results or other qualification, how do you make the most of the opportunities that come along? How do you bounce back once things go wrong? How do you believe that you can achieve?

> Over quite an extended period of time, we've had a real focus on examination results – not quite to the exclusion of all else but to a really great degree. But some schools also go on about how developing the character of the young person is absolutely core business.[16]

Schools were focusing on the educational attainments of students and encouraging competition based on succeeding and passing rather than on thinking about how failure can be seen more positively. For this reason, competitive sports were seen as important – not in terms of emulating the success of Britain's Olympic team the previous summer – but for children to learn that 'not everybody is going to win everything'. The head of the All-Party group argued that 'failure is going to happen at some point in life. The question is how early you start being prepared for it'.[17]

This snapshot of resilience as a policy approach tells us a few things about the rise of resilience-thinking. First, there is the appearance of an intractable and complex policy problem – in this case, that of 'social mobility'. The problem is understood to indicate lessons for governance through tracing this problem as the outcome of processes of social interaction. Second, rather than starting at the top of the policy ladder, reactively intervening to attempt to address the consequences, resilience traces these processes backwards to deal with them at the level of root causes. These roots are seen to lie deep within the social texture of society. Social problems are thereby re-presented as problems which are deeply social, rather than as problems of social policy-making at the level of state regulation or intervention. This is why schooling is often considered a vital area of governance intervention today. Third, resilience policies seek to work with existing capabilities and practices and to enable them to operate more efficiently and effectively.

The implication is that children have capacities that are not being developed adequately in schools – which merely focus on upon achieving exam results or on the acquisition of knowledge – these are the vital personal and emotional qualities of resilience. So what is resilience and why is it needed? According to the All-Party group, acquiring knowledge can be seen as a core educational value in a modernist world, which is assumed to remain static. However, in a rapidly changing world, success is not based so much upon a store of acquired knowledge but upon the capacities for self-reflection and reflexive understanding of how one needs to adapt in an ever shifting environment. The experts thought that children from deprived backgrounds were not being adequately taught how to develop these qualities of self-reflexivity and therefore could not cope with failure. In a complex world, the limits of what we know and expect are seen to be more important than what we know: coping with these limits – with failure – enables us to see 'failure' as part of the learning process based on adaptation and self-reflexivity. Failure plays an entirely different role in this approach to the subject, to knowledge and to the world. Not only is failure to be expected in a complex world, but the key point is how we use failure or limits to enable progress. Failure is the starting point for personal and societal growth. We learn more about ourselves and how to govern from failure than we do from success, which merely defers this process of learning and growth.

Classical and post-classical resilience

There is very little consensus on the concept of resilience. This lack of consensus reflects our difficulties in coming to terms with the limits of knowledge and with the implications of these limits for how we rethink the world and our relationship to it. Despite its ubiquitous use in policy documents, it seems to have manifold meanings. Is it about responding ('bouncing back') from disaster or crisis?[18] Is it a process through which crises make us stronger, more flexible, and more open to new opportunities?[19] Is it about how we can act preventively and proactively to minimise the effects of crises or problems?[20] What is the relationship between resilience and the event, crisis or problem?[21] How does resilience understand the subject?[22] Is the subject interpellated as strong and independent, capable of surviving the toughest tests? Is the subject seen as flexible, adaptable and autotelic, thriving on self-growth and self-direction? Is the subject passive and reactive, disciplined to adapt to external changes and dictates? How we understand resilience depends a lot on the disciplinary fields in which we work and, to a certain extent, on the era in which we were brought up.

Resilience appears to cover a wide spectrum of meanings, in terms of both its temporal relation to the event, crisis or threat and its interpellation of the subject from active and self-creating to passive and responsibilised. This is no coincidence because the concept of resilience has itself been transformed: this transformation can be read through different understandings of the relation between the human subject and his or her environment. A concept that started out as clearly distinguishing the subject and its inner strengths and capacities has become transmuted into a concept which emphasises the interrelationship between subject and object. This is somewhat counterintuitive as resilience in its initial formulations was very much subject-centred. This is clear in classical understandings of the resilient subject as an isolated individual withstanding the severe tests and pressures of nature. Think, for example, of the Robinson Crusoe figure, the resilient shipwrecked sailor living off his own wits and resources on a deserted island, or an Arctic explorer, surviving the extreme cold and hunger, traversing a barren wilderness. The resilient subjects overcame the barriers of the environment (classically constructed in natural terms rather than social) through their inner strengths and capacities. In social terms, the resilient subject could withstand oppressive conditions. In these cases it was usually women who were understood to be resilient, withstanding the pressures of poverty and abuse, calling upon their inner strengths and capacities to cope with pain or deprivation.

These human or subject-based understandings of inner capacities for survival – through inner strengths and capacities to withstand trauma or pressure – came to be applied to objects or to nature in the engineering and environmental sciences. When these concepts were transferred, it was this classical understanding that was taken on board. External pressures could be withstood through inner strengths. In this framing, especially in psychology and engineering, resilience came to mean 'bounce-back ability' – the tensions of metal to withstand stress or the capacity of individuals to recover from loss or trauma. In ecology, it came to mean the rejuvenating capacities of ecosystems to withstand both natural and human stresses. The etymological history of resilience is therefore one of a strong subject/object divide and thereby reflective of the world of liberal modernity. The focus was on the subject's internal capacity to withstand pressures or stresses which were understood to be externally generated. This – let us call it 'classical' – understanding of resilience also came to the fore in security discourses, especially in relation to post-9/11 discussions of the impact of terrorist attacks. These discussions concerned the possibility of preparedness and response to possible attacks, causing major social disruption, and focused upon the ability of society to 'bounce back', to maintain basic operational capacity and to cope with disaster, which was seen to be as inevitable as it was unpredictable.[23]

The rise of resilience would have been limited, however, if it had merely reflected the need to cope or to survive in a world of fluidity and uncertainty: if the concept was merely about inculcating and developing the capacities and properties needed for subjects to cope with external shocks and setbacks. This book is essentially about 'post-classical' or 'post-liberal' understandings of resilience, which deploy the concept of resilience in ways which challenge the 'classical' understandings with their clear subject/object division. The etymological roots of classical understandings of resilience are framed in terms of the inner resources and capacities of the autonomous individual and therefore are implicitly linked to the classical liberal subject of modernity. In these understandings, the isolated individual was the 'natural' starting point for the framing of law, politics and the market, as spheres in which rational and morally autonomous subjects interacted.

The etymological basis of 'post-classical' framings of resilience can be found in a much more relationally embedded understanding of the subject (the genealogy of resilience as a political concept will be dealt with in Chapter 3). This understanding of the subject stems from conceptual concern with dynamic and nonlinear systems in the natural and environmental sciences, particularly in terms of the understanding of resilience through adaptation. In this framing, the subject/object divide is overcome through understanding resilience as an interactive process of relational adaptation. The subject does not survive merely through its own 'inner' resources, the subject survives and thrives on the basis of its ability to adapt or dynamically relate to its socio-ecological environment. This dynamic of systemic interaction is ontologically and epistemologically distinct from the earlier use of resilience, whereby the subject either actively conquered or controlled its external environment or passively survived and coped with it (as in the gendered framings of classical approaches outlined above). Resilience, in the post-classical framing, is therefore an emergent and adaptive process of subject/object interrelations. Both subject and object are immersed in and are products of complex adaptive processes. Resilience still remains an 'inner' attribute, but an 'inner' or relational attribute of a system or assemblage. In as far as the human subject is part of this system of interconnection, resilience becomes an ongoing process of responding through a self-reflective awareness that the subject is both producer and product of the world. Resilience is thereby both about adapting to the external world and about being aware that in this process of adaptation the world is being reshaped. Adaptation is thus a process, in which how we adapt shapes the context in which our ongoing adaptation will take place. We increasingly understand adaptation to the world as being inseparable from the world in which we adapt.

In this framing, there is no juxtaposition of subject and object, of human and nature or of culture and environment. These 'liberal' binaries are instead understood as legacies of modernist approaches, which are 'reductionist' – reducing the complexity of the world to separate and discrete objects rather than looking at the dynamic relationships involved. This reductionist perspective is thereby understood to be a barrier to resilience as a set of practices and policies which foreground politics in an age of complexity. To clarify how this works, let us look at an indicative example: that of the relationship between the human subject and risks, dangers or threats. In classical resilience approaches, the question would be how the subject responds or 'bounces back' from the trauma or danger. Two points may be highlighted in this framing: first, spatially, the risk or threat is external, caused by external factors or agents; second, temporally, the threat, risk or trauma is manifested prior to the response of resilience. In post-classical approaches – or in how we understand resilience in a world of complexity – these two key aspects no longer apply. Post-classical understandings of resilience do not view the threat or crisis as external to the subject, and resilience is no longer purely *post hoc* after the event.

In post-classical framings of resilience, there is no longer a spatial or temporal divide between the subject and object. The transformative work in this area was done mainly through debates within the natural and environmental sciences. As noted earlier, the importation of 'liberal' subject–object understandings into ecology and the environmental sciences was initially reflected in formulations of the protection of 'nature' or the 'environment' from human influences (seen as external to nature). Nature was anthropomorphised as if it was a separate autonomous subject with 'needs' and 'interests', which required 'protecting' or 'preserving'.[24] The extent to which natural or environmental processes were able to sustain themselves against (in most cases) human pressures and threats was thereby a measure of 'ecosystem resilience'. This view of a 'natural' equilibrium was challenged as post-classical frameworks of resilience were introduced which no longer 'anthropomorphised' nature or the environment, as somehow a separate subject which needed to be maintained in a natural state of 'balance' or 'harmony'.

Threats, dangers or disruptions were increasingly not seen as 'external' but as 'internal' to the subject–object relationship or socioecological system. They were also no longer seen as problematically disrupting a 'natural balance' but as part of a relational process of change and adaptation.

The work of Crawford Stanley Holling is often seen as the turning point in moving beyond classical or 'engineering' understandings of resilience in ecology, with the introduction of non-linear population dynamics. In 1973 Holling published a much-cited paper on resilience and the stability of ecosystems, articulating system resilience in distinction to 'stability' understandings of return to equilibrium after an external shock or disturbance.[25] For Holling, resilient systems involved complex adaptivity, with the existence of multiple stable states or regimes. Resilience now acquired a dynamic, relational aspect which, as we shall see, will be key in considering how resilience-thinking operates in terms of the governance of a complex, globalised world.

This dynamic, relational framing of resilience has generally displaced classical understandings of resilience as an internal attribute of the subject, although in policy-practice resilience is not always used in ways which clarify the conceptual framework underlying the approach. Perhaps a good example of this ambiguity is the one mentioned at the beginning of this chapter, concerning the teaching of resilience in UK schools. At one level it appears that resilience is being taught to enable the development of character and coping mechanisms as inner attributes enabling individuals to 'bounce back' from disappointments. At another level, the inner character traits are not those of fortitude or of self-determination which assume a fixed subject/object relationship but of self-reflexivity and openness to the world. Such traits suggest a much deeper entanglement with the world and the need for greater humility. Rather than strong subject understandings of character, the inner traits required suggest a set of post-modern or relational sensitivities.

These new sensitivities are seen as essential once it is understood that a complex problem, such as that of social and economic equality, cannot be addressed through macro-level government economic and social policy, attempting to steer or direct the economy. Rather, such a problem can only be tackled by working on the inner mechanisms and social dynamics which are seen to reproduce poverty and exclusion. The approach advocated suggests that governments cannot effectively 'touch' the problem through top-down policy mechanisms but need to understand the real processes at work at the level of the society and the individual and to enable these inner mechanisms. In the same way, these inner mechanisms of subject/object interconnection need to be revealed at the level of the individual's 'government of the self', which also requires an inner reflexivity. Both the relation between government and society and between the subject and the external world are thus reconceived in a post-modern or more relational ontology.

Non-linearity

It is very important to highlight how resilience enables a coherent understanding of the necessary connection between social understandings of interconnection – relational ontologies – and the consequent need for work on the self and self-reflexivity. Resilience has played a transitional role of shifting from a modernist subject-centred perspective (of a strong subject) to a relational ontology of system dynamics (with a relational, embedded subject) through its focus on non-linearity (unexpected outcomes). Resilience in its classical framing of inner attributes of the subject, such as character, fortitude, and patience, was used to highlight the non-linear outcomes of societal interactions. Men of fortitude did not cave in to extreme environmental conditions. Neither did women, whose inner strength enabled them to cope under the harshest domestic conditions: social outcomes were not necessarily structurally determined. Resilience was a challenge to deterministic understandings of the causal power of nature or of socioeconomic structures. There was no direct, reductionist, or mechanical relationship between cause and effect or input and output. Resilience as a concept, even in its restricted 'classical' sense, already indicated the importance of the contingent power of agency in the construction of a non-linear world.

This classical understanding of resilience was often used in managing Britain's sense of post-imperial decline, where the inner strength of character of a people was held to explain how Britain could 'bat above its weight' in international affairs. In the UK narrative, there was always plenty of self-praise for plucky little Britain withstanding the firepower of the German military-industrial complex in the early years of the Second World War, described in recent BBC commemoration programming as: 'Finest Hour: The Resilience of Churchill and the British People'.[26] Britain was resilient because the superior firepower of the German air force failed to achieve its aim of defeating and demoralising the British people during the Blitz. Their inner qualities of grit and determination enabled a non-linear outcome. Similarly, in psychology, work on resilience demonstrated that people can respond very differently to traumas and disappointment according to their internal mental states: there was no universal or linear outcome or effect of trauma. A strong 'bulldog' spirit could enable positive outcomes under the most pressing and direst of circumstances.

In the era of liberal modernity, non-linear outcomes, understood in terms of resilience, were seen as positive, especially in the fields of engineering and psychology. It was in those fields that the ability to withstand pressure, to cope and to bounce back clearly had progressive connotations. However, as will be analysed in the following two chapters, non-linearity was already developing a dark side. In the discipline of economics, the focus on the inner qualities of the subject and on differential individual responses to external stimuli was often being used to undermine or to challenge liberal assumptions of universal reason and the possibilities of progress and development. (Generally, these obstructionist efforts were made by conservative or neoliberal commentators who were also keen to stress the importance of non-linear outcomes.) The non-linear framing, emphasising the inner attributes of the subject, could be positively cast in terms of resilience or understood more negatively in the language of new institutionalist economics which stressed the internal cognitive and societal barriers to liberal progress. Nevertheless, both neoliberal constructions of non-linearity as a limit and resilience constructions of positive non-linear outcomes focused on the internal world of the subject rather than on adoption of broader relational or open system ontologies. Both constructions of non-linearity also operated outside the dominant Western political paradigm of governing: post-classical or new institutionalist economics was influential mainly in explaining the limits of non-Western growth and psychological approaches operated at the level of the individual in the private sphere.

It was only with the problematising of the liberal modernist understanding of politics, with the decline of the politics of the Left and Right and the rise of globalisation, that states seemed to lose their ability to rule in the old ways and governmental practices became increasingly attuned to the non-linear outcomes of a world of complexity. The rise of resilience-thinking could thereby also be understood as the rise of non-linearity or of our awareness of contingency and complexity. Complexity and non-linearity seem to encourage resilience-thinking, and resilience-thinking seems to indicate that non-linearity can be used as an agenda for governance, thus drawing upon classical positive connotations of resilience as a non-linear process of generating positive outcomes.

In post-classical understandings of resilience, these positive outcomes are generated by attention to the systemic processes and interactions at play rather than by the inner properties of discrete subjects. Resilience increasingly concerns the emergent attributes of processes of subject–object relations: the understanding of relational or system dynamics. These dynamics are understood to be constantly in the process of emergence and transformation. Whereas in classical understandings of resilience security could be strengthened through overcoming vulnerabilities and adaptation, for post-classical understandings, these adaptations would merely produce new and unforeseen consequences: new vulnerabilities. Attempts to achieve security would thereby be understood to be the source of new (and unexpected) insecurities. The goal then becomes not security but a self-reflective awareness of the unintended consequences or secondary effects (side effects) of any securitising measures. In this process of self-reflective awareness, the resilient subject emerges not as a secure subject but as a self-aware subject: self-aware not only of its own internal capacities and attributes and the need to be constantly adaptive but also increasingly aware of its own relational vulnerabilities and how these are reproduced through different embedded relational systems – through cultural, social, economic and environmental processes of emergent causality, operating across a range of interrelated and overlapping levels from the local to the global.

This shift from subject-centred to relational understanding is of fundamental importance to how we understand politics in an age of complexity. Resilience-understandings point towards a different set of strategies and processes of governance. Rather than governance around certain goals – such as modern liberal aspirations of knowledge, security, development or democracy – resilience suggests that goals cannot be imposed upon complex relational systems. Indeed, policy-making is a process of learning about those relations and adapting to them rather than imposing upon them from above, as if they could be shaped or directed. Governing complexity is thereby understood to be a process whereby failures or unintended outcomes can be seen as an inevitable part of that process and the key aspect is how failure is reflected upon to shape future policy-making.[27] In a complex and fluid reality, failing better is seen to be a much more realistic goal than narrow short-term understandings of policy 'success'.[28]

Reality versus artifice

Whereas the liberal world strictly divided humanity from nature in terms of active subject and passive and compliant object, the world of resilience-thinking seeks to overcome this reductionist and binary approach that is at the heart of liberal governmental assumptions. The one binary that could be said to shape the problematic of resilience as a technique of governing complexity is that between an awareness and a sensitivity of 'real' complex processes of causation and the tendency to impose reductionist, abstract or teleological understandings which reflect the artifice of liberal forms of top-down imposition. In a non-linear world of interactive or emergent causality, any top-down attempts to direct or control the social world fly in the face of the 'real' processes of social causation, leading to counterproductive or unintended outcomes. Resilience-thinking is thereby constantly drawing lessons from the real and complex appearances of the world to learn that liberal artifice – the constructed world of linear cause and effect and reductionist binaries – is a barrier to be overcome through new ways of conceiving the world that is to be governed.

Resilience approaches today tend to understand the world as a complex set of overlapping emerging processes in which all subject–objects are embedded. There is nothing 'natural' about nature or the human subject. Politics in an age of complexity has to be sensitive to the fact that we no longer live in a linear or binary world of liberal and modernist certainties. We are no more separate from the world than individuals are separate from societies or states are separate from international relations or humanity is separate from nature. This post-classical understanding does not view resilience as an inner capacity or attribute of a separate subject or agent but as a governing ethos or relational attribute emerging from the complexity and interdependence of the modern world, as an assemblage in which both subjects and objects (or subject–object relations) are embedded. Resilience, in this sense, is always relational and context-dependent: threats or dangers are as inherent in this relationality as much as positive outcomes might be. Resilience is thus not a matter of a separate subject adapting to an external world but of the reflexive management of contingent outcomes of different assemblages or relational ensembles (of varying degrees of transiency).

Politics in an age of complexity is discursively constructed in terms of complex adaptive systems, 'emergent causality', 'post-humanism', actor network theory, 'new' or 'non-equilibrium' ecology, 'new materialism' and other conceptual frameworks which attempt to come to grips with the embeddedness of subjects in complex processes and interrelationships. Not all these framings necessarily put the concept of resilience at the centre of their concerns, but they all share the ontological premises of the need for a new understanding of politics informed by the erosion or attenuation of traditional liberal constructions of the political and particularly of the liberal binaries of human/nature, culture/environment and subject/object. They all assert that in a fluid and globalised world the liberal modernist conceptions of power, politics and agency need to be reconsidered. There is no doubt that the rise of resilience-thinking plays a formative role in this process of reworking the problematic of governance in an age of complexity.

Therefore, if resilience is to be defined, it would perhaps be useful to understand resilience as the discursive field through which we negotiate the emerging problem of governing complexity. Resilience appears to be a process of learning the lessons of governance failures: of how to live with the end of the modernist promise of linear modes of governing and understanding. Resilience is thereby less a final goal than a mode of thinking and acting in the world, which starts from the appearance of limits to traditional forms of governing and of liberal modernist politics of representation. Resilience approaches operate to draw attention to how governance can operate as a process of governing through the 'reality' of processes and relations rather than as a top-down imposition seeking to direct, manage or assert control over things.

The structure of the book

This book is divided into three sections. Part I deals with the most important conceptual frameworks that have shaped the discussion of resilience as an approach to governance in a world of complexity. Chapter 2 analyses the implications of understanding life as complex. Here complexity approaches are drawn upon to illustrate how complexity is understood to be ontologically distinct from understanding life as either complicated or as chaotic. Complex life is life understood as having the emergent properties of order.

Thus, although life is then seen as non-amenable to linear, top-down understandings of cause and effect, it can be governed through an understanding of interactive emergent, organic and autonomous processes. Chapter 3 charts the development of analogous understandings of life as emergent and self-ordering in the political discourses of the post-1968, post-Marxist and autonomous Marxist framings of the Left. It will be argued that while neoliberal constructions of complexity operated to understand (and naturalise) the limits to government, it was the critique of liberal modernist frameworks from the post-foundational and post-structuralist Left which enabled these limits to be reworked as positive and emancipatory possibilities and to facilitate the emergence of resilience-thinking as a coherent programme of postmodern or post-liberal governance.

Part II contains three chapters, which analyse the shifts in thinking about policy-intervention in the international sphere. Chapter 4 considers the rise of complexity as a response to the growing perception of the limits to liberal internationalist aspirations of exporting liberal understandings of peace, development, democracy and human rights in the 1990s. Critiques of 'liberal peace' thereby shifted from criticisms of the lack of liberalism of the interveners (the fact that they selectively pursued the interests of power) to criticisms of intervention precisely because of its universal assumptions and teleological understandings. Critics therefore focused on the limits of liberal forms of knowledge and the complex, non-linear and hybrid outcomes of intervention. Chapter 5 analyses how the problems of complexity and non-linearity gradually shifted from merely naturalising the limits to external intervention to attempting to articulate forms of intervention which operated within a non-linear problematic, transforming social interaction in ways which were seen to facilitate liberal forms of rationality. Using the example of the shifting approaches to the war on drugs in the Americas, it flags up the paradoxes of intervention on the basis of instrumental approaches which problematised and essentialised cultural understandings and how resilience approaches have increasingly focused upon practices and interactions at the local level. Chapter 6 takes the analysis of resilience approaches to global problems beyond the discourses of intervention to understandings of the indirect consequences of relational embeddedness and the need for reflexive governance of the self at both institutional and individual levels. In this framing, governing actors are always and already understood to be relationally entangled with the emergent problem. Intervention can therefore only work indirectly through retracing the chains of emergent interaction.

Part III contains three chapters, which analyse different facets of the political–ethical approach of resilience-thinking, building upon the shared ontology of the governance of others and of the self. Chapter 7 concerns the revelation of the public and its interactive bonds of interconnection through the event or the problematic appearance of the world. Rather than the public being self-constituted in the glare of the public sphere, resilience approaches argue that the reality of the public and its governance is only revealed *post hoc*, after the fact. Responsivity to the event then enables complex life to inform governance as a self-reflexive process (the response to the Utoeya Island massacre in Oslo in July 2011 is used to illustrate the process at play in the enfolding of the event into the process of governance). Chapter 8 then analyses the transformation of the public from being the collective subject of modern government in the public sphere to becoming the plural and shifting objects of resilience as governance in the social sphere. This shift is analysed through consideration of the political theorising of complexity and emergent causality in the work of pragmatist theorist John Dewey and neoliberal theorist Friedrich Hayek, and some of the shared assumptions behind resilience as a responsive and self-reflexive form of governance are drawn out. Chapter 9 completes the analysis of the politics of resilience-thinking through consideration of the rise of post-humanist, actor–network, non-representational and new materialist approaches in social theorising. These approaches take the understanding of embedded and emergent relationality to its logical conclusion in assemblage theorising and the critique of the subject/object divides of representational thought. These approaches are then analysed in terms of how they construct the human subject and the subject's relationship to the world and their claim that the encouragement of self-reflexive responsivities and sensitivities can enable progressive change. Chapter 10 concludes the book with a consideration of the promise of resilience-thinking and complexity ontologies and how this promise has helped overcome some of the problems and paradoxes of liberal and neoliberal governance. Unfortunately, this success has only come at the cost of reifying the appearances of the world and subordinating the human will to this anthropomorphic projection of human creativity onto the world itself.

Notes

1 Wales College, 2006; Neocleous, 2013.
2 OECD, 2011: p.8.
3 Demchak, 2011.
4 See, for example, the *International Journal of Disaster Resilience in the Built Environment*, established in 2010.
5 Ganson and Wennmann, 2012.
6 Nanyang Technological University, 2009.
7 OECD, 2013.

8 Wagner, 2012; Warner and Grünewald, 2012.
9 Hussain, 2013.
10 Levine *et al.*, 2012.
11 See, for example, Reghezza-Zitt *et al.*, 2012.
12 Although many such handbooks do exist, see, for example, CARE Netherlands, 2013.
13 At the All-Party Parliamentary Group on Social Mobility 'Character and Resilience Summit', 6 February 2013. Report available at: http://www.appg-socialmobility.org/.
14 All-Party Parliamentary Group, 2012: p.6.
15 Ibid.: p.32.
16 Walker, 2013.
17 Ibid.
18 Coutu, 2002; Dyer and McGuinness, 1996; Smith *et al.*, 2008.
19 Walker *et al.*, 2004; Richardson, 2002; Zautraa *et al.*, 2010; Leipold and Greve, 2009.
20 Coaffee and Wood, 2006; Menon, 2005; Paton and Johnston, 2001.
21 Norris *et al.*, 2008; Dillon, 2007; Aradau and Van Munster, 2011.
22 Gunderson and Holling, 2002. Lifton, 1999; Chandler, 2013b.
23 Ekici *et al.*, 2009.
24 See, for a critique, Latour, 2004a: p.19.
25 Holling, 1973.
26 http://www.bbc.co.uk/programmes/p009cmyn.
27 For example, Little, 2012; Harford, 2012.
28 Conner, 1993.

PART I
Thematics

2
GOVERNING COMPLEXITY

Introduction

The precondition for the rise of resilience-thinking is the understanding that a complex world requires a new approach to governing. There is therefore little point in attempting to understand resilience as a core concept at play in discussion about policy problems and policy solutions today, without considering what is assumed in the assertion that the world is now more complex. To understand the demand for resilience-thinking as a potential answer or solution, we must first grasp what is already implied in the question of the ontology of the world or life itself as 'complex'. Without complexity there would be no demand for resilience. As leading resilience theorists Brian Walker and David Salt argue, in the preface to their influential book *Resilience Thinking*, it

> should appeal to anyone interested in dealing with risk in a complex world. This includes business leaders, policy makers, resource managers, and politicians. It also includes … members of the public. … This is because, at its core, resilience is about risk and complexity, things that impact all of us. We live in a complex world. Anyone with a stake in managing some aspect of that world will benefit from a richer understanding of resilience and its implications.[1]

Core to this book is the analysis of the assumption that complexity – or life as the object of governance conceived as complex – necessarily calls forth a new 'resilience' agenda of governance for governing institutions, concerned with the government of others, and for individual members of the public, concerned with the ethical government of the self. Complexity understandings do a lot of heavy lifting for resilience-thinking as they play a key role in critiquing metaphysical assumptions of truth and justice and instrumentalist liberal 'linear' or 'reductionist' approaches to governance, substantiating new approaches to governance based on an understanding of life as complex.

This chapter seeks to unpack the nature of that 'life' which is seen to evade liberal forms of representation and of government and to dictate new forms of governing from within the framework of resilience-thinking. The following sections seek to clarify the ontology of complex life emphasising that, while it is understood in precisely the relational terminology immune to liberal reductionist and linear understandings, complex life is also understood to demand governance through other – non-linear and non-reductionist – approaches. Complex life is governable but on a very different basis than liberal 'life'.

What is complex life?

The synergy between governing, informed through resilience-thinking, and the construction of the world as complex is dependent upon the way in which we understand the complexity of life as an object of governance. If life was merely arbitrary and chaotic, it could not be the subject of governance any more than the weather could be.[2] Complex life is governable but not in the same way as life in liberal modernity was. To highlight the key points of this chapter, which will be elucidated further below, complex life is governable because, by definition, complex life is neither ordered nor chaotic. Complex life is therefore generative of self-governing order precisely because it is constantly interactively adapting, communicating and exchanging with its environment or surroundings. Complex life, as we shall analyse, brings order out of chaos through this mechanism of interactive adaptation.[3] The second crucial point about complex life is its interactive or open-ended characterisation; it is not closed off to the world or merely adapting to its environment on the basis of its initial conditions, as an autopoietic system would. The interaction between complex life and governing intervention is open and therefore full of immanent possibilities.[4]

To understand the ontology of complex life, it is first necessary to understand how life was constructed or understood in classical frameworks of liberal modernity and how these frameworks were contested by post-classical or neoliberal understandings of non-linear life. Resilience-thinking – as a solution to the problem of governing complexity – understands itself to be a radical alternative to the modernist ontology of life, held to have been dominant since the Enlightenment in the seventeenth century. The modernist approach is identified negatively today, often under the problematic rubrics of 'reductionism', 'rationalism', 'mechanical materialism' or 'Cartesianism'. The modernist ontology sought to understand life at the level of fixed relations between objects with fixed properties, subject to universal laws and understanding. Complex life, by contrast, is emergent and cannot be understood merely by a study of its parts or their properties. Reductionist approaches therefore fail to grasp that which is crucial to complexity: interaction.[5] As Paul Cilliers notes:

> [T]he interaction among constituents of the system ... are of such a nature that the system as a whole cannot be fully understood simply by analysing its components. Moreover, these relationships are not fixed, but shift and change, often as a result of self-organisation. This can result in novel features, usually referred to in terms of emergent properties. The brain, natural language and social systems are complex.[6]

According to René Descartes, who is often considered to be the founder of modern philosophy, complex problems needed to be broken down into as many parts as possible and then reassembled, beginning with knowledge of the most simple parts and then building up to the most complex.[7] It is Descartes' view of subject/object representation[8] that is seen as the starting point for the modernist reductionist ontology of fixed properties and interactions which, during the seventeenth century, spread to the sciences, with Galileo, Kepler and Newton – with the classical mechanics of fixed laws – and to political philosophy, with Hobbes and Locke – with calls for stable and centralized power and a reductionist understanding of individuals and states as autonomous entities. This linear, mechanistic, ontology of natural order and natural law dominated both the social and the natural sciences. As Stephen Toulmin argues, the period from the late seventeenth century to the outbreak of the First World War in 1914 could be understood to be the high tide of modernist or rationalist thinking.[9]

From the 1920s onwards, important intellectual currents in both the natural sciences (especially in theoretical physics) and the social sciences (particularly in historical sociology, continental philosophy and economics) challenged this rationalist ontology; yet the modernist world (in terms of dominant political understandings) clung on until the collapse of the Cold War Left/Right divisions some quarter of a century ago. From the vantage point of today, it may seem strange that modernist ontologies managed to dominate political and philosophical thinking for three hundred years when they were based on simplifying and abstract understandings rather than on the concrete complex reality of human and societal experience.

Toulmin's classic treatment is useful in this respect, suggesting that the desire for stability and order, particularly after the Thirty Years War (1618–48) and the English Civil War (1642–51), underlay the rise and success of this framework.[10] Other theorists have suggested that the modernist age of mass manufacturing also suited simplified linear understandings,[11] or, following the prescient claims of Walter Lippmann and John Dewey,[12] that simplifying and reductionist assumptions have great appeal to governments seeking to win votes by promising easy solutions to problems (and therefore also appeal to the public, who do not have the time or interest to consider politics more seriously).

However, the three-hundred-odd year reign of modernist thinking is now declared to be over, either because the world has changed – to become quicker, more fluid and more interconnected and complex – thereby making reductionist rationalist assumptions even less workable,[13] or because these assumptions were never workable and the decline of the politics of Left and Right (and the sensibilities and attachments which these political commitments brought with them) has left this reality much more clearly exposed.[14] For a more balanced view, Ilya Prigogine and Isabelle Stengers suggest that we need to understand both the ontological reality of life as complex and the importance given to this in the cultural and social context of our time, when it appears that the world is in increasing flux.[15] With the crisis of modernist framings, complexity is the leading contender as an alternative ontological vision of the world – of how life can be conceived as the object of governance. In this sense, complexity approaches could be seen as reinforcing the new materialist 'ontological turn' in the social sciences (considered further in the next chapter), which highlights how a complex ontology constitutes radical possibilities foreclosed by liberal forms of governance.

As stated above, complex life is not amenable to reductive and linear reasoning because the whole is not reducible to the sum of its parts. Complex or non-reductionist ontologies are by definition non-linear: changes in causal elements do not produce proportionate outcomes. There is not necessarily a fixed, linear relationship between inputs and outputs – between cause and effect – because causation is complex and relational. Changes in effects or outcomes may be radically disproportional to changes in causal elements. Small variations in initial parameters can have a major effect which could not be known in advance, i.e. there may be tipping points or thresholds, which mean that quantity can rapidly turn into quality – a new stable regime or state. This framing brings in a radically different understanding of agency. For closed systems, such as weather systems, chaos theory has highlighted this radical redistribution of agency in terms of the 'butterfly effect', whereby a butterfly flapping its wings can 'cause' a hurricane, once this tiny variation of wind speed is inserted in the development of a deterministically chaotic system.

With this radical diffusion of potential agency, complex life (human and non-human) is no longer conceived as passively subject to the timeless laws of mechanical physics but constantly, 'becoming', in process, 'alive': it is therefore impossible to determine in advance which direction causation will take. So while planning is impossible, it is possible to govern life by being attuned to how life spontaneously self-organises to bring order out of disorder. This ontology of 'life' is central to resilience as a mode of governing complexity. There are no reductionist understandings of rationalist individuals, where unit- and system-levels are distinct: the system connections at any concrete moment need to be traced, whether we are dealing with understanding the ant colony or the capitalised ANT of actor-network theory, which articulates a very similar ontology of human social interaction: that of emergent collectivities rather than directed ones. The point is not necessarily that ants and humans are the same but that complex emerging order occurs as much in the social as in the natural world. Human actors are not aware of the end consequences of the myriad interactions they are involved in every day, any more than the body's immune system cells or individual ants are acting consciously and intentionally to achieve the system outcomes of their interactive activity. How complex life works is held to be beyond the planning, control or comprehension of any individual, no matter how clever they are or what position of power they might occupy. Nevertheless, order emerges from these simple, often rule-based, interactions without intentional causation, planning or structure.[16]

Complexity is vital to resilience-thinking, as the ontological understanding of life as complex is understood to pose reality – the complexity of life – in such a way as to enable or make necessary an alternative form of governance. In this respect, the ontology of complexity could be understood as a 'Third Way' approach, beyond both Left and Right: a critique of both hierarchical understandings of the state-based politics of the Left as well as of the chaos of the unregulated free market of the Right. Complexity ontologies do not understand life in the liberal binaries of either hierarchy (where there is order and progress) or anarchy (without order and progress) but in non-liberal or post-liberal understandings of governance through self-organising adaptivity. Complexity approaches of resilience-thinking enable life to order governance by insisting that reality – life itself – contains an immanent process of emergent order which can inform the aims and practices of its governance.

The emergence of complexity

This understanding, that complex life is not bound by fixed laws or structures, lies in direct opposition to Enlightenment understandings of knowable laws which can be understood and put to human purposes – setting up the liberal distinction between human as subject and the instrumentalisation of nature as a passive and malleable object. This subject/object divide was based on the classical mechanics approach to natural laws, exemplified in Isaac Newton's discovery of the universal laws of force and mass, held to be applicable to the whole of the universe. God was no longer needed once rationalist science produced a picture of a 'clockwork universe' running its mechanical course on the basis of universal laws, enabling the possible prediction of all future events. The operating laws of the universe were not easy to understand, and it was held to take a lot of work to acquire the knowledge needed to predict this future, but nature – and life in general – was not 'complex' in the sense of complexity theory and resilience-thinking.

As intimated above, life began to be conceived as complex, in both the natural and social sciences, in the 1920s – after the shock to liberal modernist confidence in progress caused by the carnage of the First World War (1914–18) and the fears unleashed by the Bolshevik Revolution of 1917. Complexity theorists often locate this shift less in cultural and political sensitivities than in scientific discoveries such as Werner Heisenberg's discovery of the uncertainty principle in quantum mechanics in 1927 – where at the quantum level of tiny particles it was impossible to measure both mass and momentum simultaneously. Since the 1920s, classical mechanical understandings have increasingly given way to emphasis on the growth of 'uncertainty': the theorisation of the limits to understanding processes of interaction in order to predict outcomes.

Prior to the recent influence of complexity-thinking on the social sciences, the extension of the logic of Heisenberg's 'uncertainty principle' – chaos theory – was the most widely cited scientific theory of the limits of knowledge. In 1987, James Gleick's *Chaos: Making a New Science*, became a best-seller, introducing the general principles of chaos theory as well as its history to the broader public.[17] Essentially, the fact that it was impossible to accurately measure, at the same time, the position, mass and momentum of particles was, over the long term, held to lead to unpredictable variations in outcomes. Chaos theory thus emphasised the importance of sensitivity to initial conditions, which meant that tiny, unobservable, differences could – over repeated iterations – have major effects in the long term. Chaos theory is ontologically distinct to complexity theory as it emphasises the importance of differences, which undermine universal assumptions, but, nevertheless, the apparent randomness – caused by tiny variations in initial conditions – can be understood as driven by an underlying mechanical conception of a law-bound world. In this sense, chaos theory does not directly challenge liberal assumptions of linearity. In chaos theory, systems are closed, and the problem is an epistemological one of the difficulty of knowing the initial conditions in order to predict the future.

Whereas chaos theory still operates under a liberal episteme of law-bound determinism, complexity theory introduces a different ontology of objective unknowability beyond merely epistemic limits. The radical implications of this shift were already recognised and highlighted by Jean-François Lyotard in the late 1970s. In Lyotard's understanding, for chaos theory it is *de facto* impossible to have a complete definition of the initial state of a system (or all the independent variables) because of the resources this would take up. It would be analogous to an emperor wishing to have a perfectly accurate map of the empire, making the entire country devote its energy to cartography and therefore leading it to economic ruin because there are no resources for anything else.[18] However:

> this limitation only calls into question the practicability of exact knowledge and the power that would result from it. They remain possible in theory. Classical determinism continues to work within the framework of the unreachable – but conceivable – limit of the total knowledge of a system. … Quantum theory and microphysics require a far more radical revision of the idea of a continuous and predictable path. The quest for precision is not limited by its cost, but by the very nature of matter.[19]

It is difficult to underestimate the importance of the distinction between the deterministic ontology of chaos and the understanding of emergent causality of complexity theory. Calculation or control and direction become impossible in complexity theory, but the unknowable is not a result of hidden determinism (as in chaos theory), nor can it be the result of blind chance or luck. Lyotard insightfully flagged up how a complexity approach transformed the ontology of knowledge and unknowability and its implications for modernist subject/object distinctions. In a liberal episteme, there is the necessary assumption of hidden determination – as Einstein argued, it was impossible that 'God plays with dice.' In complexity theory – where statistical regularities (orders) occur without 'the supreme Determinant' – nature or life reveals itself as an emergent power, neither determined nor merely arbitrary:

If God played bridge, then the level of 'primary chance' encountered by science could no longer be imputed to the indifference of the die toward which face is up, but would have to be attributed to cunning – in other words, to a choice, itself left up to chance, between a number of possible, pure strategies.[20]

Complexity has a different ontology to chaos theory, which drew on theoretical developments in quantum mechanics. Complexity's roots are in the laws of thermodynamics, evolutionary science and computational mathematics. What follows may sound a little technical but is actually crucial to understanding how complexity (unlike chaos) provides a means of operationalising 'life' as a technology of governance. While in chaos theory order produces disorder, in complexity theory, life – by definition – produces order.[21] Order emerges through life itself: it is self-governing and by virtue of being self-governing provides frameworks for thinking about how human life can be self-governed. The self-government of complex life, it should be clarified, has no connection with the self-government of liberal political philosophy involving the formal constitution of a governing order. Liberal orders only have hierarchy – under a sovereign – or anarchy – the pre-social contract state of nature. The order and governance of complex life is emergent – complexity can therefore not be conceived in terms of anarchy or hierarchy.

Chaos theory and complexity theory, as stated, are distinct in that in the latter order rather than entropy emerges from a dissipative system. This is vital for the understanding of complex life as a key to resilience as a governance rationality. However, this is not the whole picture for those interested in complexity in the social sciences rather than in the natural sciences. Complexity theory itself provides a conceptual field in which emergent causality can be understood to work at different levels. At the most basic level, the object of governance can be understood as being shaped through emergent causality – often articulated in terms of cultural evolution or path-dependencies – which then pose a problem for governing intervention into these processes. In this understanding of complexity, there is still a division between the subject (the governing actor) and the object (now understood as complex). Under simple complexity, there is still a liberal subject external to the problematic – much like a scientist observing complexity in ecosystems or a liberal observer considering how to intervene in a non-liberal (complex) social order. In a more extended understanding of complexity, this divide between subject and object is effaced through understanding that the governing/knowing subject is not external to the problematic but always and already 'entangled' or embedded in this relationship.

Complexity-thinking in the social sciences could thus be understood as being on a continuum between a problematic of complexity for intervention with instrumental governance goals – for example, to bring peace, democracy or security – and complexity understandings which would dispute the possibility of such a subject/object separation. The two ends of this continuum could be heuristically framed in terms of the governing rationalities of neoliberalism (where the object of intervention is constructed in terms of complexity) and resilience-thinking (where governance is no longer a matter of intervening in an external problematic but of self-reflexive understandings of entanglement). It is heuristically useful, therefore, to make an analytical distinction between neoliberal and resilience ontologies and their analogous methodological configurations in complexity theory. In this regard, I follow Byrne and Callaghan in their distinction between 'simple' and 'general' complexity, and in their intimation that simple complexity lends itself to neoliberal understandings of emergent order, while general complexity provides a fundamental challenge to both liberal and neoliberal framings of the governance of life.[22] For understanding complex life as the subject of governance, this distinction is therefore crucial.

Simple complexity theory focuses on complexity as an epistemological problem of knowledge of emergent causality in a closed system, understood as operating externally to (and independently of) the governing actor. As we shall examine, this understanding of an emergent order through closed or endogenous interactions between agents has much in common with neoliberal or new institutionalist accounts of the endogenous emergence of difference, used to explain the reproduction of economic and social differences despite the universalising tendencies of the market or globalisation. The neoliberal governance perspective is one of 'bottom-up' emergent agency, which constitutes the world in plural and multiple ways but within different and distinct social systems – it is these emergent interactions which constitute the problem for governance – the problems of conflict, poverty, state failure, and so on. At the level of simple complexity, emerging domestic or endogenous orders, which develop in a complex emergent way, can then explain at a higher level where the international system meets this domestic system, nonlinear outcomes, such as different responses to the same economic stimuli or to natural disasters.

General complexity, on the other hand, does not work on the basis of closed systems, which endogenously develop emerging internal orders, but on the basis of the impossibility of such a closure marking off a subject or territory from the world. For general complexity theory, this closure would essentially reproduce a liberal modernist ontology of potentially knowable relations of cause and effect, which could enable instrumental means-ends understandings of policy governance. General complexity, therefore, does not pose the problem at the level of knowledge of these emergent interactions and therefore pose policy solutions at the level of interventions to alter or change endogenously determined development paths ('path-dependencies' in the language of new institutionalist economics). For general complexity theory, the problem of governance does not presuppose a modernist subject/object divide; policy interventions have to be based upon understanding problems as a result of already interconnected relations between agents. There can be no 'intervention' from one system to another system or reductionist perspective of lower and higher levels of causation. General complexity, like simple complexity, understands the possibility of order emerging from unplanned interaction but this is dependent on a very different type of governance intervention, attuned to the constant creative possibilities of interactive life in which governance interventions are reflexively imbricated.

In non-social science analytics of complexity, the distinction between closed and open systems of interactive or emergent order is rarely a concern. This is problematic as the ontological assumption of complexity theorists working in the natural sciences, mathematics and computation analysis is that they are operating in a closed (but interactive) system where the reiteration of simple rule-bound interactions enables order to emerge from complex life.[23] However, it is vital to stress that while the ontology of simple complexity has little to add, technically, to social science understandings – historically demarcated from the natural sciences precisely because of the role of the contingencies of 'life' in the interactive world of politics – simple complexity has been extremely influential in enabling a rethinking of traditional cause-and-effect understandings which were much more dominant in the 'hard' sciences. However, the knock-on effect on the social sciences should not be underestimated. Traditionally, the contingencies of the human subject matter of the social sciences were understood to be a product of conscious political struggle and economic competition, but now another component could be added: the contingent outcomes that seemed to flow from 'complex life' itself. This new component was not just a minor add-on. The 'soft' social sciences had always been understood to be subordinate in status to the 'hard' natural sciences. If complexity theory could demonstrate that even the 'hard' sciences could be undermined by the creative self-organising power of life itself, then there was every reason to think that this must have an impact on the linear assumptions and reductionist scientific 'pretensions' now seen to be underlying social and political theory.

For these reasons, the understanding of how order emerged through self-organisation, under the conditions of simple complexity, was of major importance to future developments in social theory. How order emerges is, in fact, still hotly contested within the scientific community, but the fact that it does is held to be scientifically proven through the laws of thermodynamics. In thermodynamics, disorder or decay is conceptualised as 'entropy'. The most important law in thermodynamics is the law of entropy (the second law of thermodynamics), which states that in isolated systems (which do not exchange energy with an outside entity) entropy or disorder will always increase until it reaches its maximum possible value and will never decrease unless an outside agent works to decrease it.[24] This law is said to define the 'arrow of time', proving that there are processes which cannot be reversed in time: the future is defined as the direction of time in which entropy increases. This law is the only fundamental law of physics which distinguishes a direction of time; all other laws are reversible in time, meaning that they would hold true whether time was moving forwards or backwards.

Thermodynamic systems are open and dynamic, exchanging and transforming energy and matter, being pushed away from the stability and equilibrium states of classical mechanics. While the second law of thermodynamics states that entropy will always increase until it reaches its maximum value, complex life seems to provide a counter example existing in a middle ground between order and disorder. Complex life is understood as becoming more efficient and adaptive rather than more disordered and entropic. Life seems to be evolving towards greater order and complexity through a process of evolution through natural selection, first elucidated by Charles Darwin in *On the Origin of Species* in 1859. Here, it seemed there was the appearance of greater order, of expert design, but there was no God and, even more importantly (for resilience-thinking as it subsequently developed), no mechanical clock with fixed laws. Entropy appeared to decrease as life became increasingly ordered through evolution as a process of emergent causality.

While Darwin's theory of evolution was important for the emergence of complexity theory, there was little understanding of how natural selection worked to enable life to adapt and allow order to emerge until after the discovery of DNA in the 1940s. The processes at stake are still hotly debated today, for example, with Stephen J. Gould's view of evolution as a process of punctuated equilibria rather than of gradual change and his critique of 'strict adaptationists' who see little room for historical contingency and unintended effects in a story of continual evolutionary progress.[25] Nevertheless, science had established the existence of complex life: life that self-organised to produce emergent order through the process of adaptation. This formulation of complex life as order through emergence has since become increasingly important in the computational sciences, especially in the desire to create artificial or emergent intelligence – a 'living' computer capable of thinking for itself, i.e., capable of using its own resources to mirror complex life through producing order out of disorder.

It has now been established that computers can be self-adaptive: that they can be programmed through genetic algorithms (simple step-by-step procedures which can be repeated to process data) to 'learn' and to develop solutions to set problems that human programmers are unable to beat or to fully understand. The developments in the computational sciences and understandings of how simple programme codes can produce order – enabling computers to be artificially intelligent – has also led to further thinking about how simple actions of individual elements in nature can produce order at a higher level: how complex life itself possesses 'non-artificial intelligence'. Central in drawing out these connections was the work of Alan Turing in the early 1950s; Turing had developed the blueprints for the first computer programme codes and then sought to analyse 'morphogenesis' – how life emerged – through the use of similar simple mathematical formulae.[26]

The development of computer algorithms of complex adaptation, as a means of problem solving, has enabled computer programmers to simulate complex life as a process of simple step-by-step procedures generating order from disorder. These simulations depend upon understanding natural systems as analogous to computer systems: through the processing of information. Complex life – at the level of immune system cells, collective insect colonies or the synapses of the human brain – can thereby be understood to adapt through networks or relations whereby information is exchanged through chemical and sensory stimuli. The development of the immune system in the body makes a good example as its adaptation to threats, such as diseases, has nothing to do with the brain's conscious decision-making; nevertheless, the immune system is constantly working on the detection and eradication of pathogens, through the interaction of the body's different types of cells which 'communicate' and respond to each other's signals in order to work efficiently. Ant and bee colonies are also increasingly understood to work in this way, with emergent intelligence through simple communication between individuals, rather than some sort of direction or imposed order.

The emergent order of life as complexity is held to be neither the product of the free will of autonomous subjects (immune system cells or insects do not think autonomously – they are not free to take other decisions or to make other choices) nor linearly determined by structures, mechanical laws or sovereign power. How, for example, immune system cells and social insects respond depends on the concrete context: they adapt to solve specific problems, developing ways of detecting and dealing with new pathogens or responding to specific situations of resource availability or external threat. These systems thus appear to be 'conscious' – or to be the result of a process of ordering – but this order is emergent without the autonomous rationality associated with the human subject.[27] For social sciences, this power of emergent ordering is not limited to nature but can also be seen in the development of social units, such as cities, for example, which can be understood as a complex set of self-organising clusters, where initial developments soon become self-amplifying.[28] Work has also been done in the history of the development of scientific and technological advances, in which contingency and unintentional outcomes seemingly played a larger role than planning and narrow instrumental thinking.[29]

Computer modelling of human collective information processing, under conditions of simple complexity, is held to put human rationality in a poor light compared to the modelling of emergent intelligence in computers and in nature, which still exceeds full human understanding. Under simple complexity, emergent causality can also be simulated through game-playing models of reiterated choice-making, which reveal that the pursuit of rational self-interest can lead to less than optimum overall outcomes; perhaps the most famous model is the 'prisoner's dilemma', which highlights the difficulty of sustaining cooperation and avoiding entropy or disorder.[30] The problem of the 'prisoner's dilemma' as an iterative model cannot be understood by merely considering the individuals concerned but only by considering the interactions between them; these problems and ways of resolving them through emergent intelligence are increasingly understood in terms of network modelling. In a world of complexity, it seems that rationalist approaches are less capable of creating order than approaches based upon understanding how order emerges in simulations of reality.

Given the power of complex life, it often appears that complexity becomes a problem for governance because the emerging rationality of self-organising life, both human and non-human, can clash – with unexpected and disastrous effect – with the simplistic and reductionist understandings of governments and markets, seeking short-term and narrow instrumentalist ends on the basis of linear understandings of mechanical causality. The dangers posed by this clash of rationalities are held to be increasingly apparent with the expansion of human interconnection and the rapid development of information technology. This problem was highlighted, literally as I write this paragraph, in August 2013, with the top story on the *Guardian* website, one of complex life and the problem of 'digital infrastructure exceeding the limits of human control'. The data information systems set up to make life more secure produced their own emergent causality, creating new forms of unanticipated and less manageable insecurity.[31] A three-hour network shutdown had paralysed the New York Nasdaq stock market on 22 August 2013 and, in consequence, a third fewer shares were traded in the United States on that day. High-frequency trading by computers, built to automate buying and selling high volumes of shares by hedge funds and banks, was intended to speed up and facilitate trading but had triggered and magnified the impact of IT failures on stock markets. According to Neil MacDonald, a fellow at technology research firm Gartner:

> These outages are absolutely going to continue. There has been an explosion in data across all types of enterprises. The complexity of the systems created to support big data is beyond the understanding of a single person and they also fail in ways that are beyond the comprehension of a single person. ... You get under the covers and high frequency trading algorithms are beyond understanding. Sub-millisecond trades taking place, tens of thousands per second, and when that fails it fails spectacularly. That is what you are seeing manifested in Nasdaq.[32]

In the same month, networked failures at the *New York Times*, Google, Amazon and Microsoft also caused service breakdowns. MacDonald, quoted in the *Guardian*, articulated clearly the logic at play: 'The outage at Amazon last year was traced back to some of the processes and technologies they had put in place to make it more resilient. It is almost like an auto-immune disease, where the systems they created to make it more resilient actually spread the failure more rapidly.'[33] It seems that computers, networks, nature and eco-social systems and more and more areas of socio-political life are understood to be revealing a logic or life of their own: an emergent causality which evades human control as long as we think in old ways about mechanical means-ends causation and linear outcomes while ignoring the unintended 'side-effects' and 'externalities' of systems designed to improve and develop our capacities for controlling and securing ourselves in the face of the complexity of life. Even attempts to make life 'resilient' will fail if the real and ever-changing interrelations of emergent causality are ignored.

For many complexity theorists, life therefore always trumps human attempts to constrain and to order it. The powers of life – understood as an emergent system of ordering – always dwarf the artifice of human understanding and construction: this is clear in the case of nature itself but is also increasingly clear in the power of technology and computing. In the face of emergent life, human governance faces one central task: that of adaption to this superior power. While the power of liberal forms of knowing and governing seems to be dissipating, our appreciation of the real source of power – life itself – appears to be growing. The process of governing complexity through adapting to life as emergent causality means rejecting modern liberal understandings of life as inert, passive and governable in 'top-down' ways, from above. The problem for governance is that of understanding the power of life and how complexity – as a technology of emergent order – operates.

How can complex life be governed?

Complex life can thereby be seen positively, unlike chaos, because its inner logics are alleged to provide ways of understanding that can save us from our hubris, enabling us to think and to govern differently. One leading analyst of emergent order in the thermodynamics of physical and chemical processes was Ilya Prigogine, who won the Nobel Prize in Chemistry in 1977. His work has been widely influential in the social sciences through his collaborations with philosopher Isabelle Stengers, investigating both historically and scientifically how order may arise within self-organising or dissipative systems.[34] Prigogine's work has been central in demonstrating how simple behaviour at a lower level can result in complex ordering at a higher level, with examples throughout the natural sciences of the emergence of order without any deterministic structure or organising centre. In this framing, crucially, time is understood to be open rather than closed: the world becomes full of creative possibilities, which are sidelined in a liberal mechanistic view of deterministic causality. Another world becomes possible, because the possibility of a different future becomes 'real' – grounded in the reality of emergence – rather than excluded by the stable world of the laws of classical mechanics.[35]

Theoretical biologist Stuart Kauffman, renowned for his work on the natural origin of order and on the importance of the emergent properties of dynamic systems for understanding 'complex life', is probably one of the most fervent advocates of the power of life over human hubris.[36] His 2008 book, *Reinventing the Sacred: A New View of Science, Reason, and Religion*,[37] contrapositions the 'reductionism' of Enlightenment reason to the 'real' of complex emergent life.[38] For Kauffman, 'real' life has the capacity to overcome the scientific/religious divide as: 'Reason itself has finally led us to see the inadequacy of reason.' It is life's 'wondrous radical creativity' that humbles human achievements and is 'stunning, awesome and worthy of reverence'.[39] Life – as complex emergent reality – is more efficient, more imaginative and more creative than the human mind can ever be. Kauffman is by no means alone in asserting that 'life' is much cleverer than humans are.[40]

In simple complexity theorising, the emergence of complex order is understood in the language of 'system parameters', 'attractors', 'feedback loops', 'basins of attraction', 'self-organised criticality', 'punctuated equilibria', 'cascades', 'thresholds' and 'tipping-points'. The maps of complexity theory are not of states and continents, in the geo-political framing of liberal modernity, but of 'fitness landscapes' with peaks and troughs, upon which diverse actors, often modelled through evolutionary algorithms, take 'adaptive journeys'.[41] These journeys can be between different peaks of achievement or collapses into various 'basins of attraction' depending on feedback mechanisms.[42] The importance of processes of interactive feedback loops, both positive and negative, and the understanding that different development paths are shaped by a 'lumpy' rather than a flat or linear landscape has enabled frameworks of simple complexity to understand non-linear outcomes which apparently demonstrate the 'truth' of post-classical neoliberal economic theorising. Applying these non-linear ontologies of emergent order, neoliberal advocates warn that government interventions in the economy will have counterproductive and unintended consequences as well as restricting the emergence of more positive outcomes through limiting choice and innovation.

Thus, simple complex life in closed systems of interaction is held to be cleverer than governments working on the basis of universal understandings and attempting to impose or to export these frameworks in traditional 'top-down' ways. In this paradigm, government top-down interventions in complex life will have perverse consequences if they act 'against' life in a restrictive manner because 'economic evolution will find the loopholes':

> This is why sensible-seeming environmental rules can produce perverse results: rainforest chopped down to produce palm oil; trucks laden with woodchips braving the congestion of central London; the rise and rise of SUV. Evolution is smarter than we are, and economic evolution tends to outsmart the rules we erect to guide it.[43]

Where the general complexity of open systems is important is in understanding that complex life does not have to be a problem or barrier to governance interventions. Resilience-thinking agrees with simple complexity theorists that complex life is creative and productive, but argues that governments can intervene to harness this power if they appreciate that this cannot be done through directives and impositions. Complex life is thus transformed from being a limit to governance to being a resource that enables the extension of governance into new realms of 'real' complex life.

Whereas the neoliberal problematic is that of caution regarding intervention in complex life, perceiving it as an external barrier to governance, the problematic of resilience-thinking is that of welcoming complexity. Resilience-thinking holds out the promise of harnessing the reality of complex life to enable governance through it rather than 'over' or 'against' it. Complex life is clever, resourceful and serendipitous, able to produce solutions from the most unexpected sources. In reductionist linear thinking there is little room for the side-effects and externalities which are the tell-tale signs of complex life: yet complexity tells us that linear ways of securing, and making life safer, will produce more and more problematic ways in which life becomes insecure. Life is cleverer than humans. Examples of cascading emergent failure abound whenever new, faster, more efficient mechanisms of securing top-down goals are implemented in ways which do not consider the inherent problems of the new interactions and combinations they institute; from credit default swaps to computer systems to international intervention in the cause of democracy and human rights, the reductionist hubris of linear thinking increasingly stands exposed.

Resilience seeks to enable complex life to govern through its own mechanisms of creative problem-solving. Thereby, it does not just question classical modernist ontologies of the world; it can also be understood as a challenge to (or a development upon) the post-classical critique of liberal aspirations for progress and the limits of human reasoning posed by neoliberal or new institutionalist frameworks, which were increasingly popular in the policy-world from the 1980s to the 2000s. Neoliberal understandings of limits emphasized the determinist hold of the past on the present, posing life as a limit to governing attempts to transform or develop society. The most prominent articulation of neoliberal understandings of life as a limit is the idea of endogenous path-dependencies: self-reinforcing feedback loops of social interaction, which lead to differential and sub-optimal outcomes. Neoliberal understandings share much with simple complexity theory, in that starting from what appear to be very similar points of socioeconomic development, cultural and institutional interactions – influencing governing structures, social organisation, values and culture – can have accumulated consequences which result in major differences. These differential outcomes are understood in terms of stable (but sub-optimum) orders or regimes of socioeconomic life. From very similar socioeconomic conditions – very different forms of order can endogenously develop – the reproduction and intensification of international developmental inequalities are a prime example of neoliberal understandings of closed or endogenous systems, held to self-reproduce differences which, once established or stabilised – trapped in a 'basin of attraction' – can be very difficult to overcome.

A neoliberal ontology of life therefore is keen to flag up the power of closed interactive systems to produce non-linear outcomes at a higher level through processes endogenous to the subject or system itself. Friedrich Hayek, writing in the 1950s, fully appreciated the political importance of simple complexity theorising for the development of neoliberal understandings of governance. His driving concern was the need to counteract the Keynesian influence of state-led development perspectives, seen as a dangerous approach to governing intervention in the market, which could reinforce the claims of socialist and communist parties, seeking power on the basis of the possibility of a state-led transformation of socioeconomic conditions.[44] In order to combat this, Hayek sought to reintroduce difference as ontologically prior to universality and to emphasise the non-linearity of human sociopolitical organisation on the basis of interactive evolutionary characteristics, which become self-amplifying to produce different regimes of order. In his *The Sensory Order: An Inquiry into the Foundations of Theoretical Psychology* (1952) he emphasized the importance of understanding human subjects themselves as unique, differentiated and emergent outcomes of complex evolutionary processes.[45]

According to Hayek, behavioural responses depended less on the universal 'reality' we were confronted with than on the previous psychological preconditioning of our minds.[46] Human consciousness, in fact, prevented engagement with the world in a universal reasoned and rational way.[47] Just as individuals were held to respond in differential non-linear ways, which fed-back and magnified differences in behavioural responses, so too did nations and states, depending upon their endogenous ecosocial conditions. For neoliberal development economists, these path-dependencies meant that, even if the world was becoming more interdependent and globalised, the impacts of these universalising tendencies would be non-linear – differences in ecosocial developments would be magnified rather than become ameliorated (as in a classical linear liberal understanding).[48] For neoliberal theorising, closed systems could self-reproduce different forms of emerging order despite seemingly universal starting conditions. Interactive and iterative processes meant that small differences could produce different socioeconomic orders – in the same way as evolution produced differences in species if they were isolated from each other – such as Darwin's finches on the Galapagos.

Neoliberal understandings of the spontaneous production of order, in closed systems, guide policy governance in terms of the need to intervene in the interactive social processes, which are held to reproduce problematic path-dependencies and enable societies to adapt to market rationalities.[49] Feedback and adaptation are crucial here. Simple complexity provides a purchase for a particular type of intervention designed to impact on the system through work at lower levels of interactive behaviour. These perspectives view complex life as an external barrier to governance and caution against any attempts to impose linear understandings. Nevertheless, the problem is posed as a problem of external governance, with the assumption being that it is possible to intervene instrumentally to shape the outcomes of these processes and to realign them to liberal rationalist understandings of progress and development. The problem is that of understanding the interactive process of emergent causality and of strategic intervention to transform path-dependent and bounded rationalities which are alleged to fail to rationally read and respond to market signals.[50] In contrast, resilience approaches share with general complexity understandings of open systems the understanding that the problem is ontological – there is thereby no possibility of intervening to readjust governing processes or 'set them on the right track', governance interventions are not based on hierarchical claims to knowledge of what is 'right' and then encouraging others to adapt to international norms and prescriptions.

From the perspective of resilience-thinking, the governance of complexity therefore – of necessity – needs to reject the artifice of imposing goals and direction on the world and instead seeks to find its goals in the processes, practices and communicative interactions of the world itself. Resilience-thinking seeks to access, tap into and instrumentalise the 'real' power of life as complexity rather than either hubristically ignoring the realities of the complex post-modern world or seeing governance as impossible in the face of a turbulent and uncertain world. The conceptual understanding of system dynamics enables governance through interventions which increasingly seek to channel 'real' processes of emergent adaptivity rather than imposing liberal or neoliberal means-ends understandings upon them. The open system of exchange and communication is crucial here vis-à-vis a neoliberal focus on the adaptation of a closed system to external environmental influences (such as globalising market forces). For neoliberal framings, the understandings of the individual or community need to be changed to adapt to an external market logic or to internationally accepted norms and values,[51] for resilience-thinking the powers and knowledge of the individual or community are needed to enable the 'real' system to work better.

For resilience-thinking, complex life is not just to be celebrated or problematised as 'sacred' in its power to constitute regimes of order, but has to be understood as amenable to governance in ways which can accentuate the lessons gained from governance through life as a 'real' process of ordering. In this way complexity as a governance framework can be linked to Third

Way thinking (which assumed neither the capacities of the state to order
from above nor the market to order from below), to encourage life to be
self-governing.[52] It is recognised that both states and markets can tend to
increase disorder rather than order. State interventions to shape and direct
economic forces or to socially engineer communities are understood to be
doomed to fail in their linear assumptions of means-ends outcomes and ignorance of unintended consequences.[53] Perhaps less noticed is the growing
understanding of markets as similarly 'hubristic' or 'unreal' in their expectations and behaviour, blinded by a reductionist approach to growth and profitability. Rather than providing clear feedback, equalising risk and distributing
opportunity, the global financial crisis of 2007–8 seems to have highlighted
the fact that market behaviour is highly unstable, exaggerating boom-bust
tendencies rather than alleviating them.

It appears that the best ways for order to emerge are through technologies
of adaption, which cannot be grasped in terms of liberal binaries of state and
market rationalities. Perhaps, rather than understanding complexity in terms
of moving beyond the binaries of the social and the natural or of the state and
the market, the clearest way of articulating the shift in terms of governance
is in the increased centrality of a new binary: the 'real' and the 'artificial'.[54]
Resilience-thinking governs complexity through attention to (and construction of) the 'real' processes underpinning appearances rather than through
attempts to shape and direct according to preconceived goals, an approach
now understood to be 'artificial' and reductionist.

The governance focus on the interactions of the present – freed from
the neoliberal determinism of the past and the classical liberal reductionism
of linear constructions of the future – has largely centered on the power of
networks to symbolise the growth of complex interconnections. Networked
understandings are particularly important as they suggest much broader
chains of overlapping connection and the construction of publics and communities of interest, which are free from the rationalist liberal model of representation. The institutional setting for resilience-thinking and governance
through complexity is neither state frameworks of representation nor the
competition of the market but the construction or recognition of 'negotiated moral communities' capable of self-organising in relation to the shared
world.[55] These communities of interconnection become resilient in their
capacities to work with the reality of emergent order only when they are
able to be self-reflective enough to be aware of their embedded productive
agency at multiple levels of interconnectivity.

This sensitivity to relational embeddedness is the key to resilience-thinking
rather than the development of a specific rationality (conscious or otherwise).
It is alleged that only by returning power to the individuals and communities,

who really have the power to self-organise in relation to the problem, can complexity become a force for governance rather than a barrier to it. Often, examples of self-organising order are given in relation to communities on the World Wide Web, which are self-ordering, driven neither by profits nor by instrumental ends but through the construction of a shared community. One such example could be eBay where the trustworthiness of the site is driven by reviewer feedback.[56] As we shall see below and in the following chapters, this networked construction of community is dependent upon understanding a relationship of communicative feedback (both materially and immaterially) through connection to a specific local issue (for example, of flood risk) or a global concern (such as global warming or international human rights).

Adaptive life as the solution to complexity

If the world of complexity is not amenable to liberal modernist understandings or practices, it nevertheless seems to promise alternative approaches to governance which can be learnt from understanding the mechanisms and processes of life as complexity. As we have seen above, complex life forms an adaptive system which can evolve and develop using more 'natural', 'innate', or 'intuitive' approaches. Complex life appears to 'think' and to 'act' and to 'problem solve' very differently to linear and reductive modernist understandings. Complex life appears to be self-governing at the level of the individual and the collectivity or assemblage. There is no directing centre or controller, no agent who possesses superior knowledge or information. Importantly, the actors in these complex webs of interdependence or collectivities, whether they are insect colonies, immune systems or ecosocial systems, are not necessarily acting consciously or instrumentally.

While complexity seems to undermine liberal forms of government, seeking to represent, to know, to direct and to control, it also seems to be able to construct new possibilities and new forms of agency, which can be governed in a non-linear world. In this way, the erosion of old forms of governing and old forms of constructing subjects of governance is not seen to be problematic but positive. It seems that even the most hierarchical of organisations are learning the lessons of 'reality', diversifying decision-making and no longer imposing top-down 'big-picture' understandings of the world. Tim Harford's best-selling book, *Adapt*, provides useful insights here, focusing particularly on the change in US military strategy to deal with the insurgency in Iraq.[57] Resilience-thinking tells us that for governance to mirror the achievements of complex emerging order, it is better to allow for flexibility and variation in approaches to problems; in this way 'life' produces the strategies of governance from the micro-tactics of actors at the lower levels of engagement. For complex order to emerge, the problem is not one of leaders pursuing mistaken strategy but one of top-down hierarchy per se. Complex life cannot be governed through the imposition of policy-directives as the best strategy cannot be known in advance. Governance needs to evolve in the same way as complex life itself – through local adaptation.

The key to complex life as a framework for governance through resilience is the understanding of dissipative systems as generative of order rather than disorder through interactive adaptation. Ulrich Beck provided an early insight into the transformation of politics in the age of non-linearity. Rather than complain about the breakdown in traditional forms of association, Beck argued that the only solution was to encourage this process of greater freedom:

> What astonishes and angers me is that the conservative wailing about the alleged decline of values is not only completely false, it also obstructs the view of precisely the sources and movements from which can be created a readiness to take on the tasks of the future. The much demonized decline of values actually produces the orientations and prerequisites which, if anything can, will put this society in a position to master the future.[58]

Beck reformulated the loss of modernist framings of centralised power and shared frameworks of traditional values and meaning, as a crisis for old ways of governing but an opportunity for new understandings of governing through complexity. Rather than resisting change or looking back to the past, resilience-thinking suggests forward-looking approaches to governance, through adapting to and facilitating society's own inner rhythms and drives, and encouraging the 'reality' of complex life as a diversification of power and responsibility and the growth of more empowered individuals:

> The basic idea is that without the expansion and strengthening of political freedom and its social form, civil society, nothing will work in the future. In this regard, it is important first of all to recognize that changing values and acceptance of democracy go hand in hand. An inner kinship exists between the values of self-development and the ideal of democracy.[59]

Resilience-thinking develops as the reinterpretation of problems of the 'first modernity' as solutions to the 'second modernity'. The decline of 'first modernity' forms of representation can therefore be reinterpreted as the rise of 'second modernity' forms of empowerment. Beck powerfully argues the case that governments should make the most of 'real' life processes rather than resist them:

Personal responsibility, self-organization and personal politics are getting an enlightened and realistic chance to redistribute responsibility and power in society, but this opportunity must now be seized by a politics that is hitting its limits in every respect.[60]

Resilience thereby asserts that the implosion of the governing artifice of modernity is an act of serendipity because apparently: 'People are better adapted to the future than are social institutions and their representatives.'[61] Complex life can only be governed through the micro-knowledge and micro-tactics of those most 'in-touch' with this 'reality': those with the innate or tacit knowledge required to respond and adapt.[62] The fact that people are considered better at governing complexity than governments is the starting point for resilience-thinking as 'life-politics'. Complex life is, in fact, amazingly governance-friendly once it is appreciated rather than problematised. The reason for this is that 'agency is everywhere at every social level', and not just human actors (as if this was not enough) but non-human agents also involved in collective, networked, understandings and practices and the actions and interactions of these assemblages or collectivities at different and overlapping levels.[63] In non-linear systems, the demand for governance is unlimited, once it is understood that governance can only take place through 'agency' rather than as a directing or controlling power over or against agency.

Conclusion

The importance of contextual knowledge in governing complex life is understood to give time and space back their active importance, rather than being understood as 'empty'. Whereas for simple complexity understandings, external governance interventions, to adjust or rectify on the basis of the knowledge of these interactive processes is conceptually possible; under conditions of general complexity this knowledge can only be provisional and ongoing through a relational process itself. Here, the knowledge acquired through complex life is inseparable from the process of governing it and cannot be developed outside of this relational process. It is important to note that the ontological framing of interactive emergence challenges both modernist linear understandings and neoliberal and post-structuralist views that the human subject can externally intervene in and understand the real processes at play or reveal the hidden workings of power behind phenomenological constructions.

For resilience-thinking, the type of knowledge that is possible is necessarily concrete rather than abstract; therefore, complexity- and resilience-thinking lends itself to action-research methods engaging with actors in the situation, rather than to expert knowledge generated by liberal and neoliberal policy-approaches. This blurs the line between policy-work and research and researcher and research subject as the praxis of local engagement, and 'giving voice' becomes transformative in its own right.[64] In resilience-framings, parochial or local knowledges are not a limit but a policy goal, once it is understood that all knowledge can only be local, contextual and time and place specific. This is the reality of the world, seemingly reflected in the 'ontological turn' of social theory: the pluralist growth of different knowledges (and forms of knowing) is not merely a pragmatic response to the unknowability of the world but is a result of knowing the world, as it is, in its complex reality.[65]

This understanding probably goes furthest in the work of post-humanist or non-representational theory, which suggests that we need to reject not only the ontology of liberal reductionist thought but also the idea that rationalist thought is the key to practices of governance. Nigel Thrift and other non-representational theorists have done much work over recent years suggesting that the role of conscious representation in human interaction has been overemphasised at the expense of the role of embodied practices. In his chapter 'Life, But Not as We Know It', Thrift draws upon the general thematic presented in this book, of life as both resistance to liberal representation and as opening up new political potentials, calling new publics and new forms of politics into existence.[66] This perspective is equally prevalent in resilience policy advocacy. For example, the postscript to Walker and Salt's *Resilience Thinking* discusses the lessons of Hurricane Katrina, which hit New Orleans in September 2004.[67] The problem is constructed in terms of the dangers of artifice over life: the pursuit of short-term demands of residential, tourist and commercial development, which undermined the 'natural buffers' in place. The solution is to return the power of governing to 'life' itself – to a community, empowered and self-reflexively aware of their relational embeddedness:

> If the local communities had known more about the ecological drivers of the regions in which they lived, had they embraced the processes of natural change rather than attempted to control them for short-term returns, had they been empowered to make their own decisions about what type of developments were appropriate for their area, and had they been given responsibility to learn to adapt to the changes happening around them then it's likely they would have been much better prepared for the disturbances that hit them.[68]

The life politics of complexity and resilience call attention to the importance of diversifying decision-making power and shifting from centralised 'big-picture' understandings. Here, as we shall see later in the book, the rise of the local is important as local knowledge becomes a vital resource. Attention to diverse cultural values and understandings is also increasingly valuable as often these are more attuned to the 'reality' of complex life than the abstract and reductionist understandings of top-down rationalist approaches. It also suggests that rather than depending upon received wisdom, 'life' itself should be regularly consulted and engaged in the policy-process, through the use of randomised or controlled clinical trials and other methods of engagement. These processes of involvement can then enable complex life to reveal or represent itself and to suggest methods of governance which 'artificial' reductionist understandings of governance are unable to see or to comprehend.[69]

Notes

1 Walker and Salt, 2006: p.xiv.
2 At least at our current level of understanding and technological development.
3 Prigogine and Stengers, 1984: p.292.
4 See, for example, the treatment in Byrne and Callaghan, 2014: pp.86–106.
5 Ibid.: pp.4–5; Toffler, 1984: p.xi.
6 Cilliers, 1998: pp.viii–ix.
7 See, Mitchell, 2009: p.ix.
8 René Descartes, *Meditations* and *Discourse on Method*, originally published in the 1630s.
9 Toulmin, 1990: p.139.
10 Ibid. This instrumental view of the power interests behind modernity is also forwarded by Bruno Latour, 1993, 2004a.
11 Naím, 2013: pp.35–50.
12 Lippmann, 1993; Dewey, 1927.
13 See, for example, Beck, 1992; Giddens, 1994.
14 See, for example, the writings of Beck and Latour regarding whether the collapse of (the 'first') modernity is a matter of a changing material reality or a shift in the ways in which this reality is interpreted; see especially Latour, 2003.
15 Prigogine and Stengers, 1984: p.309.
16 See, for example, Harford, 2012: pp.3–8. The next section considers this emergent view of complexity as vital to the focus on the power of 'life', essential to resilience-thinking as a governing rationality.
17 Gleick, 1998.
18 Lyotard, 1984: p.55.
19 Ibid.: 56.
20 Ibid.: 57.
21 As noted by Norman Farmer and J. Doyne Packard, complexity theory for this reason is the 'related opposite' of chaos theory (cited in Resnick, 1999: p.14).
22 Byrne and Callaghan, *Complexity Theory and the Social Sciences*. Whereas they argue for the importance of the ontology of life as general complexity, it is precisely this paradigm, and the policy practices and understandings stemming from it, that this book seeks to critically analyse.

23 For this reason Prigogine and Stengers are too reductive in stating that
evolutionary paradigms can be distinguished from each other, as they include
'isolated systems that evolve to disorder and open systems that evolve to higher
and higher forms of complexity' (1984: p.298). This works in terms of their
concern of distinguishing complexity from chaos theory but does not assist in
social science analysis, where it is important to distinguish simple complexity –
where the closed nature of systemic interaction is essential for an external
subject position of governance intervention into the problematic – from general
complexity where no such separation between analyst or policy-maker and the
problem to be governed is possible.

24 See discussion in Mitchell, 2009: pp.40–55.

25 See, for example, Gould, 2007.

26 Mitchell, 2009: pp.60–70.

27 Of course, there are major ontological claims at stake here in the level of
'agency' associated with micro-level 'actants', such as cells and individual insects;
nevertheless, at this point it is only necessary to set out the claims themselves
and note their increasingly widespread acceptance.

28 See, for example, the treatment in Johnson, 2001: pp.33–41.

29 For example, Harford, 2012: pp.83–114.

30 The prisoner's dilemma is a canonical example of a game analyzed in game
theory that shows why two individuals might not cooperate, even if it appears
that it is in their best interests to do so. Examples have been extended to the
analysis of international conflict and to problems of cooperation to deal with
global warming.

31 Garside, 2013.

32 Ibid.

33 Ibid. It is important to note the governing rationality at work rather than
the simple use of the word 'resilience'. As this quote makes clear, classical
understandings of resilience as a fixed property clash with post-classical
understandings of resilience as the product of a contingent relational process.

34 Prigogine and Stengers, 1984, 1997.

35 See, in particular, Prigogine and Stengers, 1997.

36 See, for example, Kauffman, 1993.

37 Kauffman, 2008.

38 Ibid.: p.x.

39 Ibid.: p.xi.

40 Evolutionary biologist Leslie Orgel was famous for his second rule of evolution:
'Evolution is cleverer than you are.' See, for example, the discussion in Dennett,
2005.

41 Room, 2011: pp.33–49.

42 See further, Holling, 1973.

43 Harford, 2012: p.175.

44 Plehwe, 2009.

45 Hayek, 1952.

46 Mirowski, 2002: pp.232–40.

47 Hayek, *The Sensory Order*, 1952: p.25.

48 See, for example, North, 1990, 1999, 2005.

49 As Byrne and Callaghan note (2014: p.9), this form of reductionist or restricted complexity theorising is predominant in US discourse, relying largely on directly applying methods developed in physics and applied mathematics to the social world, popularly exemplified in the work of Melanie Mitchell and Stuart Kauffman, whose works are cited above.

50 Perhaps the most extreme social theorising in terms of closed autopoietic processes is that of Niklas Luhmann, where social actors can have no privileged knowledge of their environment; see, for example, Luhmann, 1995.

51 See Chandler, 2013a.

52 Giddens, 1994.

53 The most often cited examples being those of Stalin's ambitious industrialisation initiatives in the 1930s, such as the construction of the Lenin Dam or the steel mills of Magnitogorsk, both of which resulted in human and environmental disaster; see, for example, Harford, 2012.

54 See Khalil, 1996; Schmidt, 2013.

55 Ostrom, 1990.

56 See further, Johnson, 2001: p.222.

57 Harford, 2012: pp.43–79.

58 Beck, 2002: p.161.

59 Ibid.

60 Ibid.: p.163.

61 Ibid.: p.162.

62 See also Scott, 1998.

63 See, for example, Byrne and Callaghan, 2014: p.193.

64 See, for example, Bang, 2004.

65 As in the development of new materialist analyses, see, for example, Connolly, 2011; Bennett, 2010.

66 Thrift, 2008: p.3

67 Walker and Salt, 2006: pp.153–4.

68 Ibid.

69 Harford, 2012: pp.120–31; Room, 2011: pp.306–10.

3
RESILIENCE

Putting life to work

Introduction

In the face of our growing awareness of complexity, resilience seems to be
an increasingly ubiquitous concept. There is a good chance that any policy
document about international relations, development, conflict-resolution or
environmental degradation will give the term a prominent role, let alone policy interventions in domestic politics, concerning educational performance,
welfare and social needs. However (as noted in the introductory chapter), the
fact that the concept appears to be everywhere does not mean that it is clear
exactly what it is doing or why so many different policy organisations working in so many different spheres seem to have taken it up. Nevertheless, for
many commentators, the rise of resilience is straightforward, they find a definition of resilience – 'the ability to bounce-back', to 'reflexively engage with
a complex world', etc. and then argue that this is necessary because the world
is more globalised, fluid and complex. The only mystery is why it took us so
long to realise that a policy rethink along the lines of resilience was necessary. It is not just policy advocates who are at home in the world of resilience
advocacy. For critical theorists, the rise of resilience is often straightforward as
well, once it is linked to the neoliberal needs of capitalism or the need to gov-
ernmentalise responsible or docile subjects.[1] In both policy advocacy and in
much of the critical analyses, resilience is a secondary-product of the world –
a reflection either of global complexity or of the needs of power. Resilience
itself, as a concept, is not seriously engaged with, and works on the topic
then tell us little that is new and, depending on our political perspectives,

we can make a normative case for or against resilience depending on whether we wish to think in terms of problem-solving in a world of complexity or in terms of resisting the dominant needs of power, states and markets.

This chapter takes a different approach which, while putting resilience at the centre of our understanding of politics and policy-making today, as the advocates insist, also problematises the concept on its own terms (rather than using resilience as a foil for a restatement of traditional Marxist or critical sociological exposures of power and hegemony). It understands resilience-thinking as an invitation to reconsider how we understand the world and the human subject. For this reason, it argues, resilience needs to be taken seriously as an emerging conceptual paradigm: a particular way of telling the truth of the world. Resilience can, in this way, be understood as an emerging framework that facilitates the adaption of policy-making to a world in which politics seems to be in need of radical renewal and rethinking. It is a framework that enables us to, first, accept the loss of modernist understandings and, second, to understand this as not a loss but as a positive gain, a realisation of a truth of the world, which we were somehow blind to before. Taking this more analytical view of resilience as a way of rethinking the practices and understandings of politics, we will approach resilience as a way of thinking about how we think about the being of being. This may sound a little Heideggerian or contrived: it is not. The argument of this book is that resilience-thinking can be understood as the first post-liberal or post-modern episteme: the first coherent, positive, alternative to modernist frameworks of the subject and the world.

Resilience, as a way of thinking about how we think about the being of being, can be understood in Foucauldian terms as a new 'regime of truth' or 'discourse of veridiction';[2] as a framework which enables us to reflect upon, to test, to examine and to negotiate a radically different understanding of the world. When policy advocates and academics think about resilience, they are thinking about how to think differently and about how to see the world differently. They suggest that policy actors need to open themselves up to the world as a site of empirical testing and understanding and that the world tells us that we need to learn certain types of truths or policy 'lessons': that we need to reconsider what we do when we intervene or make policy in the world. As emphasised in the previous chapter, this reflective process is often highlighted when policy problems are addressed in terms of their complex nature; an increasingly dominant issue in our fluid, fast-moving and interconnected global world. It appears that there is only one way in which we can think about governing in a world of complexity: that is through the new 'truths' about 'reality' uncovered with the help of resilience-thinking.

Resilience as a discourse of veridiction does not just allow us to think about how we govern in a world of complexity as if this was merely a technical matter of governing differently in the world. If this was the case, then there would be no problem with the two positions outlined above, in which resilience was understood unproblematically in terms of problem-solving or as amenable to traditional critiques from social and critical theory. Resilience-thinking does not just allow us to adapt to a more complex, fluid and uncertain world. Resilience-thinking enables us to understand this as a radically different world: a world in which everything we thought under liberal modernity needs to be re-evaluated. While the previous chapter dealt with this re-evaluation in terms of the shift from reductionist or linear ontologies to process-based or complex ones, this chapter is concerned with how this process of re-evaluation was engendered in political understandings of power and resistance, through concrete historical struggles over the nature and meaning of political life.

Foucault famously suggested that rather than critiquing discourses of truth as somehow based upon 'false' knowledge or as merely serving the interests of power, they should be critically interrogated to understand the practices and frameworks which enable a certain truth of the world to be constructed:[3]

> That is to say ... not how an error ... or how an illusion could be born, but how a particular regime of truth ... makes something that does not exist able to become something. It is not an illusion since it is precisely a set of practices, real practices, which established it and thus imperiously marks it out in reality.[4]

Foucault suggested a sceptical approach to truth claims, such as those of resilience-thinking, which grasps them as practices that construct an understanding of the world we live in through a very specific 'game of truth'.[5] Discourses set out the rules of the game of understanding, the game of truth-telling; but these truths are the product of the assumptions of the particular discourse. It is these assumptions, their 'conditions of possibility', their form of articulation and the practical history of struggle and contestation which produced them, that this chapter seeks to investigate. Critical understanding will be understood here neither as dependent upon disproving the discourse – for example, by denying complexity or by reasserting that we live in a modernist world of structure and agency, or a world of Cartesian subjects able to know and to control – nor as involving the assertion of the class or power-based interests being served through a particular discourse, as if the critique of liberalism or neoliberalism, capitalism or power in general, could stand in for an analytical engagement with the rise of resilience-thinking as the solution to policy-making in a world of complexity.

What this book seeks to analyse are the stakes involved in the ontologies of the world as apprehended in and through the truth discourse of resilience-thinking, particularly the ontology of the human subject and the world, provided and produced through this discourse. If the classical liberal subject is conceived as acting in a universal linear world of passive objects, open to knowledge, control and direction, and the neoliberal subject is conceived as acting in a plural and non-linear world of closed endogenous systems, tending to reproduce difference on the basis of cultural evolution and path-dependencies, then the resilient subject appears to be conceived of as acting in a complex, interactive world, where non-linearity is seen to constantly create possibilities for self-reflexive action in the world. In the complex world, it seems life is too fluid and too interactive to be governed from above through systems of formal political representation. The governance of resilience-thinking therefore concerns the informal, the social and the 'real' interactions of societal behaviour rather than our choices in the public sphere of politics and law. The reduction of the public sphere to that of societal interaction enables new forms of governance but implies a major shift in the location and meaning of politics whereby the formal barriers of liberal modernist think-ing dissolve or are overcome, such as those between the international and the domestic, the public and the private, the state and society. This chapter is therefore concerned with developing an analysis of how resilience-thinking works in constructing a world in which the complexity of life both estab-lishes the need for governance and provides a solution to the problem of governance.

The next sections recap the ontology of resilience in political terms, build on the assumptions set out in the previous chapter on complexity, and seek to unpack the resonance of the ontological framing of complex-ity and resilience, suggesting that this 'truth' of how governance operates in the world is emerging rather than entering the world fully formed as the product of a new scientific or theoretical breakthrough or strategic act of dominant power. Key to the argument will be an alternative genealogy of the rise of resilience, one that is based not on the scientific discoveries of physics, ecology, psychology or economic theorising but on the struggles and disappointments of the political sphere itself. It will be suggested that the resilience-thinking ontology of the world, where formal political power needs to be guided by the 'real' processes of the production of complex life, stems from radical and critical struggles and disappointments, especially in the experience of the post-Marxist Left after 1968 in France and Italy. It will be further argued that this shift from the formal political sphere to the focus on the power of 'real life' itself only became mainstreamed and then a dominant or 'commonsense' truth of the world with the collapse of Left/ Right understandings which gave content to liberal representative frameworks of the political.

The ontology of resilience

Resilience-thinking articulates a very different ontological understanding of the world – it sees the composition of the world in a very different way. At stake here is not merely different forms of being – giving importance to different facets of the world or different actors (individuals, families, firms, communities, states, interstate organisations, NGOs, etc.) – but the nature of being itself. For resilience-thinking, the nature of being is complex, relational, embedded and contextual. The world is not amenable to appropriation within liberal frameworks of representation with their attention to the autonomy of distinct, separate, individual actors and universal understandings of causal connections, structures and rationalities. For resilience-thinking, there is no problematic of the universal and the particular: there are neither fixed universals nor isolated particular subjects. There is no reductionist divide between subject and object, between culture and environment, between agent and structure, between public and private, between politics and economics, between production and consumption or between facts and values: resilience works on a different and very distinct ontological basis.

As noted in the previous chapter, resilience as a paradigm of policy-making and academic understanding operates to provide a positive agenda for governance through a radical reworking of neoliberal understandings of the limits to liberal modernist frameworks of representation. The ontology of complexity transforms a neoliberal critique of the rationalist promise of liberalism into a positive project of managing change. It does this because non-linear understandings go from being a limit, explaining difference in a linear world, to being an asset in a world now conceived as complex and non-linear. Whereas neoliberal thought sought to naturalise or essentialise limits to liberal aspirations for universal progress, resilience-thinking radicalises the neoliberal episteme to argue that these limits need to be reposed as resources to be drawn upon.

The neoliberal episteme critiqued the epistemological assumptions of classical liberalism, based upon understanding the human subject as a Cartesian subject – universal, rational and autonomous. These assumptions formed the basis for legitimising both the liberal regimes of universal democracy and legal equality and the assumptions of market equilibrium and perfect competition. Neoliberalism instead highlighted the limits to the free operation of democracy and the market and located these limits in the bounded, relational and context-dependent rationality of the subject. Differential, bounded and limited rationalities meant that there was no natural tendency towards understanding, progress or development and that the reproduction of social and economic inequalities could be understood as a product of human social, historical and cultural path-dependencies, rather than as a problem with the market relations of capitalism per se.[6]

Schematically put, classical liberal modernist understandings articulated a discourse of sovereign power – a rationalist, top-down, state-based, view of political dominion of humanity over nature where, with the growth of science and technology, the secrets of life would be revealed and natural laws put to the service of human benefit. Neoliberal critiques of liberal universal assumptions questioned the capacity of human reason to shape and direct life, arguing that human understandings and responses to the world were shaped by embedded social relations, norms, ideas and cultural path-dependencies and that there was no such thing as a universal rationality. Where liberalism posited a linear understanding of the world, amenable to human understanding and capable of human transformation, neoliberalism argued that human social interaction was much less amenable to scientific understanding or social engineering and that policy-making led to non-linear outcomes, shaped by the specific rationalities and understandings of individuals and societies.[7]

Essentially this was an epistemological critique of liberalism, understanding human rationality as the barrier to universal progress. This epistemological focus on differential understandings and rationalities has been radicalised through resilience-thinking, which draws upon a different ontological understanding of the human and the world, arguing that the world is not amenable to rationalist approaches and understandings which set the human apart from the world and that our experiential, differentiated responses and rationalities serve us much better than attempts to transform these rationalities or adapt them to liberal reason. In effect, rather than a liberal understanding of human political collectivities ruling over life, resilience-thinking insists that life has to rule or govern policy-making.

Whereas life – the plural and embedded nature of human reasoning – was understood to be the limit or problem for neoliberalism, for resilience-thinking, human relational embeddedness and plural rationalities enable interactive adaptation to a fluid complex world once the problem of the liberal episteme has been overcome. Resilience-thinking does not problematise those who are suffering from economic and social exclusion, conflict or underdevelopment and naturalise the problems as a product of their differentiated or limited rationality. Rather, it sees the most marginal or oppressed as the agents of policy solutions through the understanding and channelling of their differentiated rationalities and local knowledges and understandings (as discussed in the conclusion to the previous chapter). The limits for neoliberal framings become transformed into a positive programme of governance, into assets or solutions under the rubric of resilience. Parochial or localised understandings are no longer a limit factor but are to be encouraged and facilitated as a policy goal, once it is understood that there can be no universal top-down solution to problems but only ever plural and differentiated, context-dependent, bottom-up solutions. Whereas neoliberalism argues that transformative projects of socialism or communism will inevitably end in failure, the radical inversion of neoliberalism argues that all projects of governing have to cope with failure as a positive process of learning and development.[8]

The 'resonance' of resilience and complexity

It is useful to consider resilience-thinking along the lines of William Connolly's conception of a 'resonance machine'.[9] Resilience-thinking emerges from today's cultural and political context without having been designed by any central agent, theorist or institution of power, but is self-amplifying, seemingly driven by its own dynamic.[10] Resilience-thinking is a 'resonance machine' in this respect: sucking in traditional understandings of cause and effect, of subjects and structures, and belching out new conceptions of complexity, non-linearity and relational dynamics. For Connolly, the resonance machine of 'evangelical-capitalism' involved the amplification and positive-feedback between evangelical Christianity and 'cowboy capitalism', fed by the electronic news media, but not consciously planned or manipulated by the needs of either political economy or religion, constituting a 'qualitative assemblage resistant to classical models of explanation' based on self-interest and means-ends instrumentality.[11] The binding together of these different constituencies is understood more on the lines of a shared and developing set of sensitivities or a 'circulating ethos' rather than anything thought through or concretised.[12]

I think Connolly's points about the lack of instrumentality and systemisation are important here, for, as has been highlighted already, resilience-thinking does not emerge from a clear conceptual framework or set of generalisable practices and seems to be driven by a compulsion which is expressed more as an ethos or sensitivity – an awareness that power or government cannot work in the old way and that problems in the world (complexity) appear to call forth or elicit a new approach to governance which is in the process of being negotiated and formulated clearly. The world of resilience-thinking and complexity is more like a 'condition' which we find ourselves in, than something produced through political contestation or instrumentality. It seems to have emerged without a political subject bringing it into existence. In this sense, resilience can be understood as a 'resonance machine', which is self-amplifying: where commentators continually appear to learn policy-lessons making them more aware of what resilience might mean and how life can be governed differently through this knowledge. The 'truths' of resilience-thinking seem to be emerging from our engagement with the world rather than appearing as a consequence of a new theory or discovery or coherent political or ideological project.

Resilience-thinking appears to be developing in a self-amplifying way as our experience of the world makes theories of adaption, emergence and complexity seem sensible to us – makes them even appear as necessary – and thereby to reflect the world in a better way than the liberal episteme, with all its reductionist and linear assumptions. This 'resonance machine', operating below the level of conceptual and political or ideological clarity and contestation, reflects a certain synergy between dominant trends of critical and neoliberal thinking which would otherwise be considered separate. In the same way that Connolly argues that although there may not have seemed to be a lot of conscious or ideological connection between evangelical Christians and corporate bankers, certain shared synergies of sentiment and ethos are held to have created a powerful basis of reasoning. The rest of this chapter fleshes out how this approach can be used in analysis of how resilience-thinking has developed through a powerful set of cultural sensitivities to become an almost 'natural' or 'commonsense' way of looking at the world, bringing together both policy-makers and radical critics.

The resilience 'machine' appears to be drawing more and more areas and themes into itself, transforming their understandings of power and subjectivity and producing new theories of the world: enabling more and more policy actors to see the world in terms of 'new materialism', actor-networks, philosophical pragmatism, post-humanism, complexity, emergent causality, adaptive systems and non-linearity. Resilience is thereby transformative: a 'machine' which transforms our understandings of ourselves and our world. In Nietzschean terms, the emergence of resilience-thinking enables the revaluation or 'transvaluation' of modernist values, much as Christianity was able to turn over or invert humanist values, exalting the weak against the strong and suffering over pleasure.[13] Resilience-thinking can be understood as transvaluing modernist values in a similarly nihilist manner, celebrating incapacity over capacity, unknowability over knowledge and failure over success. It is held that in a world of ontological complexity, liberal modernist attempts to understand, to shape, to direct and to transform the world for human ends are hubristic and dangerous. Even liberal attempts to set humans up as distinct from the world, through the twin fields of science and politics, are seen to be barriers to governing in a world of complexity.

Resilience transvalues liberal aspirations to constitute new understandings of what it means to govern in a complex world. This transvaluation can be grasped as an inversion of liberal understandings, which sought to construct an artificial human world of politics – of constitutions, representation, rights, law and decision-making – over and above the complexities of the natural or real world. In resilience frameworks, the world of politics cannot sit external to the world and cannot operate somehow over or above the complexities of our relations and embeddedness. The formal politics of the public sphere are therefore seen as much less relevant to governing – to power and to decision-making – than under liberal framings. The public sphere is useful to discuss and debate and reflect upon our ethical commitments but not in terms of constituting a power over the world, a power of law-making and a power of directing or controlling social forces. Politics, it appears, is liberated or freed from the artifices of liberalism and is no longer seen as somehow separate to the spheres of culture, economics and social life. Under resilience, politics returns to 'the people', to the sphere of our 'everyday' practices, interactions and understandings.

The hidden genealogy of resilience

While some work is critical of the concept of resilience – predominately by asserting that it is a framework for neoliberal understanding - for many radical or critical thinkers ambiguity seems to dominate, arguing that resilience is problematic when used by hegemonic power but that understandings of adaptive complexity can be useful tools of oppositional critique.[14] Jeremy Walker and Melinda Cooper raise the interesting question of why – despite its prevalence as a policy concept – there is so little critical engagement with the assumptions of resilience-thinking on their own terms. They argue that:

> Almost by definition, complex systems internalize and neutralize all external challenges to their existence, transforming perturbation into an endogenous feature of the system and a catalyst to further self-differentiation. ... In its tendency to metabolize all countervailing forces and inoculate itself against critique, 'resilience thinking' cannot be challenged from within the terms of complex systems theory but must be contested, if at all, on completely different terms, by a movement of thought that is truly counter-systemic.[15]

Unfortunately, Walker and Cooper do not elaborate on what a 'truly counter-systemic' movement of thought could look like, perhaps because of the obvious difficulties of countering resilience-thinking with reductionist frameworks of linear cause and effect. In fact, sensitivity to systemic understandings – the interactive nature of the 'human condition'[16] and the necessarily contingent nature of sociopolitical outcomes – has meant that the social sciences traditionally had demarcated themselves from the natural sciences on this point in particular.[17] In fact, it is precisely the rich awareness of the importance of systemic understandings – in particular, for the history of Marxist progressive and anti-capitalist thought – that is vital in understanding the conundrum which resilience-thinking poses for radical and critical theorists. Here, it is important to draw out the synergies between neoliberal and critical sociological critiques of classical liberal ontological and epistemological claims and their shared concerns with drawing attention to the limits of the constituted power of government.

Rather than seek to achieve power, radical political and social thought, especially since the intellectual disillusionment with official Communist Party positions and attitudes after the Soviet crushing of the Hungarian uprising of 1956 or the Prague Spring and the student movements of 1968, has sought to expose, to deconstruct and to reveal the limits of power. Power, especially state power, became increasingly presented as an artificial barrier to social progress rather than its means. With the end of the Cold War in 1989, the world rapidly caught up with the disillusioned post-Marxist Left. Immediately after the end of the Cold War, it appeared that the world was 'globalised', and it was held that globalisation weakened the coherence and power of formally constituted government at the state level, and over the last quarter of a century this power has seemingly continued to wane.[18] In a complex, fluid and indeterminate world, it appears that governing in the old ways is not just no longer possible but actually is a barrier to governing complexity.

It would appear that in a world where constituted power is necessarily doomed to fail, all we can do is 'learn to fail better':[19] learn to fail through not attempting anything too ambitious and learn to fail through being continually self-reflective about the unintended and unexpected consequences of any policy-interventions. The failure of constituted power is written into the psyche of critical social thought in the late twentieth and early twenty-first centuries. Foucault is seen to have taught us that power creates resistance – that power continually works against and constitutes its own limits.[20] Many critical post-Marxists have asserted that, in fact, resistance preexists power and drives power,[21] or that power depends on critique and resistance.[22] Ernesto Laclau and Chantal Mouffe inform us that hegemony can never be complete, that power will always be challenged.[23] For Laclau, any discourse of power will contain its own contradiction and aporias – power doesn't fail by accident, or even because of resistance, but because of the necessary flaws of any discourse of power.[24] Today, the limits of power are conceived not merely in terms of the inability of constituted power to contain resistance, but also in terms of the ontological limits of power to act in the world. Things, objects, the world – as complex life itself – resist power or are recalcitrant to its commands.[25]

For Anthony Giddens and Ulrich Beck, the inability of power to rule in the world is a recent product of globalisation, of manufactured risk and uncertainty, reflecting the closure of the liberal telos of progress, with the realisation that all attempts to resolve problems through the advancement of science and technology will have unintended 'side-effects' which merely re-create problems on a new level.[26] While Giddens and Beck follow Walter Lippmann and John Dewey in suggesting that it is the new technological age of globalised complexity which compels governance to shift in approach, others have gone much further.[27] Bruno Latour, for example, argues that this problem is not new and that modernity itself was always an illusion.[28] Discourses of resilience therefore take the form of radical and thorough critique – a critique which seems to be confirmed by the world itself. In fact, this critique seems to be so fitted to our world of complexity that even the idea of theorising beneath the surface to find hidden structures and social forces is held to be hubristic. If reductionist or linear views of determination are no longer viable, then the focus on interactive or emergent outcomes necessarily deals with the concrete surface of the world as it appears, and can be traced *post hoc* through identifying the specific contingent interconnections. As Jessica Schmidt argues: 'the critique of artifice is launched from a phenomenological perspective of reality in which surface appearances are construed as the secondary product of contingent processes of interaction';[29] thus any search for hidden structures becomes pointless.

Thereby, resilience-thinking, in its transvaluation of modernist values, understands critique as not to be about unearthing 'essences' or structures but about tracing surface connections and following the actors in their everyday practices and understandings. Empiricism is the new method of critique because the reality of the world is seen to have been obscured by social science, which has attempted to set itself up above the world. Critique is a reflective appreciation of the appearances of the world rather than an elitist project of revealing hidden truths, to which ordinary people are apparently blind.[30] This appreciation of the surface appearances depends on the ontological understanding that these appearances, often ignored by social scientists, reveal the hidden truths of social relationality and the power of micro-practices to produce the world. Reflective understanding of appearances is seen to lead to a greater grasp of 'reality' than working from abstract (fictional) structures or social forces to attempt to understand the concrete or 'real'.

On this basis, it seems possible to offer an alternative understanding and genealogy of resilience using the Nietzschean analytics of ressentiment. Ressentiment, in the framework of Nietzsche, is not merely a negative reaction against power but a creative act of revaluation; the construction of a different moral ordering based upon the inversion of dominant understandings but with the aim of still achieving the original goal of progress or transformation. It is important to draw out the positive and creative aspects of ressentiment as a heuristic mechanism for analysing the 'resonance machine' of resilience. Resilience, in its creative reordering of modernist liberal values, does not just reject power; it also posits the possibility of achieving social goals through this rejection. This analytic will be used to distinguish resilience approaches from neoliberalism – pointing out how resilience-thinking goes beyond neoliberal discourses (which themselves range from a defensive argument against the possibility of change towards a more active and interventionist approach of adaptation).[31] Resilience increasingly points to a move beyond active and interventionist neoliberal understandings of resilience as adaptation to a more generalised inculcation of adaptivity and self-reflexivity. Resilience (unlike neoliberalism) has a potentially coherent programme of governing in order to achieve emergent goals in an age of complexity rather than just seeking to maintain the status quo or suggesting that it is hard to go beyond this – it is this positive governing agenda which enables the discourse to be so dynamic in its transvaluation of modernist values.

If resilience was merely a brand of non-linear or agent-based modelling, as proposed in neoliberal or new institutionalist understandings, it would lack this transformative dynamic. The epistemological critique mounted by neoliberalism is a rejection of modernist values and mechanisms but lacks a progressive agenda.[32] The neoliberal framing is more akin to the tale of the fox in Aesop's fable of 'the fox and the grapes', where the hungry fox tries to obtain the ripe black grapes hanging from a vine and cannot reach them, satisfying itself in the belief that 'those grapes are sour, not as ripe as I thought'.[33] Resilience is not merely the rejection of the possibility of modernist aspirations for progress and development or the rejection of the state as a mechanism for wielding collective political power. Resilience transvalues the values of modernity. If the fox was expressing the ressentiment of resilience she would not merely reject the grapes as sour but would revalue her aims themselves and state that 'sweetness is a fiction'. The fox would thereby regard its impotence as positive, not as problematic or as embarrassing.

For Nietzsche, what he called a 'slave' or a 'herd' mentality – a morality that says 'no' to what is 'outside itself', to what is 'different from itself' and 'not itself' – was also a creative impulse, giving birth to new values.[34] Resilience is a negative rejection but one recast as a positive view of the values of the self as a reaction against weakness or failure. Not only are values transvalued but this transvaluation serves as a last-ditch attempt to achieve that which was denied. The weak therefore believe that they will triumph over the strong: that in the 'last judgement' there will be a victory for the righteous and the good and that the 'meek shall inherit the earth'.[35] However, resilience does not come from a rejection of power per se, or a rejection of the values of the ruling class or the aristocratic establishment. As in Nietzsche's 'slave mentality', the creative aspects of ressentiment, which provide the transformative capacities for resilience as a 'resonance machine', have their roots in a historically specific form of disappointment: the ressentiment of the Left.[36]

The creativity of resilience, as an understanding of the limits and impossibilities of constituted power and of reductionist social science, was generated from a groundswell of disaffection and disillusionment with the politics of the official Communist Parties, particularly the two dominant influences of the French Communist Party (PCF) and the Italian Communist Party (PCI).[37] In Italy, this creative rejection could be seen in the development of the workerist (Operaismo) movements after the Hungarian uprising in 1956 and the shift from workerism to the understanding of society as a 'social factory' in the 1970s.[38] In France, we see this rejection cohere in disappointment with the PCF's support for the colonial war against Algeria and attempts to constrict and limit the potential of the 1968 student radical movements. In response, the post-68 or post-Marxist Left cohered around a rejection of linear and reductionist understandings (especially those of economic determinism). This sensibility was clearly reflected in the critical work of radical thinkers like Jacques Rancière, Pierre Bourdieu, Jean-François Lyotard, Jacques Derrida and Michel Foucault, among others. The struggle for a radical alternative to the conservative hold of official Communist Party dogma was not just sought in the different spaces and constituencies, outside the heavily politicised and unionised workplace, but also through the rejection of the 'science' of social laws and processes, which was wielded against any opponents and enabled the hide-bound party elites to claim political legitimacy as the official 'heirs' of Marx and Lenin.

The Italian and French intellectual Left, in their rejection of the Communist Party, developed an alternative creative vision of the possibilities for change and transformation. The product of this intellectual ferment, under these specific political conditions of struggle, was both a clear alternative to state-based modernist aspirations of control and direction (monopolised, both in theory and in practice, by the official Communist Parties) and one which was quite distinct from the pro-market conservative discussion of the limits to state power, articulated by neoliberal critics of social progress. The core aspects of resilience as a 'resonance machine' can be drawn from this rejection of the official Communist Party's domination of progressive or oppositional politics. First, the state-centric telos of economic determinist laws and linear understanding of material progress and development was rejected. The dynamic of change was no longer understood to be linear and homogenous and the view of progress was pluralized into a variety of forms of life-style satisfaction, not merely the material acquisition of wealth. Second, power was also transvalued, away from hierarchical and linear understandings with top-down 'elitist' assumptions of management and control from above. Power was decentred and constructed in much more non-linear, contingent, circulatory and relational ways. Thus power was conceived as a social product, emanating from below, rather than something to be instrumentalised and owned by an elite above society. Third, the role of organisation and theory was also transvalued and democratised; there was no need for a revolutionary party and revolutionary ideologues dictating a party 'line'. The workers movement and the social or student movement could, through their own spontaneous or autonomous self-activity, challenge and resist power by recognising themselves as the 'real' power at work in producing wealth and reproducing the world.

Rather than potentially liberating society, the official Communist Parties were held to be the barrier to change and to be part of the system of control and regulation. In the radical rejection of the politics of the Communist Parties, these understandings were transvalued – rejected at the deepest ontological level. This inversion can be most clearly understood in the development of two fundamentally different conceptions of politics, intentionally contrapositioned: one to indicate the old formal and failed politics of the Communist Party based on the fictional understanding of power, and the other to indicate the real, living (but in some readings, rare and sporadic) politics of social resistance. In Jean-Luc Nancy's work, the distinction between 'la politique', politics on the formal surface or institutional level, and 'le politique', the political on a deeper ontological or philosophical level of the contestation of the meaning of community, draws out this bifurcation clearly.[39] The distinction between artificial and constraining, reductionist understandings of politics and the real politics of the life world is clear in the non-foundationalist or Left Heideggerian critique of formal politics for its fictional and phenomenological nature, for its failure to ever capture the reality of the community at the real or ontological level.[40] This distinction between the limits and artifice of formal politics and the real sphere of political power is also apparent in the radical distinction between potestas/pouvoir, power over, and potentia/puissance, potential, possible or virtual power, derived from Spinoza and rearticulated in the work of Gilles Deleuze as well as in Michael Hardt and Antonio Negri's distinction between constituted power (formal power) and constituent or constitutive power (the power of the potential of the Multitude).[41] As Negri writes: 'potestas' refers to power in its fixed, institutional or 'constituted form', while potentia refers to power in its fluid, dynamic or 'constitutive' form'.[42]

In this rejection of official party politics and government for 'the political' as autonomous potentiality, the post-68 Left transvalued the official dogmas of Marxism and with this transvaluation removed the deterministic foundations of critique on the basis of the economic contradictions of capitalism. The contradictions and limits of modernity concerned the mystification of the surface of appearances, not so much the hidden process of production itself. Liberal forms of power were fictions that needed to be opposed not through struggle on the terms of liberal representation but through bringing into existence the power which really existed in life itself: this real power could change the world without 'taking power'.[43] The problem was the ideational structures of power, which sought to rule over and regulate social processes. The rule of power or of capital was based upon the reification of life – its reduction to the liberal binaries of the formal political and legal sphere, of the collective representative of the state and the atomised individual, the citizen as a bourgeois individual. It was the sphere of representation – how life was understood – that was problematic, not 'real' life itself. Representational understandings mystified the world and were the products of power and ideology, enabling capitalism to rule over real life on the basis of artificial constructions – the reified product of past (dead) labour;[44] freezing, reifying and subverting the ever fluid and creative 'real' values and understandings of those under its rule.[45] The contradictions of capitalism appear as the contradiction between the formal and the informal, representation and that which is (but can never be fully) represented.

This understanding transvalued dogmatic Marxism and in so doing inverted the classical Marxist ontology: capitalism was a surface phenomenon, a secondary and contingent reification of 'real' social processes. The radical, non-Communist Left no longer thereby needed the 'revolutionary science' of elite Party intellectuals – possessors of the 'hidden' truths of the production process and hidden 'laws' of economic determinism and crisis. Instead, power needed to be returned to the people seen as the real power of the world – as its producers and reproducers – through the removal of the superficial and artificial surface constructions of power and ideology. Thus transvalued, people (not just male factory workers) needed to be liberated from the Communist Party as well as from the reductionist representations of the world as presented by liberal capitalist elites. The potential (potentia) power of the people needed to be freed from the formal frameworks of representation (potestas) which the Communist Party attempted to govern through as much as any other reinforcers of bourgeois rule. Emancipation was to be the task of the people themselves – an internal process of self-realisation or self-valorisation – rather than achieved through their subordination to the bureaucrats and ideologues of the official Party. Emancipation was the task of freeing life from representation. This is captured well by Mouffe and Laclau in their classic summation of post-Marxist understandings, *Hegemony and Socialist Strategy*, first published in 1985, in which it is clear that hegemony is a product of representation. Instead of a 'topographical concept', where top-down conceptions of capitalist state power conceive hegemony 'as an irradiation of effects from a privileged point',[46] critical resistance takes the form of a radical pluralist project of self-emancipation, based on 'the logic of autonomy',[47] or the 'logic of the social', rather than that of 'intelligible totalities', 'explicable laws' and fixed frameworks of representation:[48]

> Pluralism is *radical* only to the extent that each term of this plurality of identities finds within itself the principle of its own validity, without this having to be sought in a transcendent or underlying positive ground for the hierarchy of meaning of them all and the source and guarantee of their legitimacy. And this radical pluralism is *democratic* to the extent that the autoconstitutivity of each one of its terms is the result of displacements of the egalitarian imaginary. Hence, the project for a radical and plural democracy, *in a primary sense*, is nothing other than the struggle for a maximum autonomization of spheres on the basis of the generalization of the equivalential-egalitarian logic.[49]

For Laclau and Mouffe, the scientificism of theory-building dogmatic Marxism was clearly at odds with the fluid, plural social world: 'If society is not sutured by any single unitary and positive logic, our understanding of it cannot provide that logic. A "scientific" approach attempting to determine the "essence" of the social would, in actual fact, be the height of utopianism.'[50] The problem becomes reductionist forms of representation which are seen to constrain and limit the autonomous and pluralised power of life constantly in flux and struggle.

The radical, non-foundationalist, Left's rejectionist critique of the modernist fictions of the Communist Party was to form the basis of a new postmodern ontological understanding of the world and of politics. In fact, the problematic of resilience as the way of governing in a world of complexity is the problematic of governing life understood as autonomous. In this world, the limits to constituted power are no longer understood as external to power itself. Constituted power is increasingly understood as a 'fiction': power can only exist as potentia – as constituent or constitutive power – the becoming power 'to' rather than the reified and formal power 'over'. It is over power as 'potentia' that critical theorists are increasingly divided. Some argue that the power of 'real life' is a plural human product of struggle and resistance to power – citing, for example, the Foucauldian 'fact' that power always elicits or incites resistance, or Hardt and Negri's assertion that the Multitude always resists Empire, or Mouffe and Laclau's view that hegemony is necessarily limited and never complete. From this perspective, the autonomous life practices of people will always constitute the reality of power.[51] Hardt and Negri's ontology is clear in their understanding of the Multitude as emergent self-organising life, which stands opposed to 'parasitical' constituted sovereign power:

> [Today] rulers become ever more parasitical and sovereignty becomes increasingly unnecessary. Correspondingly, the ruled become increasingly autonomous, capable of forming society on their own. ... [N]ew forms of labour ... present new possibilities for economic self-management ... but also political and social self-organization ... economic production immediately implies a kind of political production, or the production of society itself. ... The power of the multitude to create social relationships in common stands between sovereignty and anarchy, and it thus presents a new possibility for politics.[52]

The Multitude produces the world itself but in the social sphere of interconnection, not the formal political sphere. The real social interconnections of the people therefore produce not just economic life but political and social life as well. This real power is increasingly becoming autonomous and self-organising – no longer requiring parasitical and artificial power over it. As Hardt and Negri state, this is a new conception of politics – where the sphere of organisation and expression is not the formal sphere of public representation nor the private sphere of individual interests – but that of social interconnection. The Multitude thereby needs no programme or direction to both challenge old forms of political power and to constitute itself as the real power in the world.

   Other theorists argue for the extension of autonomous understandings to a deeper ontological level, maintaining that the power of potentia – the field of autonomy – is not a merely human field, and that the former perspective still clings to a problematic, hubristic Left 'humanism'.[53] For the post-humanist Left, the self-organising power of life as potentia exists as an ontological fact independently of human understandings, as it is increasingly understood that the world itself operates on the basis of autonomous self-activity and self-reproduction, not merely the human world (as discussed in the previous chapter on complexity). This position expands upon earlier critical understandings of autonomy and the limits to constituted power. What are complex adaptive systems other than an extension of an understanding of autonomous politics? What is Latour's recalcitrance of objects other than an extension of the 'everyday' resistance of humans? In the extension of autonomous politics to complex life itself the transvaluation of values through the 'resonance machine' of resilience reaches its culmination. Resilience-thinking has enabled, reflected and self-amplified this fundamental transvaluation – cohering current understandings that the formal politics of representation are a problematic artifice, limiting the possibility of change and progress, and that social interactivity has a powerful creative potential which needs to be self-realised as a way of governing in a complex world. This dynamic from linear to non-linear understandings of governance can be traced through this process of transvaluation, as the agency of progress shifts from being the vanguard party to autonomous workers to society more broadly to the marginal and finally to life itself both human and non-human, and the work of critique shifts from the task of party intellectuals, to collective self-organisation, to individual self-realisation and finally to the work of life itself.

Governing through life

The problematic of resilience is ontological complexity: the contingent constraints on human freedom, creativity and action, which are not recognised in liberal reductionist framings of representation. The limits to liberal aspirations for progress cannot be resolved in neoliberal framings enabling the poor or excluded to adapt to the 'natural' workings and rationalities of free markets and representative democracy. For resilience-thinking there is no natural liberal world that can be adapted to. There is no liberal or universal rationality operating somehow independently of real living people and which can be in some way 'adapted' to. There is no external rationality, which democracy and the market require obedience to. In the world of resilience-thinking, reductionist representations such as the requirements of society, democracy or the market no longer exist separately to the reality of the complex social processes of everyday life.

Resilience-thinking thereby constantly articulates the alternative way of governing through life's vitality and creative emergent powers of possibility. This helps to explain why resilience-thinking can easily lend itself to critical reproduction in radical social theorising, such as assemblage theory and new materialisms.[54] The concern is not with rescuing modernist 'anthropomorphic' or instrumentalist understandings of fixed essences or properties but with the multiplicity of relations and processes, which are creatively productive of contingent outcomes.[55] The radical ontology of resilience-thinking is concerned with understanding the fragility of objects and meanings rather than their fixity.[56] Like Nigel Thrift's non-representational theory, John Holloway's 'scream' or Hardt and Negri's 'Multitude',[57] resilience-thinking understands that our everyday practices and experiences promise the immanent possibility of alternatives: in the here and now.

The political binaries of resilience-thinking:

Properties of Complex Life	Properties of Liberal Power
non-linear	linear
relational	reductionist
open	closed
bottom-up	top-down
flat	hierarchy
mobile/fluid	fixed
concrete	abstract
autonomy	control
becoming	being
real	artificial
plurality	singularity
autopoiesis	direction
contingency	certainty
excess	limit

Real complex life is a rich assemblage of complex, concrete, multiple interactions, never fixed or final, and thus is necessarily immune to the power of representation. Drawing on the 'reality' of life thereby has a tremendous appeal, especially if reductionist short-termism is seen as palpably unable to govern the world today. In the life-politics of resilience-thinking – as in Heidegger and Nietzsche's understanding of 'the-will-to-power' of life,[58] the biopolitics of Hardt and Negri or the pragmatism of John Dewey[59] – people rule through their constituent multiplicity rather than being ruled over through constituted structures, ideologies, states or cultures. Life is always in excess of what was life and is now reified and mystified as having some power of its own – like culture, ideology or markets.[60]

It would be a mistake to think that resilience-thinking, with its alternative ontology of the complexity of life-politics, rose to be a mainstream approach to governance because of the dynamism of radical critical thought. The hidden genealogy of resilience, presented in this chapter, describes the historical conditions in which this specific political ontology arose, not how it became attractive to much broader sections of society and to power itself. In the early 1990s, with the end of the legitimising structure of Left–Right political representation, resilience-thinking appeared to be overdetermined by the dynamics of the world itself: complex life immediately came to the fore in the problematic of 'globalisation': where once there was order, fixed meanings and state direction, now life ruled through complexity and interdependence, allegedly minimising the importance and accountability of power.[61] In the mid-1990s, the power of complex life, as the limit of liberal power, was articulated in terms of the birth of 'risk society' and 'manufactured uncertainty', where side-effects and unintended outcomes took precedence over the strategic instrumentalism of constituted power,[62] and it became clear to many that a globalised world was not amenable to liberal forms of progress, knowledge, representation and intervention.

Today, it is hardly even a provocation to suggest that liberal modernity itself was a fiction.[63] Even governments appear to have bought in to the power of complex life and the consequences which this 'reality' has for reductionist ideas of liberal representation and linear understandings of policy-making. The final redoubts of constituted power, governments themselves, are much more reluctant to claim that they 'represent' 'the people' rather than being a constituent power among many others. As a constituent power, government can no longer govern as liberal government but instead must partake in governance: in the understanding and facilitation of life itself. Resilience-thinking enables power to rule as the governance of life: enabling, empowering, facilitating and capacity-building. Governments cannot rule over life but only through life. Ruling 'through' rather than ruling 'over' implies a much flatter ontological relation between governing and being governed. Policy goals – if they are not to be undermined – need to come from life itself. Life is the means and ends of governance with practice-based policy-making, self-reflexivity, feedback-loops, reflexive law-making and the inculcation of community capacities and resilience.

Conclusion

The key point about resilience-thinking is that there is no outside to an interactive, interdependent and interconnected world and therefore no way of imposing government as a form of direction and control over a complex life which will always escape its intentions. This removal or displacement of power is the product of a particular regime of truth telling or discourse of veridiction, which cannot easily be grasped within traditional liberal or modernist framings. The truth discourse of resilience-thinking is ontological in that the problem of complexity is understood to be a reality against which power is powerless. This 'reality' is not understood as a social construct or discourse of power but as an incontestable fact.

In this truth discourse, the content of political critique is transvalued and its form inverted. To attempt to critique power as hegemonic or as reflective of and as reinforcing structures of economic and social domination would be seen as bolstering power rather than challenging it. It would be problematic, uncritical and essentialising to ignore the radical resistance of life itself. There has therefore been a marked shift from critical Marxist or Foucauldian thinking which tended to emphasise the reality of power, hegemony and domination through the reproduction of hierarchical structures. For resilience-thinking, life is always in excess of power's attempts to control it. It is now common to argue that critical theorists, such as Foucault and Giorgio Agamben,[64] even though focusing on the importance of 'life' and the biopolitical for liberal regimes of power, failed to fully appreciate how life continually evades power's appropriation.[65] Critical Foucauldian theorists of biopolitics, such as Julian Reid and Mick Dillon, are now all too easily criticised for failing to realise that liberal regimes of power always fail to contain life, which is necessarily 'open, complex and interdependent'.[66] Critical understandings increasingly argue that rather than liberal regimes of power governing life, life in fact governs power, continually tests it and finds it wanting:

> At the heart of biopower (at the heart of all governance) ... is the insecurity of life itself. And it is precisely the ungovernability of life itself that demands governance. To use Agamben's language, we are all *Homo sacer* because we are always already exposed to death. But the reason for this exposure is not because our natural life has been illicitly encircled by the state. On the contrary, it is because the state can only fail to secure the life it promises to protect.[67]

Life ontologically, 'really', always forces liberal, linear, forms of governing to fail. Life demands to be governed, but it cannot be governed 'over' by liberal regimes of power. Life defies all power, and so resilience-thinking argues that post-liberal regimes need to govern through the power of life rather than by setting themselves up 'over' or 'against it'. The truth regime of resilience is that governance can only govern through complexity, through the ontological unknowability of the constituent power of life.

The appearance of the world reveals the reality of complex life as a framework for governance but also provides a world full of agency capable of transformation in a non-linear world where agency is distributed widely and with it the responsibilities of power. The following chapters will consider how life provides the material basis for governance – for example, in terms of the interconnectivity of the market, social interconnections of Norwegian society or the micro-practices of the poor in the Americas. In these chapters, the rise of interactive and relational understandings of agency is seen to provide a range of new possibilities for thinking about the place and mechanisms of politics – whether opening up new possibilities for individual actors to influence outcomes on the other side of the world, for local communities to take action in order to prevent acts of carnage and terror or for international actors to intervene in social and political problems with new understandings and new techniques, equipped with life-friendly worldviews which understand complexity as a way forward rather than as a barrier to governance.

Notes

1 There is a large and burgeoning literature on resilience as an instrumental discourse of neoliberal capitalism; see, for example, Walker and Cooper, 2011; Neocleous, 2013; Evans and Reid, 2013; Joseph, 2013.
2 Foucault, 2010: p.309.
3 Ibid.: pp.309–10.
4 Foucault, 2008: p.19.
5 Foucault, 2010: p.310.
6 See further Chandler, 2013a; 2013c.
7 Neoliberal analyses, focusing on the role of institutions in reproducing path-dependencies, initially rose to prominence to explain the inequalities of international development in the 1970s and have since become mainstream in historical and economic analysis of development; see, for example, Forest and Mehier, 2001; North, 1990, 2005; Mahoney and Thelen, 2010; Guy Peters, 2005; Steinmo et al., 1992.
8 This reassessment of failure (as more beneficial than success) was already intimated at the start of the introductory chapter on the call to mainstream the teaching of resilience in schools.
9 Connolly, 2011: p.135; see also Connolly, 2005: p.869.
10 Ibid.: p.136.
11 Connolly, 2005: p.870.
12 Ibid.: p.877.
13 Nietzsche, 2007.
14 See, for example, Grove (2013) on different types of resilience.
15 Walker and Cooper, 2011: p.157.

16   Arendt, 1998.
17   It is usually understood that the main shift has been that within the natural sciences. The ontological construction of the world as complex allows for a shared approach, which is much more open to the contingencies of systemic interaction and bridging the modernist gap between the natural and social sciences, in terms of both subject matter and methodological frameworks. See the discussion in Chapter 2 on the dissipation of the distinction between 'hard' natural science and 'soft' social science.
18   See, for example, Naím, 2013.
19   'Ever tried. Ever failed. No matter. Try again. Fail again. Fail better.' As the much-cited quote from Irish playwright Samuel Beckett would have it.
20   Foucault, 1981: p.95.
21   See, for example, Hardt and Negri, 2005;Virno, 2004.
22   Boltanski and Chiapello, 2007; Boltanski, 2011.
23   Laclau and Mouffe, 2001.
24   Laclau, 1996.
25   Latour, 2004a: p.216; pp.155–6. See also, for example, Connolly, 2011; Bennett, 2010.
26   Beck, 1992; Giddens, 1994.
27   Lippmann, 1993; Dewey, 1927.
28   Latour, 1993.
29   Schmidt, 2013.
30   For social science's 'hermeneutics of suspicion' of life, see Ricoeur, 1970: p.27; see also Rancière, 2011; Boltanski, 2011.
31   As discussed in the previous chapter, non-linear understandings of simple complexity enable the understanding of endogenous, path-determined regimes of order as open to potential external intervention to alter emergent outcomes by intervention at lower levels.
32   See Chandler, 2013a: pp.15–18.
33   Taken from Harrison Weir's 1884 English translation, which claims to be 'from original sources'. Available at: http://www.phrases.org.uk/meanings/sour-grapes.html.
34   Nietzsche, 2003: p.19.
35   Ibid.: p.28; see also Reginster, 2008: pp.256–9.
36   This sensitivity to the historical specificity of ressentiment, as a framework of transvaluation seeking to still achieve positive goals, can also be seen in much of Karl Marx's and Frederick Engels's work, especially in their analysis of how the frustrations of the German bourgeoisie, in the face of English and French economic development, enabled their transvaluation of materialism and projection of the goals of progress in abstract idealist forms. See, for example, Marx, 1975; Marx and Engels, 1970.
37   See Heartfield, 2002: pp.111–28.
38   See further, Wright, 2002.
39   See the excellent discussion on Nancy in Marchart, 2007: pp.67–69.
40   See, for example, Dallmayr, 1993.
41   See, for example, Deleuze, 1988; Negri, 1999, 2004; Hardt and Negri, 2000: p.358.
42   Negri, 2004: p.xv.
43   As reflected in the title of Holloway, 2002: *Change the World Without Taking Power.*

44 Post-Marxism critiques the hold of the past, through representation – the reductionist reification of concepts and ideas. This mirrors, on the surface level, the classical Marxist understanding of the hold of dead (objectified) labour over living labour. Dead labour – in the sense of machinery and technology, where profits have already been realised – raises the organic composition of capital, squeezing the productive life of living labour ever more tightly and objectifying (consuming and converting) living labour into commodities, see, for example, Marx, 1954: pp.574–89; 1974: pp.297–304.
45 As Rancière, one of the sharpest critics of Althusserian structuralism and official PCF dogma, argued in 1974, the task was 'to shake up the theoretical and political apparatus of representation that blocks the autonomous expression of revolt' (2011: p.123).
46 Laclau and Mouffe, 2001: p.141.
47 Ibid.: p.184.
48 Ibid.: p.3.
49 Ibid.: p.167.
50 Ibid.: p.143.
51 As Maurizio Lazzarato writes: 'social labour power is independent and able to organise both its own work and its relations.... Industry does not form or create this new labour power but simply takes it on board and adapts it' (cited in Thrift, 2008: p.48).
52 Hardt and Negri, 2005: p.336.
53 See, for example, Connolly, 2011; Bennett, 2010; Thrift, 2008.
54 Resilience-thinking, and its reflection in assemblage theory and new materialist theorising, can be understood as heavily influenced by the political philosophy of Gilles Deleuze, in terms of self-organising material systems, the importance of relational exteriority rather than fixed essences and the refusal to subordinate difference to identity. See, for example, Deleuze and Guattari, 2004; and, for an influential rereading, see DeLanda, 2006.
55 For a good overview, see Srnicek, 2012: pp.25–52.
56 See, for example, Connolly, 2013b.
57 Thrift, 2008; Holloway, 2002; Hardt and Negri, 2005.
58 For an excellent analysis, see de Beistegui, 2007.
59 See, for example, his classic statement, Dewey, 1927.
60 To locate the heritage of resilience-thinking in critical constructivist understandings, see further, Berger and Luckmann, 1979; Giddens, 1984.
61 See, for example, Rosenau and Czempiel, 1992; Baylis and Smith, 2006; Chandler, 2009.
62 Beck, 1992; Giddens, 1994.
63 Latour, 1993.
64 Even theorists of resistance, such as James Scott or Michel de Certeau, are increasingly criticised for their 'residual humanism', in seeing resistant life and the practice of the everyday as hidden or obscured rather than as central (Thrift, 2008: p.77).
65 Rose, 2013.
66 See, for example, Lundborg and Vaughan-Williams, 2011: p.378.
67 Rose, 2013.

PART II
Resilience and the international

4
THE POLITICS OF LIMITS
The rise of complexity in peacebuilding

Introduction

For much of the 1990s it seemed as if international relations had lost the pluralism that demarcated the discipline from political theory since its birth in the post-colonial era of an enlarged international society of states based on international regimes of formal sovereign equality. With the end of the Cold War division of the international sphere and the emergence of hegemonic liberal interpretations of international law and binding norms, it appeared that the international arena might be moving to a new universalist order, dominated by Western liberal democracies. In this new regime of understanding, sovereignty was no longer understood to be a barrier to universal conceptions of rights and, if necessary, the intervention of international forces to protect or enforce these against regimes held to be unwilling or unable to do so themselves. A new era of interventionist policy-making opened up once the internal political processes of states, now considered to be problematic, were considered a matter of international concern. The new post-international world was considered to be a liberal one, amenable to universal, linear, top-down, policy solutions, capable of being developed in the capitals of the West and imposed through detachments of military personnel and civil administrative experts deployed into conflict and post-conflict zones.

Problems of peacebuilding in post-conflict interventions were seen as largely technical questions, concerned with the export and establishment of certain institutional frameworks – in which case, problems of peace were narrowly understood in terms of exporting universal understandings of democracy and good governance. The barriers or limits to success were seen essentially from two interlinked perspectives: first concerning the limits of Western will, resources or coordination; and, second, as the illegitimate blockages of local elites concerned to maintain their control of power, patronage and resources. This reductionist or technocratic approach to democracy promotion and peacebuilding worked on the basis that local elites were not truly representative of their societies' needs or interests; elites were seen as illegitimate claimants for power, influencing society but manufacturing their support through illegitimate means of patronage, media manipulation and corruption. The universal assumption was the hubristic one that the populations concerned had real interests in supporting Western aspirations for reform and that therefore these reforms would work smoothly once blocking elites were removed, undermined or constrained by the policies of conditionality.

By the end of the 1990s, these 'top-down' approaches – based on linear or reductionist assumptions that the Western powers and international institutions could just impose a set of international policy-prescriptions through bargaining, bypassing or constraining local elites – were seen in a much more negative light. These approaches were seen to be externally driven and hubristic – in their assumptions of external actors having the right policies and the means to attain them – and to express a limited understanding of politics as a linear or hierarchical process, focusing solely on the limited and artificial formal or public political sphere. Approaches which appreciate the limits of the 'linear' approach have increasingly emphasised that international peacebuilding is not a technical question of application or implementation but a complex 'political' question, involving a problematic which is not open to easy calculation and 'elite bargaining'. The 'non-linear' understanding of the limits to peacebuilding interventions started not with international designs and blueprints but with the understandings of simple complexity theory, focusing on the problematic of the local or societal agents and actors and the processes, practices and interrelationships that shape ideas and understandings. These non-linear approaches emphasised the importance of system- and process-based thinking and emphasised the contingent and unknown factors involved in the peacebuilding process; in particular, they sought to highlight the importance of local agency (often hidden or unrecognised) in resistance to international aspirations.[1]

This chapter reflects upon the shift away from linear understandings of peacebuilding, which assumed that Western 'blueprints' could be imposed upon non-compliant elites. Today, it is increasingly suggested, in both policy and academic literatures, that there should be a shift towards non-linear approaches of complexity theory. Rather than focusing upon Western policy prescriptions, intra-elite bargaining and formal institutional structures, these understandings stress non-linearity, hybridity, endogenous local societal processes and practices and the importance of 'hidden' agency and resistance. This chapter shows that, while these approaches set up a critique of liberal linear approaches, they tend to reify complex, hybrid, non-liberal or non-linear outcomes as the product of interaction within closed systems amenable to external understanding and interventionist practices. In this way, they reproduce the external subject position of governing power which is so prevalent in liberal peace approaches, but locate the problems or barriers to peace and development at the micro-level of iterative processes of interaction rather than understanding the barrier at the level of elites.

From linearity to non-linearity

The civil conflicts of the 1990s unleashed by the collapse of the Cold War divide, which impelled the transformation of Soviet-style regimes in Central and Eastern Europe and the removal of superpower clientelism in sub-Saharan Africa, provided the backdrop against which understandings of peacebuilding interventions and their limits were developed in linear ways. Perhaps paradigmatic of linear understandings of peacebuilding, in terms of compliance with international blueprints, was Mary Kaldor's highly influential analysis of 'New Wars'. Using this framing, she described conflicts in ways which constructed a moral divide between the understanding of war and conflict in the West and in the non-West. The binary of old and new war had little to do with the spatial framing of conflict as intrastate rather than interstate, for example, the US or Spanish civil wars would be construed as old wars rather than new wars.[2] Following Kalevi Holsti's analysis of 'wars of the third kind',[3] Kaldor drew a conceptual distinction in which old wars were rational – constitutive of a collective or public interest and politically legitimate – whereas new wars were understood to be irrational – driven by private interest and politically illegitimate. This conceptual divide enabled Kaldor to argue that illegitimate political elites had no right to hide behind the rights of sovereignty and that external peacebuilding interventions were morally necessary and legitimate, casting international interveners as interest-free enforcers of emerging international peacebuilding norms which could be universally applied.

Another leading example of the linear framing of international intervention in the cause of peace, with its implicit liberal telos, was Keck and Sikkink's influential book *Activists beyond Borders*. Keck and Sikkink argued that, to diffuse liberal norms of democracy and human rights, illegitimate state-based or interest-based barriers to communicative interaction needed to be removed.[4] The overcoming of barriers, seen to be at the level of state government resistance, was construed in terms of the 'boomerang effect', which allowed the spread of liberal norms as international actors 'removed the blockage' of the narrow interest-based action of repressive regimes, 'prying open space' for domestic civil society actors which were bearers of these democratic aspirations:

> Voices that are suppressed in their own countries may find that networks can project and amplify their concerns into an international arena, which in turn can echo back into their own countries ... networks open channels for bringing alternative visions and information into international debate. ... At the core of network activity is the production, exchange and strategic use of information.[5]

In these linear discourses, peacebuilding transformation was understood to be primarily the task of international institutions and powerful Western states, acting to remove the narrow 'interest' blockages of entrenched power elites and thus freeing the local agency of civil society, understood to be unproblematic. This framing was perhaps most clearly exemplified by those advocating international intervention in the break-up of Yugoslavia, particularly in the Bosnia War of 1992–95, which was one of the key foreign policy focuses of the mid-1990s. It was held that international interveners were acting in support of local civil-society actors in seeking to preserve multicultural Bosnia against the machinations of unrepresentative nationalist elites who were acting in their own narrow and criminal interests.[6] Once international intervention had removed the nationalist leaders from power, through prosecutions for war crimes and the oversight of free and fair post-war democratic elections, it was assumed that the population of Bosnia would express their support for universal liberal democratic norms in voting for non-nationalist political representatives.

In these 1990s framings of linearity, formal political processes at the local level were often problematised – for example, in terms of local elite resistance – but these problematic blockages to liberal international norms were understood as amenable to resolution through a combination of top-down international carrots and sticks. Once local elites were removed from power or constrained, it was assumed that the externally drawn up plans for democracy-promotion or for peacebuilding could continue unhindered. However, these linear liberal interventionist aspirations have since dimmed – in the wake of failures in the Balkans and in other post-conflict scenarios from Afghanistan to Iraq. The understanding of political blockages has shifted from the more easily accessible formal level of local state institutions to concern with the less accessible level of societal relations. With this shift, the emphasis has moved from linear ends-based or goal-orientated interventions to understanding the limits to change in the non-linear or 'hybrid' politics of social or everyday practices and interactions.

Rather than being understood to be resisting through the political motivations of self-interest, elites are today more likely to be understood as lacking the capacity or the authority to implement Western policy-making goals. A recent book which upholds the linear approach, advocating that international actors should assert more leverage over recalcitrant elites, stands as an exception to the general trend of thinking in the post-conflict literature.[7] Critical international relations theorising – focused on the Western export of 'Liberal Peace' and the problematic nature of 'top-down' frameworks which ignore local societal influences – stresses the need for 'bottom-up' theorising; giving a much larger role to local agency and the spaces and mechanisms which need to be accessed in order to understand, empower and transform local actors. Rather than focusing on the formal public political sphere of domestic elites, analysts argue that researchers needed to go deeper into the societal sphere, particularly to those actors capable of expressing, influencing and shaping 'grass roots' opinion.

This understanding of 'politics' works in a very different register to the 'top-down' liberal institutionalist frameworks, which had tended to ignore the societal sphere. In the early post-Cold War years of intervention, liberal statebuilding approaches envisaged states being constructed on the Western, or 'Weberian', model, focusing on the export of liberal institutions standing above society, assumed to operate independently from social forces. Assuming the universal nature of the liberal subject, these approaches understood the institutional framework as determining the outcomes of social interaction. Liberal peace would thereby be assured through the introduction of a liberal state: through attention to the construction or reform of neutral constitutional arrangements, political party representation, civil service appointments, the army and policing, and the courts and judiciary.[8]

The failure of these experiments in exporting liberalism led to attention shifting to the societal sphere and a critique of institutionalist assumptions regarding state–society relations and the universality of the liberal subject. Today's approaches reverse liberal institutionalist frameworks, understanding states as operating upon and through the societal sphere rather than standing neutrally above it, as if the state was purely a technocratic and administrative body along Weberian lines. Work on the institutional level is increasingly seen to be purely formal and superficial when it comes to post-conflict governance for sustainable peace. For non-linear approaches, work purely on the level of elites and state-institutions is seen as mistaking a part for the whole and assumes the successful top-down or linear imposition of the end goals of Western peace and democracy-promotion.

As Körppen and Ropers note:'systemic approaches understand phenomena as an emergent property of an interrelated whole; hence, a phenomena cannot be fully comprehended by analysing its constituent parts'.[9] Roger Mac Ginty has similarly argued that linear approaches ignore the local relational and contextual aspects; for this reason he deploys the concept of 'hybridisation' to bring clearly into question top-down understandings of temporality and linearity.[10] 'Bringing the local back in' thereby indicates a shift from a linear approach to a non-linear or systems approach focused upon societal relationships and interactions at both the local-local level and local-international level.[11] In this way, academic commentators have focused on the 'hybrid' outcomes produced by attempts to impose formal liberal institutional frameworks on what is argued to be non- or a-liberal societies.[12] These hybrid outcomes are held to indicate that the 'top-down' shaping of state institutions has little broader social impact and that liberal aspirations are easily undermined or blocked by 'resisting' or countervailing societal practices and institutions.[13] Non-linear approaches thereby seek to work at the societal level, focusing on addressing the transformation of societal processes and understanding the social reproduction of resistances to democracy and peace, allegedly ignored by liberal universalist 'top-down' policy-making.[14]

The problematic of how states can be strengthened through accessing and influencing social or societal processes has thereby become positioned at the heart of the peacebuilding problematic.[15] Non-linear approaches seek to highlight how attention to societal processes, instead of the formal institutional frameworks of government, necessitates a different form of interventionary practices and understandings. In focusing on the peacebuilding shift to society and societal processes, non-linear conceptions build upon the growing interest in the shift to governance approaches of societal intervention.[16] This framework of governance, and the focus on the ways in which external actors can influence the societal environment in which individuals make choices and take decisions, fundamentally challenges the traditional liberal assumptions on which the division of the public and private spheres were based – the societal sphere becomes problematised and 'life' becomes the subject of governance.[17]

In this respect, Michel Foucault's work on shifting liberal governing rationalities and the birth of biopolitics serves as a useful starting point for the non-linear analysis of the barriers or 'resistances' involved in the social practices which produce and institutionalise cognitive and ideational understandings. As Foucault indicated, this shift away from state-based, sovereign and disciplinary power to a biopolitical or 'society-centred' approach constituted 'the population as a political problem' and, within this, focused on the real lives or the everyday of individuals and communities 'and their environment, the milieu in which they live … to the extent that it is not a natural environment, that it has been created by the population and therefore has effects on that population'.[18] It is this interactive 'milieu' that is understood to shape social and individual behavioural choices and to account 'for action at a distance of one body on another' and thereby 'appears as a field of intervention' for governance policy-making.[19] In this framework, any external peacebuilding intervention can only operate on society indirectly, through connecting to, understanding and facilitating the interactive processes of societal life itself, rather than through the formal framework of public law in relation to individuals as citizens: 'action is brought to bear on the rules of the game rather than on the players' as Foucault states in *The Birth of Biopolitics*.[20] In this shift, liberal understandings of linear politics with the state (as representing and directing society from above) and the subject (as universal, rational and autonomous) are fundamentally altered.

The discovery of the 'local'

The shift from linear to non-linear understandings, together with the shift from the formal sphere of government institutions and elite interactions to a sustained focus on the local or societal level is captured well in the pioneering work of Paul Lederach. His work has been crucial in establishing this approach in the policy literature.[21] Lederach was the first leading policy-academic to problematise 'top-down' or linear approaches to peace and democracy. Lederach took the emphasis away from international diplomatic agendas and local elites to focus on a societal approach. This approach is also known as a 'relationship-', 'practice-' or 'process-orientated' understanding. In this framework, the role of external actors is to assist in establishing an 'infrastructure that empowers the resources for reconciliation from within that society'.[22] In his focus upon 'the experiential and subjective realities shaping people's perspectives and needs', Lederach argued that institutional structures and elite settlements were not the key concern:

[T]raditional mechanisms relying solely on statist diplomacy and real-politik have not demonstrated a capacity to control these conflicts, much less transform them toward constructive, peaceful outcomes. Contemporary conflict thus demands innovation, the development of ideas and practices that go beyond the negotiation of substantive interests and issues. This innovation, I believe, pushes us to probe into the realm of the subjective-generationally accumulated perceptions and deep-rooted hatred and fear.[23]

Lederach's approach was to point towards the dominant understandings of the 2000s. His key break with existing practices was not merely to reject the focus on state-level elites but to insist that Western policy-conceptions, posed in linear terms of 'conflict management' or 'conflict resolution', were misplaced. Instead of linear thinking of the imposition of external blueprints, he argued that social scientists needed to learn from the new thinking of natural scientists, particularly in physics, where both quantum and chaos theory indicated that the system itself was more important than looking at its individual parts.[24] Rather than understanding politics in terms of leaders, elites and political programmes, or 'throwing money at problems', he suggested that societal spaces, practices and processes should become the starting point for transforming social subjectivities.[25] In this focus on societal processes, the concern is with social practices and relationships, rather than the external design or imposition of some alleged 'solution' to conflict.[26]

It is useful to consider how, in this framework, the space of politics – the space of blockages to peace and their removal – shifted from the formal institutional sphere to the informal social sphere. For Lederach, the formal political sphere of elite politics lacked representational legitimacy, not in the 'linear' sense of Mary Kaldor's 'new wars' analysis – where, as we have seen, elites were seen to be criminal and corrupt, and to lack legitimacy – but in the sense of elites no longer being understood as 'representative' of, or as fully connected to, society. Local elites were seen to represent the formal machinations of government; elites in this understanding, precisely because of their public visibility, were inevitably conservative upholders of the status quo, dependent on military, political or media power for their standing, and thereby were less connected to society itself.[27] For the non-linear, societal or process-based approach it is the social milieus of everyday life which are crucial, not formal politics operating in the rarefied sphere of international-elite diplomacy and negotiation.

The sense of a 'disconnect' between formal political authority and social processes and practices is central to non-linear approaches to peacebuilding.

In these framings, international policy-makers need to connect with, to understand and to enable or influence local agency, now seen as key to successful peacebuilding outcomes. For Lederach, the key to peacebuilding was not Western knowledge or resources but local agency: 'The greatest resource for sustaining peace in the long term is always rooted in the local people and culture.'[28] In this framework, locals were foregrounded, not in terms of formal political representation but the social processes and relationships in which they were embedded. In which case, the approach to the local is transformed to 'see people in the setting as resources, not recipients'.[29] In this way, there was a 'move beyond a simple prescription of answers and modalities from outside the setting' to 'empowering the resources, modalities, and mechanisms for building peace that exist within the context.[30] There was no quick diplomatic solution to conflicts which could be agreed on and somehow imposed from the top-down; rather, it was 'the healing of people and the rebuilding of the web of their relationships' which took centre stage.[31]

Lederach is worth quoting at length to gain an understanding of the distinctive nature of 'non-linear' as opposed to 'linear-thinking' regarding the 'infra-politics of peace':

> An infrastructure for peacebuilding should be understood as a process-structure, in the way that quantum theory has proposed. A process-structure is made up of systems that maintain form over time yet have no hard rigidity of structure. ... In more specific terms ... a process-structure for peacebuilding transforms a *war-system* characterized by deeply divided, hostile, and violent relationships into a *peace-system* characterized by just and interdependent relationships with the capacity to find nonviolent mechanisms for expressing and handling conflict. The goal is not stasis, but rather the generation of continuous, dynamic, self-regenerating processes that maintain form over time and are able to adapt to environmental changes. Such an infrastructure is made up of a web of people, their relationships and activities, and the social mechanisms necessary to sustain the change sought. This takes place at all levels of the society.[32]

Non-linear, systems-based approaches seek to transform social practices and behaviours understood as self-reproducing processes. Understood as systems of societal reproduction, there can be no 'solution' which fixes some settlement. It is a matter of ensuring that societal reproduction through practices and relationships becomes sustainable at a level at which conflicts are managed peaceably. As the Berghof Conflict Research think tank director, Hans Giessman, notes:

> The inter-linkages of causes, intervening variables and consequences of conflict dynamics are still widely under-researched. In complex conflict scenarios it can be hard to distinguish between causes and consequences, and the borders between both become fuzzy, if not blurred. Goal-seeking linear approaches will most likely fail in such scenarios. . . . The actual matter of transforming (violent) conflict into constructive interaction is about people internalising the chances for socialising alternative non-violent patterns of beliefs, behaviour and relations.[33]

While Lederach stressed the need to engage with community leaders with well-established links and reputations, 'chosen not for their expertise or profession, but for who they are in the network',[34] other, more critical, academics have argued that societal transformation needs to operate at a deeper level still. Thania Paffenholz, for example, argues for a more comprehensive approach to conflict transformation, with greater emphasis on context sensitivity and local agency.[35]

This may have seemed a radical departure from traditional theorising but non-linear or systems-based approaches tend not to focus on transforming economic and social relations but on the social associations, spaces and practices which are understood to reproduce them. Here, societal problems are addressed at the level of practices, ideas and cognitive frameworks held to produce the problematic reality or problematic responses to the stresses of post-conflict transformation. By shifting 'politics' to society, these approaches open up 'a new object, a new domain or field' for policy intervention:[36] the 'local'.[37]

In non-linear approaches, the focus of the problematic is the local level, understood as the sphere within which political agency operates in the production and reproduction of barriers to – as well as the facilitation of – peace. This radical understanding of the societal or informal reproduction of social identities and practices, which can be seen as 'resistance' or as a barrier to liberal statebuilding aspirations, owes much to Louis Althusser's conception of the individual subject as always and already ideologically embedded through its insertion into material social practices.[38] He argued that these social practices were shaped by the 'Ideological State Apparatuses' of religion, culture, the family, communicative media etc. – operating in both the public and private spheres and, through which, cognitive and ideational understandings were continually formed.[39] Contra Marx, therefore, individual understandings were not shaped by the real conditions of existence but, instead, dominant ideological framings 'represent to them there [through social practices] … the imaginary relation of those individuals to the real relations in which they live'.[40] Imaginary, false or 'ideological' understandings were therefore inescapable 'material' products of the social practices of everyday life, through which subjects were always and already interpellated intersubjectively.[41] It is here that different 'rationalities' or 'temporalities' are held to be in play, which resist or contest the linear demands of liberal peace.

The local production and reproduction of difference through micropractices, spaces and relationships is at the heart of non-linear understandings and the 'embedded' understanding of the subject. Liberal linear approaches necessarily were dependent upon universal presumptions of the rational subject, which merely needed to be 'freed', in terms of the removal of elite blockages. The non-linear subject can no longer 'be' freed by peacebuilding interventions as if the 'blockages' somehow existed outside the subject and its relations and understandings. Thus, the shift away from rationalist approaches – which were held to ignore the societal relations shaping cognitive understandings – toward attention to the deeper social practices of 'everyday life' shaping cognitive and behavioural choices, is fundamental to understanding current academic and policy perspectives criticising linear peacebuilding rationalities of intervention. Althusser's work on ideology thereby provides a template for critical and post-Marxist approaches, which have considered informal social practices more in terms of the active reproduction of ideas and cognitive frameworks than as the products of social and economic relations.

The 'local', 'bottom-up' attention to 'the hidden' processes of the societal sphere' focuses on this sphere as the problematic barrier, preventing better, more effective, more adaptive responses to post-conflict stresses. This ontological framework, centered on the real lives of local actors and their 'everyday' practices, thereby assumes that social practices are much less open to transformation through external intervention which focuses on the formal, public and political sphere. It is through this construction of the 'local' – as self-producing of emergent rationalities and temporalities of difference – that external peacebuilding interventions become inevitably understood to produce non-linear or hybrid outcomes.

The 'hidden' politics of resistance

As long as liberal rationalist approaches to politics were the dominant framework for understanding peacebuilding, the formal political sphere of inter-elite bargaining was seen to be the sphere through which problems could be understood and overcome, for example, by forcing illegitimate elite practices to change through compliance practices, such as conditionality. In non-linear, hybrid, approaches there is a very different approach to politics and the space and mechanisms of its action. In these understandings, politics is primarily understood in terms of societal processes held to be self-reproducing. For Coleman et al. (2011), for example, politics is seen to operate through social practices in a form that is more analogous to the reproduction of cancer – operating beneath the surface and transforming from the inside – than a clash of political interests or structural contradictions:

> An intractable conflict can be looked upon as a 'malignant' social rela-
> tion. Cancer works by penetrating the structure of the organism and
> enslaving essential elements of the body, which then lose their original
> functions and begin working in the service of the structure of cancer. …
> The richness and multidimensionality of all the processes occurring in
> a healthy society become entrained in the structure, leaving no oppor-
> tunity for positive interactions.[42]

Here, systems come to the fore, with complex mechanisms of interaction below the surface. In this new framework, in the words of EU High Representative for Common Foreign and Security Policy, Javier Solana, 'domestic politics matter'.[43] He explains:

> Domestic politics matter because they limit what is achievable. … This
> is never more the case than when the problem is a dispute over the
> control and legitimacy of the state. … In the Balkans and elsewhere,
> the aim of crisis management has been to create the space for politics
> to work. But functioning politics is one thing that foreigners cannot
> provide; only the locals can do that.[44]

Traditional, linear, 'top-down' or technical approaches assumed that the West could bring democracy and sustainable peace through the removal of blockages and opening the 'space for politics to work'. Today's understandings suggest that the problem is precisely that of 'politics' itself. 'Politics', in this sense, is not merely a matter of establishing or imposing technical solutions but refers to the area outside of external or Western influence. As the UK government Foreign Office and Department for International Development now argue, 'politics is central to stability'.[45] The British government sees this as a shift from previous approaches of the international community, which merely 'looked for technical fixes, to conflict'.[46] What the West cannot easily influence through external interventions is the social space in which 'politics' is now seen to operate. In this space, there are blockages which do not appear to be amenable to Western influence. This is the space in which resistance works and where 'only the locals' can take responsibility.

It seems that the discovery of 'hybridity' has brought back 'politics', but not the linear politics of representation, with its linear understanding of state-society interactions. The politics of 'the local' operates in the informal and societal sphere, out of the reach or vision of Western policy-makers and linear social theorists. This shift is reflected in Mary Kaldor's view of the increasing importance of 'subterranean politics' where political contestation (in all its xenophobic, populist and emancipatory forms) is seen to operate below the surface. The important point is that, using this framework, social mobilizations and collective activities are reinterpreted as 'public displays of subterranean politics'.[47] In these analyses, trying to understand politics through a focus on elites would miss the bigger and more important picture, which can only be found through engaging with society itself. Kaldor argues that, with hindsight, this blind-spot can be clearly seen in relation to the 1989 'velvet revolutions' of Central and Eastern Europe. Policy- and academic-analysts were caught blindsided because they were only studying elite and inter-elite relations.[48]

For authors such as Oliver Richmond, it is precisely here that we see the limits of linear, top-down understandings of liberal peace 'compliance': in the hidden or neglected political agency of the masses:

> How do we know these agencies exist if they are hidden? Where is their empirical proof? An easy response to this counter-critique is because power, state and sovereignty, as well as international blueprints for which IR maintains compliance – an enormous gathering of the power of liberal modernity – have not had their way so far. This has been one of the lessons of modernity. ... How do the 'powerless' engage in politics and international relations should be its starting question, not whether they do.[49]

Here, there is no understanding of the economic and social structures beyond the reach of local agency. In fact, any such structures are explicitly written out of the picture once the gap between asserted aims and policy outcomes is entirely the product of hidden agency. With the dismissal of social and economic relations, all that is left is 'politics'. However, this is no longer politics understood in terms of the rational pursuit of self-interest and as amenable to top-down 'solutions' or 'settlements'. Nor does the return of politics imply a focus on the public politics of the formal sphere of representation. The politics of hidden agencies and resistances operates in the social sphere and is, by necessity, not amenable to traditional liberal political theory, with its episteme of linearity and means–ends relations. This shifting conception of resistance has already been well noted and is usefully highlighted by Hollander and Einwohner in their discussion of resistance literature, considering resistance as both political and formal or public as well as identity-based and therefore stemming from the informal or private sphere of interaction.[50]

James C. Scott has probably had more influence than any other author on our understanding of resistance as below the surface of formal political processes, for example, through emphasising the importance of access to non-public 'hidden transcripts' – the cognitive and sociological institutional contexts in which shared meanings are produced and transmitted at the local societal level.[51] Scott, in his focus on resistance under authoritarian rule, where open political contestation was impossible, articulated a conflation of the political and the social which speaks powerfully to us today, through his emphasis on the 'infra-politics' of resistance and his location of political understandings in the spaces, practices and relationships of 'everyday life'.

As Scott argued, social science has failed to understand the politics and conflicts of the societies it examined as it has 'focused resolutely on the official or formal relations between the powerful and the weak'[52] and, essentially, in focusing on the formal level, was 'looking in the wrong place for political conflict'.[53] Scott articulated the hidden, subterranean, societal space for politics in the socially-embedded practices, relationships and networks of the informal sphere set apart from power.[54] It was the 'infrapolitics' of these relations which provided 'the cultural and structural underpinning of the more visible political action'[55] and enables us to understand how political conflicts can escalate in ways that social movement approaches or public choice theory fail to grasp.[56]

The blockages of politics thus shift from the resistance of elites, seen to be easily amenable to international resolution, to the blockages of the 'local' or social sphere which, by their very virtue of being 'hidden', are much less amenable to understanding or to external influence. It is here that Scott's critical anthropology begins to resonate with current policy understandings of the difficulties of overcoming the barriers of local resistance, which does not necessarily take public or formal political forms. Scott thereby suggests that it is the 'infrapolitics' which are key to understanding the blockages to democracy-promotion and peacebuilding, as here:

> There are no leaders to round up, no membership lists to investigate,
> no manifestos to denounce, no public activities to draw attention …
> infrapolitics is … the realm of informal leadership and nonelites, of
> conversation and oral discourse, and of surreptitious resistance. The
> logic of infrapolitics is to leave few traces in the wake of its passage.
> By covering its tracks it not only minimizes the risk its practitioners
> run but it also eliminates much of the documentary evidence that
> might convince social scientists and historians that real politics was
> taking place.[57]

Non-linear and systems-based approaches appeal increasingly as external
interventions at the level of formal politics are seen to be ineffective. This
understanding is confirmed by academic work in the areas of democracy
promotion and peacebuilding. Elena Semenova, in a survey of Central and
East European political elites, has highlighted the problem, noting that: 'We
can't use parties to identify elites. The party system is quite unstable.'[58] A similar finding is confirmed by Christoph Zürcher from research in post-conflict
states where, similarly, there seems to be a breakdown between political elites
and social or political processes: 'We have no idea who really are the power
holders in these regions. In post-war contexts we have no clue who these
people are. We just don't know.'[59] The starting assumption is that local agency,
in fact, draws strength from its hidden forms of evading the liberal gaze.
'Infrapolitics' is no longer analysed as a product of weakness and repression
but as an ontological starting point for explaining the limits of peacebuilding.

The reification of 'resistance'

The assertions at play in current understandings of politics operating below
the surface and through 'hidden' agencies of resistance are quite astounding.
Resistances may be hidden, as Scott's research shows, they may be 'mobile
and transitory' as Foucault suggests and they may even become 'strategically
codified' to 'make a revolution possible', as Foucault further indicates[60] but, as
suggested above, resistance can never become the ontological limit to power
without the rejection of any understanding of the importance of structures
of economic and social relations.[61] It seems that Foucault's much quoted
statement on the imbrication of power and resistance has been turned into
a reification of resistance as marking the limit to liberal aspirations of power.
In fact, the actual articulation in his sentence is this: 'Where there is power,
there is resistance, and yet, or rather consequently, this resistance is never in a
position of exteriority in relation to power.'[62]

It seems that it is just this 'relationship of exteriority' that drives the search for 'hidden agency' in the sphere of the 'local'. This approach is probably best exemplified in the work of Oliver Richmond who argues that International Relations, as a discipline, 'needs a theory of resistance'[63] and that, along the lines of Scott, the discipline's lack of attention to 'hidden capacity and resistant agency' means that the real workings of politics are ignored. That, in fact, 'hidden resistance' is entirely exterior to liberal power: akin to the dark matter of physics, upon which the world itself depends; forming 'a massive percentage of the scale of all capacity for reform, development, justice, institutions, civil society, rights, needs, peace and emancipation'.[64] It is thereby hidden resistance which explains the limits to external projects of intervention, operating as 'a conglomeration or aggregation of fragmented and hidden everyday forms of resistance', which 'cannot be seen or easily resisted by power' or co-opted by it, yet is capable of agency and 'holds power to account and illustrates the limits of its sovereignty'.[65]

The need for theory to understand 'resistance' is thereby of prime importance; Richmond sets out the new research agenda thus:

> It has now become axiomatic in several other disciplines that the sum of disaggregated, uncoordinated and fragmented, hidden, disguised and marginal agencies represents a significant totality. It is not homogenous, unidirectional or unilevel, but still it is almost impossible to predict or to countermand. It represents decentralized, bottom-up and grass-roots forms of identity, culture and legitimacy, and a capacity that disrupts hegemony.[66]

Non-linear approaches, bringing a variety of self-reproducing frameworks of explanation to bear on the reproduction of cultural, ideational and material barriers to peacebuilding success, have increasingly come to dominate the academic and policy agendas in the 2000s. Non-linear and hybrid approaches reflect well the sense of limits in today's world. However, they tend to reify or to naturalise these limits as somehow inherent in the world and beyond the reach of liberal reason.[67] The limits of peacebuilding can therefore be understood as a product of the hubristic linear thinking of Western modernity rather than as economic and social structural problems eliciting the possibility of social transformation. Resistance articulated as the limits of liberal aspirations for democracy and peace thereby no longer needs the transformative political agency of subjects. It is for this reason that Oliver Richmond can suggest that resistant agency is a vital determining factor, much as the dark matter of space. This agency is resistant objectively, in its mode of life or being, regardless of subjective political actions or demands.

Once we understand resistance or the limits of liberal peacebuilding aspirations as objective aspects of the world, then it is easy to understand how the academic boom in 'resistance studies' articulates these assumptions.[68] Resistance as an objective characteristic of the world beyond the focus of the linear epistemes of liberal modernity needs no politics.[69] It is for this reason that complexity and new materialist approaches can further dilute our understandings of agency and resistance to suggest that non-human actors can also be seen to 'resist' and 'undermine' the linear causal assumptions at the base of international policy-making.[70] Whereas the old 'historical materialism' understood that the structuring of inequalities was amenable to conscious human transformation, the world of agency of the 'new' materialism lacks the possibilities for structural change. The actor–network framework of Bruno Latour is a good example of this approach, where social explanation needs the 'missing masses' – both human and non-human – whose 'hidden' influence is seen in the uncertainties and contingencies of the world.[71]

In this way, non-linear approaches explain the limits of liberal linear reason as a product of the objective complexity of assemblages or associations of human and non-human actors, in a flat world of 'quasi-objects and quasi-subjects'. Latour's ontology is the same as that of Richmond's in Latour's insistence that the 'dark matter' or 'plasma' of the world, untouched by the social sciences of liberal modernity, is the key to overcoming our 'astronomical ignorance' and the hubristic fantasies created by this. Latour differs merely in his understanding that this 'vast hinterland' is limited and bordered by the lack of inclusion of both human and non-human actors or agents and also in his more radical challenge to liberal linearity, in his assertion that these excluded agencies are 'not hidden, simply *unknown*'.[72] In this ontology, it is the 'recalcitrance' of being itself that resists liberal linear framings rather than conscious or intentional political activity on behalf of the subject.[73]

Conclusion

While Foucault insightfully argued that 'where there is power, there is resistance', this survey of the shift towards complexity and non-linear understandings of peacebuilding suggests that there is the danger that the power/ resistance binary may become a formalistic and reified one, explaining, rationalising and legitimating 'hybrid' outcomes. In reifying peacebuilding outcomes, the transformative aspirations of peacebuilding become muted and dissipated. The analytical focus on the 'local' and on 'hidden agency' naturalises the understanding that the limits to peace are located at the local level and are internally generated or reproduced through local ways of life or modes of being which are understood as 'resistant' to external 'liberal' forms of compliance. While it is understandable that Western assumptions of exporting external 'blueprints' should be criticised as both politically and practically problematic assertions of unaccountable power and that attention should be drawn to the importance of local agency and capacity in the face of these moralised frames of understanding, the non-linear discourses of local 'hidden' agency neither create the basis of any genuine understanding of the limits to liberal peace nor provide any emancipatory alternative.

In the first place, the power/resistance binary, as applied in the non-linear peacebuilding discourse, provides a voluntarist or idealist understanding of the limits to peacebuilding. The success or failure of liberal peacebuilding goals is seen to be determined by a clash of rationalities, cultures, cognitive frameworks and temporalities. Ironically, the non-linear approach shares much with the linear approach highlighted at the top of the chapter, which assumed that the problem was subjective elite will or understanding rather than the social and economic context. In evading the question of the material social and economic explanations for the limits to liberal universalist aspirations, non-linear approaches, in fact, share much with the conservative understandings forwarded by new institutionalist economists at the World Bank and the IMF, similarly concerned to highlight the local (rather than international) limits to economic development – understanding these limits to be endogenous, self-produced and emergent on the basis of cultural and ideational differentiation.[74]

Second, the ontological assumptions of non-linear framings tend to problematise the emancipatory objectives behind peace itself rather than the problematic imposition of external projects per se. The ontological assumptions of hybrid understandings rest on the privileging of difference, where conflict is understood as an inevitable product of temporal and cognitive clashes between different modes of being, never amenable to the homogenising gaze of liberal linear thinking. In effect, the liberal frameworks for legitimising external intervention, through the telos of the promise of peace, are rejected while the need for external intervention is accepted as long as it takes new, more reflective and less liberal or 'post-liberal' forms, which accept the need to work upon the 'hidden' agencies of the local rather than excluding them from the analysis.

Third, and perhaps more importantly, from within this framework, peacebuilding interventions can no longer be held to account through highlighting the gap between their legitimating promise and their reality in terms of outcomes. In the world of 'resistance' rather than 'compliance' the limits of Western liberal aspirations are not constructed as the effects of the market inequalities, structuring the asymmetries of intervention, but are seen instead to be the product of cultural or ideational choices of 'resisting' or 'recalcitrant' subjects. Peacebuilding interventions working on the ontological basis of hybridity would merely institutionalise lower expectations and horizons, allocating responsibility for this to local agency. Failure would be represented as success, both in recognising local agency and in rejecting the 'hubris' of the liberal past.

It is important to realise that this discourse of limits – of life as resistance – was very much an evolving product of the confluence of critical sociological thinking and the retreat of liberal internationalism. As we will see in the next chapter, although the discourse of limits deploys the ontology of complexity, this is that of simple complexity, framed as a set of endogenous understandings of how problematic or sub-optimal regimes of non-liberal order arise in closed systems of non-Western conflict-prone states. This framing understands peacebuilding policy intervention as necessary to work on transforming lower levels of societal interaction in order to achieve external goals and is thus still stuck in a liberal or neoliberal problematic of intervention understood reductively in the means-ends perspective informed by the liberal telos and the knowledge assumptions invested in it.

The critical discourses of the limits of liberal peace were largely focused on the epistemological limits of liberal understandings and how these limits manifested themselves in the non-linear outcomes of intervention. Thus, complex life (the failure of liberal universalist aspirations of transformation) was the manifestation of the limits of liberal reason – understood crudely in statist or 'top-down' terms of linear cause-and-effect. As discussed above, these critiques drew on other critical sociological frameworks but, in applying these frameworks to governance interventions, tended to initially blunt the critical insights of the relational ontology with its gradual adoption into policy discourses. Resilience approaches (as we shall discuss in the following two chapters) slowly restored the critical and relational understandings of creative life as a potential solution rather than an unknowable limit and in doing so reframed the possibilities for governance once the 'real' was no longer hidden but accessible to policy (as Latour intimates above). Increasingly, in the 2010s (as the next chapter will argue), resilience-thinking has enabled a much more positive understanding of the local and of the practices of the everyday as producing not limits to power but policy-alternatives which enable governance through complex life.

Notes

1 For the discussion of non-linear approaches in the social sciences, see, for example, Jervis, 1998; Richards, 2000; Brown, 1995; Popolo, 2011.
2 Kaldor, 1999: pp.13–30.
3 Holsti, 1996: pp.19–40.
4 Keck and Sikkink, 1998.
5 Ibid.: p.x.
6 For example, Burg, 1997; Fine, 1996; Kaldor, 1999.
7 Zürcher et al., 2013.
8 See Lemay-Hébert, 2009.
9 Körppen and Ropers, 2011: p.13.
10 Mac Ginty, 2011: p.73.
11 Ibid.: p.210.
12 For example, Roberts, 2008.
13 See, for example, Paris and Sisk, 2009; Richmond and Mitchell, 2012; Mac Ginty, 2011.
14 Woodward, 2007.
15 See also Hameiri, 2010; Joseph, 2012.
16 For example, Foucault, 2010: pp.25–40; 2008; O'Malley, 2004; Miller and Rose, 2008; Rose, 1989, 1999; Dean, 2010; Walker and Cooper, 2011; Owens, 2012.
17 See further, for example, Dillon and Reid, 2009; Chandler, 2010.
18 Foucault, 2003: p.245.
19 Foucault, 2007: pp.20–21.
20 Foucault, 2008: p.260.
21 See, for example, Lederach, 1997.
22 Ibid.: p.xvi.
23 Ibid.: p.25.
24 Ibid.: p.26.
25 Ibid.: p.87.
26 Ibid.: p.112.
27 Ibid.: pp.38–41.
28 Ibid.: p.94.
29 Ibid.
30 Ibid.: p.95.
31 Ibid.: p.78.
32 Ibid.: p.84.
33 Giessman, 2011: p.8.
34 Lederach, 1997: p.96.
35 Paffenholz, 2012.
36 Foucault, 2008: p.295.
37 See, for example, the 'Local First' development and peacebuilding initiative, launched in November 2012, led by Peace Direct, supported by the Overseas Development Institute and linked into the UK Government's Building Stability Overseas Strategy (http://www.localfirst.org.uk/).
38 Althusser, 2008: p.42.
39 Ibid.: pp.17–18.
40 Ibid.: pp.38–39.
41 Ibid.: pp.47–50.

42 Coleman *et al.*, 2011: p.46.
43 Solana, 2009.
44 Ibid.
45 DfiD, 2011: p.16.
46 Ibid.
47 Kaldor and Selchow, 2012: p.8.
48 Ibid.: p.24.
49 Richmond, 2011b: p.434.
50 Hollander and Einwohner, 2004.
51 Scott, 1990.
52 Ibid.: p.13.
53 Ibid.: p.17.
54 Ibid.: pp.151–2.
55 Ibid.: p.184.
56 Ibid.: p.203.
57 Ibid.: p.200.
58 Semenova, 2012.
59 Zürcher, 2012.
60 Foucault, 1981: p.96.
61 This logic will be drawn out further towards the end of this section.
62 Foucault, 1981: p.95.
63 Richmond, 2011b: p.421.
64 Ibid.: p.424.
65 Ibid.: p.433.
66 Ibid.: p.434.
67 See, for example, Popolo, 2011: p.128.
68 See, for example, Hollander and Einwohner, 2004; Eschler and Maiguashca, 2005; Richmond, 2010; Richmond and Kappler, 2011.
69 For example, Michael Hardt and Antonio Negri give ontological priority to resistance rather than to power, enabling the 'Multitude' to resist 'Empire' through the nature of their biopolitical being rather than traditional political forms of organization, which remain trapped in territorial understandings; see Hardt and Negri, 2005: p.315.
70 See, for example, Bennett, 2010; Connolly, 2011; Latour, 2007.
71 Latour, 2007: pp.241–6.
72 Ibid.: p.244. However, neither Richmond nor Latour renounces the possibility of knowing or tracing these hidden agents through the use of more anthropologically grounded approaches.
73 Latour, 2004a: p.81.
74 See North, 1990; IMF, 2005; World Bank, 2002; see also Chandler, 2013d.

5
THE 'EVERYDAY' POLICY SOLUTION

Culture, from limit to resource

Introduction

As analysed in the last chapter, policy analysts and critical academics involved in promoting international peace interventions increasingly focused on the 'local' as the barrier to the export of 'liberal peace' once it became clear that 1990s aspirations of transformation seemed to have failed. For the first wave of critical reassessment, the 'local' became a problematic barrier for liberal internationalist aspirations, operating as critique of the limits of international policy-making. This critique was largely an epistemological one, of the sort categorised in this book as a neoliberal framing, which understood societies as closed systems of interaction with emergent or evolutionary causality, in terms of fixed path-dependencies, and the segmentation of social and cultural differences which were difficult to overcome. In this framework, international interventions inevitably had non-linear outcomes or unintended and negative side-effects because the outcome of universal programmes and policies depended upon the nature of the society intervened upon. It seemed that in a world of complex life, in which non-linear or hybrid outcomes were inevitable, the limits to international policy needed to be accepted and little could be done.

Over the last decade, however, the understanding of the limits to international intervention has been renegotiated, away from neoliberal understandings of the 'local' – as an inaccessible barrier to the export of liberal understandings – to the understanding that, in a world of complexity, new approaches to intervention were necessary that did not necessarily start from problematising local rationalities and practices but instead viewed the 'local' as holding the key to the resolution of problems of peace and underdevelopment. This chapter looks at how this shift to a positive view of local actors and 'everyday' practices has enabled resilience-thinking to displace both liberal internationalist frameworks and the neoliberal critique of their limits. The key to this shift – from liberal internationalism (with the focus on the universal policy prescriptions of international actors) to discourses of resilience (with the focus on enhancing the already available practices and understandings of local actors) has been the way in which neoliberal appreciations of complexity and difference have confronted the problems of transforming a discourse of limits into a discourse of policy governance.

For classical neoliberal understandings, articulated well by Friedrich Hayek, local knowledges and practices were essential for efficient and adaptive responses to problems but could not be accessed by governments. Access to local and plural forms of knowledge could only be attained through market mechanisms, which were able to indirectly connect the complex plurality of choice-making preferences through the system of market prices. Thus the inability to access the understandings of the local was both a barrier to governmental intervention and an argument for the free play of market forces. Classical neoliberalism could critically articulate how complex life posed a limit to international intervention but not how to go beyond these limits, in cases where intervention was deemed necessary.[1] Neoliberal approaches were only confronted with the need to rethink how intervention might be necessary under the conditions of the post-Cold War 1990s, when these ideas became dominant at the same time as the international barriers to intervention were increasingly removed. Perhaps the clearest expression of the problem of adapting neoliberal understandings to international intervention is that articulated by Nobel Prize-winning economist and World Bank policy advisor Douglass North: 'Hayek was certainly correct that our knowledge is always fragmentary at best. ... But Hayek failed to understand that we have no choice but to undertake social engineering'.[2]

Neoliberal thought, as we shall see in this chapter, found 'social engineering' to be deeply paradoxical, and it was this problematic that shaped the discussions on the importance of culture, the 'local' and the 'everyday' in the peacebuilding discourses of the 2000s. Once liberal internationalist understandings were rejected – for the complex and non-linear approaches that underlined the importance of local rationalities and understandings – the sphere of the 'local' could not be left to the devices of the market. It was precisely in situations of international intervention, where it was held that both local government and local market solutions had failed, that the extension (rather than the restriction) of policy-making was required. The neoliberal policy response was that of adapting international policy-making to local conditions through successive processes of mediation. The first level of mediation was that of 'top-down' statebuilding (the immediate response to the difficulties of liberal internationalism). International statebuilding recognised that universal policy prescriptions could not just be exported and expected to work and that the world was complex and nonlinear. However, it was thought that differences in outcomes could be ameliorated by institutional reforms, creating structures and 'rules of the game' that would enable local practices and rationalities to change. The second stage was that of 'bottom-up' statebuilding, on the perception that change at the level of state institutions still did not touch or access the 'local' reality and that local mindsets and understandings remained unaltered. Yet, no matter how mediated the relationship of governing became, intervention was still paradoxically based upon the assumption that the external interveners could acquire the knowledge necessary to produce instrumental outcomes.

It was in negotiating the problems of 'bottom-up' statebuilding interventions that understandings of local cultural values and everyday life underwent a transformation within neoliberal constructions. As North states, this transformation operated at the level of how neoliberal thought understood 'consciousness' and 'human intentionality'.[3] For Hayek, it was not possible to rationally reflect on the evolution of cultural understandings and the 'organic' institutions, which reflected these. However, for neoliberal policy-approaches in the 2000s, access to this knowledge became vital, once neoliberalism was no longer merely a critique of governmental power but the dominant policy paradigm. Culture became the realm of policy intervention once 'top-down', linear approaches were seen to be ineffective:

> Understanding the cultural heritage of a society is a necessary condition for making 'doable' change. We must have not only a clear understanding of the belief structure underlying the existing institutions but also margins at which the belief system may be amenable to changes that will make possible the implementation of more productive institutions.[4]

The 2000s thereby saw a boom in critical understandings of 'liberal peace' approaches to international intervention, which argued that local culture held the key to the effectiveness of peace interventions.[5] In this 'bottom-up' approach, peace, reconciliation and reconstruction then become dependent on the correct understanding of and intervention in sociocultural norms and values. However, these revised and more mediated forms of peace intervention remained trapped in the neoliberal paradox: despite assumptions of complexity, they still maintained the external subject position of the liberal subject potentially able to know, direct and to control. This paradox – the inability to go beyond simple complexity framings (considered in Chapter 2) – was reflected discursively as a problem of how to go beyond the binaries of liberal universalism and cultural relativism. Either liberal framings of rights and law were seen as too abstract and distant from the 'realities' of 'everyday life', often with unintended and problematic consequences, or there was the perceived danger of cultural relativism, undermining democracy and human rights, where law was seen as problematically adapting to 'local' sociocultural differences. This chapter explains how resilience approaches have begun to enable policy-makers to overcome this neoliberal paradox, through focusing on the transformative power of local practices and understandings.

Resilience-informed policy thinking has built upon critiques of the formal, abstract, nature of liberal modernist understandings of universal constitutional and legal rights frameworks but has avoided the neoliberal policy impasse of essentialising sociocultural difference and thereby becoming caught between the Scylla and Charybdis of universalism and cultural relativism.[6] Resilience approaches do not start from the problematic of sociocultural difference but from a different set of problems, which no longer involve a focus on a 'hermeneutics of suspicion':[7] problematising the understanding or rationality of those seen to be in need of intervention. These 'resilience' framings suggest that, in a complex and flatter world, liberal forms of institutional and legal understanding are themselves problematic; that formal frameworks of law can no longer be understood to work to shape or direct social processes in a top-down or hierarchical manner. From this starting point, 'everyday life' is neither conceived of as a problem nor romanticised as 'resisting' but is seen as providing a problem-solving resource of practices to be drawn upon. This shift evades the problems of the external imposition of abstract, 'unreal', liberal universalist frameworks, but also evades cultural relativism, because there is no external yardstick or comparison at play in such understandings and thereby no articulation of an external subject position of a superior approach or rationality.[8]

This chapter takes, as an example of this shift, the recent policy discussion on the limits of international intervention with regard to the 'war on drugs' in the Americas.[9] The 'war on drugs' has been framed in the terminology of international aid for fragile states in the region and therefore serves as a good example of how international interventions have been refocused.[10] International, essentially US-led, approaches to the problem had focused primarily on drug production and distribution in Latin American states and the prominence of international criminal organisations and networks operating with relative impunity where many states have fragile frameworks of law and rights enforcement. Heuristically, it is possible to draw out three different approaches to the problem. First is what might be called a 'top-down' statebuilding approach, where resources are put into strengthening state capacity: training police and security forces, improving the operation and independence of the judiciary, increasing state-level coordination and information sharing and developing the strength of legal regimes in terms of democracy and human rights. The second, more pluralist and culturally sensitive 'bottom-up' statebuilding approach, launched amid the perceived failures of formal institutional capacity-building, has paid much more attention to sociocultural values and understandings, suggesting that success at the state level is dependent upon 'local' understandings – that norms and values change is the key to peace and the institutionalisation of a 'rule of law' regime.[11]

The third approach – beyond the neoliberal framings of mediated international intervention – is the 'resilience' approach. This does not start from the position of an external subject equipped with superior interventionist knowledge or instrumental goals. Resilience approaches seek to work through understanding the concrete context in which social practices and everyday 'tactics' produce problematic consequences: in this case, the criminal production, trafficking and consumption of drugs. Through a process-based or relational understanding of the construction of a concrete problem (or set of problems), everyday contexts and practices are seen to provide the key to mitigating both the causes and consequences of 'the drug problem' in the Americas:

> Resilience is the story of a profound change in perspective about where the solution to the hemispheric drug problem can be found. Rather than focusing primarily on suppressing drug production and trafficking, or changing the legal or regulatory regime, national and local leaders recognize that the best approach is to focus on people rather than drugs and to rebuild and strengthen communities from the grassroots level up. Like a healthy body, a healthy community fights off an 'epidemic', whether it is an epidemic of violence or of drug dependence, through its own capacity to respond effectively – its own resilience.[12]

The shift from understanding local sociocultural values as the problem or barrier to be overcome to resilience approaches, which understand local practices in the context of the production of a concrete problem and its solution, is crucial. Here, local responses and practices are seen as key to positive transformation once the relational context, through which the problem is perceived to be generated, can be understood and addressed.

The limits of culture

Whereas liberal approaches to institutional frameworks of governance assumed a universalist approach to the subject, in classical neoliberal understandings, the efficacy or capacity of state institutions and the 'rule of law' are dependent upon their sociocultural foundations.[13] As Hayek argued, modern liberal institutions could not be exported or created by edict or plans but had to emerge organically from society. In this organic or culturalist perspective, the constitutional history of Great Britain was often highlighted to argue that even without a written (codified) constitution, the rule of law had more *de facto* purchase than in the former colonies where the rule of law needed to be produced through *de jure* democratic constitutions.[14] The pluralist, 'organic' or institutionalist position involves problematic circular reasoning in attempting to explain the differences and divisions of the present as products of the cultural hold of the past. For example, Brian Tamanaha argues: 'The rule of law existed [in Britain] owing to the widespread unquestioned belief in the rule of law, in the inviolability of certain fundamental legal restraints on government, not to any specific legal mechanism.'[15] Paola Cesarine and Katherine Hite put this well in the context of Latin America:

> The persistence of authoritarian legacies in post-authoritarian democracies may be explained in terms of a combination of socially, culturally, and institutionally induced set of attitudes, perceptions, motivations, and constraints – that is, from traditions or institutions of the past as well as from present struggles within formally democratic arrangements. … As a result, democracy in much of Latin America belongs to the realm of constitutions and code books rather than reality.[16]

For neoliberal approaches, law could not provide its own legitimacy – its own basis, limits or constraints – any more than democratic theory could explain the constitution of the demos.[17] The universal, 'natural' or 'Cartesian' assumptions of the liberal rationalist autonomous subject were subject to devastating critique from these sociologically informed positions.

But while operating to highlight the limits of liberal constructions of the rule of law, there appeared to be little that could be done to overcome these limits. Once it was established that merely having legal constitutions (which can, of course, be internationally exported or externally imposed) was no longer adequate, then the sphere of sociocultural understandings appeared to pose a formidable policy challenge. As Augusto Zimmermann, law professor at Murdoch University, notes with regard to Brazil:

> Indeed, an observation of Brazil's reality reveals a society that is deeply regulated by contra-legem (anti-legal) rules. These are not the rules taught in law schools but rather are socially defined rules that vary remarkably from the state codes and statutes, and the rulings of the courts.[18]

The focus of neoliberal understandings on the gap between the formal sphere of law and constitutionalism and the social 'reality' of informal power relations and informal rules established a problematic but not a way of going beyond it.[19] This attention to cultural differences marked the impasse of the interventionist framework, which shaped international peacebuilding and statebuilding assumptions in the 1990s. The work of the sociological understanding of constitutionalism and law revealed the shallowness of the state-level or top-down focus of peace and democratisation approaches. In these frameworks, the social reality of countries undergoing democratic or post-conflict 'transition' could not be understood merely by an analysis of laws and statutes. In fact, there appeared to be an unbridgeable gap between the surface appearances or artificial constructions of legal and constitutional frameworks and the realities of everyday life, revealed in dealings between individual members of the public and state authorities.

Often this contrast between the 'reality' of the everyday and the formal framework of law was understood in terms of two – opposing – spatially constructed rationalities: that of the 'international' and the 'local'. This clash, between the formal and the real, has been captured in critical conceptual approaches (considered in the previous chapter) which have focused on hybrid outcomes of international interventions, which have attempted to transform societies through top-down mechanisms such as legal and constitutional reforms.[20] In the framings of hybridity approaches: 'the "laws" of the society can easily overrule the laws of the state'.[21] As Zimmermann argues: 'Socially speaking, the former can be far more institutionalized than the latter, which means that the state law can easily be undermined by the lack of connection between its formal precepts and observed behavior.'[22]

These 'hybrid', sociological approaches understood 'local', national or community cultures and values as socially constructed barriers to the export or development of constitutional frameworks and the rule of law.[23] The discursive framework in which these approaches developed was that of analysing and explaining the limits of external interventions based on liberal understandings. Universalist framings of law were held to fail where societies were understood to be 'non-liberal' and therefore not ready to, or incapable of, organising on the basis of law standing above social and economic conflicts. These barriers to the 'rule of law' were often understood to have deep cultural roots in the colonial era or in the parallel power structures that emerged during internal conflicts, and seen to be similarly deep-rooted. It is these deep societal roots that were held to explain the limits of liberal transition and international statebuilding. As Zimmermann concludes:

> [I]t is impossible to understand the obstacles facing the realization of the rule of law in Brazil if we confine ourselves to a purely legalistic and a less empirical analysis of the legal system. In order to comprehend the reasons for problems blocking the rule of law from taking hold in that society, we must necessarily turn our attention to the many patterns of social behaviour that inhibit normal respect for legal norms and principles.[24]

The framing of sociocultural norms and understandings, as a barrier, shifted the emphasis from the formal sphere of rights and law to the informal sociocultural understandings into which these were deployed.[25] However, while being able to process-trace understandings of these limits to the 'rule of law' backwards into the past, through the evolutionary reproduction of values, societal path-dependencies and interactive cognitive framings, these approaches offered very little in terms of being able to move forward beyond the impasse of 'culture'.

The limits of neoliberal or new institutionalist framings, which seek to promote liberal peace outcomes, through interventions at the deeper, sociocultural level, are clearly highlighted in 'culture of lawfulness' policy interventions that attempt to transform culture to enable the rule of law. These programmes have been particularly prevalent in frameworks of the 'war on drugs' in Latin America. Heavily funded by the US government and the World Bank, initiatives led by the US-based NGO, the National Strategy Information Centre (NISC), have placed the culture of lawfulness at the centre of the United States' global law enforcement strategy. According to US Under Secretary of State for Global Affairs, Paula Dobriansky: 'Government efforts to enforce the law are insufficient in and of themselves to establish the rule of law in a country. This is a result of the fact that lawlessness and corruption often stem from social norms and historic practices.'[26] For Dobriansky, historic path dependencies and sociocultural norms meant that the rule of law could not operate universally. She argued therefore that sociocultural interventions were necessary to educate and win over the 'hearts and minds' of recalcitrant subjects:

The Culture of Lawfulness Project, an international effort fostered by the National Strategy Information Center, has worked aggressively to advance this cause. An NGO that uses public and private funding, the Project has helped a growing number of governments, school systems and civil society leaders to improve public knowledge and attitudes about the rule of law. In culture of lawfulness education, the goal is to reach the next generation of students, and through them their parents and communities. Project staff and consultants help teachers develop a lawfulness education program, integrate it into the curriculum, and involve parents and the community in complementary activities. The Project also works with other critical sectors of society, often by offering training. The Project engages representatives from business and labor groups, religious institutions, local non-governmental organizations, and the media.[27]

A typical example is that of the NSIC 'culture of lawfulness' three-year project in the city of Pereira, Colombia, funded from 2008 to 2010. The project's starting presupposition was that the local culture was a central barrier to the rule of law: 'Prior to this project, rule of law principles had few public advocates and were not well understood by the people of Pereira. Apathy and fatalism were the norm for large segments of the population, and many engaged in or tolerated illicit behaviour.'[28] The project started with local knowledge and understandings, developing 'a Pereiran rule of law narrative, locally driven and cognizant of Pereira's unique history, customs and culture' and with the desire of government and civil society leaders to tackle the barriers of the local culture.[29] With the zeal of nineteenth-century missionaries, the NSIC attempted to align US Agency for International Development (USAID) and local funding, using local knowledge and access to society – at the level of government leaders, civil society organisations, faith groups, local businesses, the media and schools – to initiate awareness of the rule of law, educate and inform and begin to change ingrained patterns of behaviour.

Local culture was to be engaged with on the basis that the locals needed to adapt to and learn about universal liberal understandings of the 'rule of law':

[T]raining judges and prosecutors, rewriting laws, and building investigative facilities for police are not sufficient. To be effective, these efforts need to be accompanied by the development of societal support for rule of law principles. This entails educating citizens about the importance of the rule of law, how it enhances their quality of life, and the role they can play in making it a reality. When education and culture supportive of lawfulness are combined with enhanced law enforcement and institutional reforms, justice and order can be strengthened and crime and corruption reduced – even within one generation. However, reform efforts that do not address the culture at large, neglect a cost efficient, effective, and long-lasting way to deepen democracy.[30]

It was understood that, if the interactive process of evolving local culture could be successfully intervened in, liberal institutions and frameworks could take root 'even within one generation'. However, reforms that operated at the state and institutional level would be doomed to failure, just remaining at the superficial level of the formal framework and not touching the local reality. To this end, local leaders were encouraged to buy into the programme, and an all-out 'counter-insurgency' campaign was launched to win over the 'hearts and minds' of the community: 'A comprehensive citywide CoL [culture of lawfulness] campaign ... touched Pereirans at nearly every point of contact – at school, at work, in transit (buses, taxis, billboards), through television/radio/print, at community events and in houses of worship'.[31]

The NISC evaluated its own project very positively, arguing that over the three-year period it had a substantial impact on the community 'measured through the degree of the institutionalization of CoL in long-term community processes, activities and planning as well as significant shifts seen during the program in popular knowledge and attitudes – a foundation of behavioral change.'[32] It is important to note that new institutionalist framings operate at the level of interactive understandings – the empowerment that they offer the 'local' level is that of understanding the importance of the rule of law and their role as active citizens. These cognitive changes then lead to changes in behaviour, which enable liberal transformation, facilitating the rule of law:

> A culture of lawfulness guides citizens' relationships with one another and with the state. It can fundamentally alter the dynamics of state institutions, making them more efficient, effective, and just. Lawless behaviour, including corruption, is marginalized as more citizens begin to defend the rule of law and act according to its principles. Law enforcement and justice sector efforts to fight serious crime and corruption are reinforced by ordinary citizens who report crimes, serve as witnesses, and act as a check against corrupt and abusive practices, holding their government accountable for upholding the rule of law and respecting human rights.[33]

Although there is the language of local knowledge and resources, needs and interests and the empowerment of local people, it is clear that the agenda is very much one in which enlightened Western interveners, equipped with the external subject position of liberal universalist understandings, attempt to transform the barrier of local cultural-social frameworks. Because intervention is consciously aimed at transforming the minds and understanding of local people – and thereby necessarily setting up a hierarchy of understanding – the gap between the external perspective and the 'local' arena becomes clearer the more the international 'empowerment' agenda extends into the society.[34]

This becomes clear in projects such as the comprehensive 'multisectoral' campaign, considered here. In fact, upon reading their report, it becomes difficult not to see this work as patronising and demeaning to those they are seeking to 'empower'. Examples of good work highlighted in the report include a 60-hour Culture of Lawfulness course to be taught in schools,[35] encouraging the media to incorporate culture of lawfulness themes into documentaries, soap operas, game and talk shows,[36] therapeutic workshops for citizens to 'give voice to the obstacles and frustrations they face along their "journey" to a culture of lawfulness',[37] an annual 'Most Legal and Most Safe Neighborhood' competition,[38] culture of lawfulness supported hip hop and rap festivals – including 'The Culture of Lawfulness is an Awesome Challenge' rap contest,[39] public education billboards with personal testimonies concluding with the phrase: 'and YOU, what are YOU going to do for lawfulness?',[40] mime and theatre to discourage speeding and jay walking,[41] pledges for lawfulness by the town mayor in front of primary school children,[42] local Chamber of Commerce prize 'Culture of Lawfulness is my Business',[43] and a Culture of Lawfulness 'paint fest'.[44] Local pastors and lay preachers have even been given manuals on how to introduce rule of law themes into their services.[45] Of course, the paradox is that the more multisectoral and comprehensive the culture of lawfulness intervention is, the more artificial and patronising it becomes; while any single activity on its own seems clearly unable to tackle the task at hand, 'to transform an entire culture'.[46]

These approaches were limited by the liberal universalist framings which they explicitly drew upon (and explicitly defended). Here 'the rule of law' was consciously articulated as an external rationality, as somehow the preserve of the West (where, as noted above, it was often held that there was no cultural or societal mismatch). Thus, any attempt to 'artificially' construct rule of law regimes, even through 'culture of lawfulness' attempts to 'transform entire cultures', hardly appeared feasible. Even the best and most determined, you could even say messianic, attempts to engage with the 'local', in order to transform cultural values, seemed to fall prey to the problems of 'artificiality' (which had already beset international attempts to export the 'rule of law' through state and institutional level legal and constitutional reforms).

Furthermore, no matter how culturally sensitive these interventions were, they still – in fact, inevitably – produced hierarchical understandings, which problematised (even pathologised) local understandings and values, and came across as patronising and neocolonial.

There are clear limits to attempts to overcome the barriers to liberal peace approaches on the basis of intervention to transform 'local' sociocultural understandings.[47] However, the alternative approach to these barriers – of adapting liberal understandings of legal and constitutional practices to local sociocultural contexts – would appear to be equally problematic in terms of leaving international organisations vulnerable to accusations of providing support to 'illiberal' actors or undermining human rights norms.[48] The paradox of liberal peace advocacy is fully highlighted in attempts to defend international intervention, but which deny that local culture will be necessarily seen in these liberal, 'problematic' ways by external interveners. For more critical or radical liberal peace theorists, intervention needs to be done in more self-reflexive ways, which similarly seek to problematise Western understandings of liberal universality. These critical approaches are often drawn towards pluralist anthropological frameworks in order to develop an ethical methodology of intervention, which can break free of the hierarchical understandings explicit in liberal internationalism. Here, the plural and 'hybrid' outcomes of international intervention are seen as positive and to be encouraged. In fact, the experience of intervention, it is alleged, can be a mutual learning exchange between intervener and those intervened upon, as fixed cultural understandings on both sides can be challenged through 'unscripted conversations' and 'the spontaneity of unpredictable encounters'.[49]

The obvious problem with the 'unscripted conversations' approach is the question: 'Why then intervene in the first place?' The answer is that intervention is essentially a mechanism of intersubjective enlargement of reflexivity, enabling an emancipation of both intervener and those intervened upon, through the opening up of possibilities for both to free themselves from the sociocultural constraints of their own societies and to share a pluralised ethos of peace which, through pluralising, goes beyond both liberal universalism and non-liberalism. As Morgan Brigg and Kate Muller argue:

> Conflict resolution analysts and practitioners might facilitate this process [of increasing exchange and understanding across difference] – something which has already begun – by openly examining and discussing their own cultural values within their practice. This can generate possibilities for more dynamic conflict resolution processes by extending the practice, also already underway, of opening to and learning from local and Indigenous capacities, including different ways of knowing, approaching and managing conflict.[50]

For Richmond, this plural and emancipatory peace, based on mutual learning and exchange, is thereby 'post-liberal'.[51] Here, cultural understandings are also seen as malleable and open to intersubjective transformation, enabling liberal peace approaches to overcome the problems of conflict, crime and reconstruction but without privileging universalist understandings (although these views can be critiqued as no more than the anthropological ethics of cosmopolitan liberalism, this is not the focus here).[52]

The paradox of liberal peace is merely brought into full focus in these critical approaches, which have found it impossible to escape the focus on sociocultural norms and values. The ethics of radical liberal peace are those of cultural pluralism and the 'respect and the recognition of difference' beyond the divide of 'liberal and non-liberal contexts'.[53] However, it is clear that the problematic is one that still shares much with the liberal universalist vision, merely questioning its ability to fully accept the existence of plurality.[54] As Richmond argues: 'Behind all of this is the lurking question of whether liberal paradigms are able to engage with, and represent equitably non-liberal others – those for which it infers a lesser status'.[55] For Richmond, the liberalism of liberal peace shapes the understanding of the problem as one of pluralisation that 'requires a privileging of non-liberal voices' and the 'ongoing development of local-liberal hybrid forms of peace'.[56] As Audra Mitchell has pointed out, this framing problematically focuses on fixed or essentialised sociocultural understandings, counter-positioning an external 'liberal' internationalist subject to a 'non-liberal' local one.[57] Mitchell points beyond liberal peace framings, in articulating practices as the key to understanding outcomes of intervention rather than focusing on the binary and hybrid perspectives of liberal/non-liberal and international/local. The focus on effects rather than on cultural difference is key to the discursive moves of resilience approaches which take policy debates beyond the liberal peace and its limitations.

The starting point for resilience is a reinterpretation of the liberal discursive construction of 'culture' itself as a fixed or settled spatial community of intersubjective, constructed meanings, which interveners are somehow external to.[58] The new institutionalist or critical constructivist approach can thereby be understood to operate merely through inversing hierarchical liberal understandings of universal reason.[59] The epistemological privileging of 'local' knowledge then becomes the basis of value pluralism, but always from the standpoint of the problems of liberal democracy and universalist approaches to public institutions and the rule of law.[60] As long as the discourse stays on the level of shared rationalities of spatially differentiated intersubjective collectivities, both academic and policy discussion remains on the terrain of liberal universalism and value relativism, based upon the judgement of the intervener, self-understood as external to the problematic.[61] It is only in the sphere of practices and strategies in relation to concrete problems that there can be a shift away from spatial constructions to social practices. The 'local' or the 'everyday' then becomes the focal point, not on the basis of the epistemological differences of liberal reason but on the ontological basis of the practical production of the world.[62]

The rise of resilience

While the top-down liberal and neoliberal governance problematics deploy external standards of judgement and downplay the critical and agential capacity of actors, resilience approaches argue that the world is made 'from below',[63] through the practices of the 'everyday', and that the only purpose of external intervention can be to facilitate and respond reflexively to these practices rather than seek to remake or constrain them through either liberal universalist or cultural relativist approaches. The importance of understanding society 'from the bottom-up' rather than 'from the top-down' has been well articulated by a number of authors with a growing impact on debates on international policy-making. Perhaps the classic text in this regard is Michel de Certeau's *The Practice of Everyday Life*.[64] In his analysis of the practices of the 'everyday', de Certeau shares much with the actor-network theory of Bruno Latour and the work of the French pragmatist theorist, Luc Boltanski.[65] Just as Latour argues that 'we have never been modern' – in his devastating critique of the artificial division between science and culture[66] – so de Certeau hints at the ever-present reality of the practices of local and 'everyday' agency outside the reach of liberal representational theory.[67]

These practices of 'bottom-up', tactical, adaption and creativity 'present in fact a curious analogy, and a sort of immemorial link, to the simulations, tricks and disguises that certain fishes or plants execute with extraordinary virtuosity'.[68] And, while we, indeed, 'have never been modern', the complex global world seems to make liberal myths of institutional power and the sciences which have supported them, more and more unreal or artificial, while the tactical practices 'from below' appear to become more and more dominant: 'Cut loose from the traditional communities that circumscribed their functioning, they have begun to wander everywhere in a space which is becoming at once more homogeneous and more extensive'.[69] Rather than seeing the 'everyday' as only operating on the margins, or merely as a barrier or limit, 'altering or defeating' the instruments of power, de Certeau argues that it is the external grand narratives and strategies of power which should be seen as marginal, artificial, phenomenological constructs.[70]

What is vital about the pragmatist framework is not so much the fact that policy attention is drawn to the everyday but its methodological centrality. Authors such as James C. Scott have focused on everyday life as the sphere of resistance, but the transformative capacities of the 'everyday' remained marginal, erupting on the surface only on rare occasions.[71] What differentiates the pragmatist philosophy of authors such as de Certeau, Boltanski and Latour is their critique of the structural discursive understandings which marginalise the concrete and specific practices of the everyday.[72] As Boltanski argues, the resources of the local provide the empirical material for a 'sociology of critique', which gives agency to previously marginalised subjects, seen as constrained by discursive structures of power in the 'critical sociology' of authors such as Althusser, Foucault and Bourdieu.[73] For Boltanski, pragmatic sociology, with its rigorous empiricism can offer 'better descriptions of the activity of actors in particular situations'.[74] Rather than starting from the external subject position of critical sociological theory, pragmatic sociology 'refocused the sociologist's attention on actors en situation, as the main agencies of performance of the social'.[75] As Boltanski contends, the key intent is to go beyond both the universalist and culturalist frameworks:

> The universalist framework is explicitly rejected, because the polities are treated as historical constructs. As to the culturalist framework, it is displaced from *culture* in the sense of anthropology towards the *political*. ... The social actors whose disputes are observed by the sociologist are *realistic*. They do not demand the impossible. Their sense of reality is sustained by the way they grasp their social environment.[76]

Resilience approaches do not start from liberal universalist assumptions of the rational autonomous subject and thus are no longer concerned with explaining the limits of liberal universalism, or attempting to work on culture to overcome the 'gap' between liberal assumptions and 'everyday' reality. In fact, this methodological framework seems to speak to us much more clearly than the neoliberal or critical conceptions of some sort of 'organic' cultural connection between society and law. Today, it seems that the 'rule of law' is just as alien and 'artificial' in a Western domestic sphere as it is in the debates on democratic transition and international peacebuilding in the international context. What we apparently 'discover' in meetings with the exotic Other in post-Cold War interventions (as earlier), we can now see clearly in our own societies.[77]

Legal theorist, Professor Reza Banakar, is typical in drawing upon the radical sociological framings of globalisation theorists, Zygmunt Bauman, Anthony Giddens and Ulrich Beck, to argue that in 'late-', 'liquid' and 'reflexive' modernity, liberal framings of law no longer have an 'organic' connection to Western societies.[78] In our more fluid, reflexive, transient and networked world, the cultural institutions and social structures – through which the modernist state operated, cohered and legitimated itself – no longer bind communities together through shared frameworks of meaning. Western everyday realities, it appears, also trump any attempts to use the law for purposes of societal regulation: 'Under late modern conditions, where law's normativity can no longer find a durable foothold in fleeting social structures, legal measures aimed at generating new patterns of behaviour or social change grow evermore ineffective.'[79]

It is important to note that, in these approaches, the complexity and fluidity of social practices are highlighted and the spatial dispersal of 'communities' with networked connections, which lack a strong sense of shared intersubjective values. Law fails to connect with society but not on the basis of the structured or cohered 'gap' between culture(s) and law. In fact, it is possible to argue that the attempts to renegotiate liberal frameworks of representation, the operation of democratic institutions and legal regimes, on the basis of cultural differences and multiculturalism, can retrospectively be seen as precursors to the discussion of governing complexity in terms of resilience.[80] Resilience approaches start from the assumption that there is no 'organic', 'cultural', or intersubjective construction of community, which gives legal frameworks a purchase on social complexity, but do not problematise this. Their concern is with how societal regulation can operate on the basis of fluidity and complexity. As the Stockholm Resilience Centre argues:

> Law is traditionally characterised by 'thou shalts' rather than opening doors for new approaches. As a reaction to this, the concept of reflexive law has emerged. Reflexive law is less rule-bound and recognises that as long as certain basic procedures and organisational norms are respected, participants can arrive at positive outcomes and correct their projects along the way, basically learning by doing. In response to growing complexity, detailed rules are replaced by procedures for regulated entities to follow. Reflexive law is a social innovation which seeks to promote multi-level governance and preserve diversity and experimentation at local level.[81]

Law follows society but not because there is a clash between liberal universalism and cultural relativism but because liberal frameworks of law are understood to be the barrier to governing complexity rather than a solution. These approaches share the focus on the local societal milieu of liberal peace debates, but in these framings the milieu is seen as providing the sphere in which transformative agency is generated through practice. In effect, resilience approaches to law re-pose the problem not in terms of a 'gap' between law and society (or the abstract and the concrete) but in pragmatic terms of specific problems or consequences, which can no longer be meaningfully addressed through the mechanisms of law (or external subject positions) as a guide to practice.[82] It is the internal processes of practical relations and outcomes that need to be understood and worked upon, not the external mechanisms and frameworks which need to be refined.[83] This resilience approach evades the problems of liberal peace, neither imposing a universal framework over sociocultural difference nor recognising or privileging 'local' choices as emancipatory. According to Charles T. Call, Senior Advisor in the US State Department Bureau of Conflict and Stabilisation Operations, current approaches seek not to impose artificial external goals nor to merely accept local values, but to facilitate local transformative agency: 'to find those organic processes and plus them up.'[84]

The drug problem in the Americas

A good example of the resilience approach to law and institutional frameworks is that of the discussion with regard to the 'war on drugs', which has been re-posed not as a question of law enforcement but in terms of 'the drug problem in the Americas'.[85] What makes the report particularly interesting is that it is produced in two parts: the Analytical Report based on a series of case studies, which analyses the problem; and a Scenarios Report based on a hypothetical analysis of four possible futures. It is the Scenarios Report, which will be focused upon here. The four possible future scenarios are categorised as 'Together', 'Pathways', 'Resilience' and 'Disruption'. These different scenarios can be heuristically categorised, respectively, as liberal internationalist institution-building; cultural pluralist experimentation to align law and sociocultural norms; resilience-based approaches which are concerned with the problem in terms of the contextual framing of local practices; and the perceived status quo, which would lead to diverse responses, including compromising with criminal networks where the costs of controlling them were considered too high.

The neoliberal or statebuilding approaches to the drug problem are divided into two in the Organisation of American States (OAS) report – the 'top-down' approach, focusing on state institutional frameworks, and the 'bottom-up' cultural pluralist approach of attempting to 'organically' relate the law to social practices. The 'top-down' neoliberal approach focuses on state-level institutions, arguing that the drug problem 'is part of a larger insecurity problem, with weak state institutions unable to control organized crime and the violence and corruption it generates'.[86] The response then is to strengthen the capacity of judicial and public institutions, improving their professional status and bringing in new techniques, benchmarks and success indicators. Collectively, states in the region will then be able to launch a sustained campaign against transnational criminal organisations. In this scenario, liberal institutional changes are seen to be effective: reducing the power of criminal organisations and trafficking gangs through increasing the strength and effectiveness of democratic and legal institutions. This good governance framing would also be understood to strengthen economies in these states and to transform local values and understandings, lessening support for organised criminal groups and enabling liberal institutional frameworks, based on human rights and transparent procedures, to extend even in outlying areas where drugs are grown and produced.[87]

However, the 'top-down' approach is seen as just one possible scenario. The report argues that there is also plenty of evidence against such approaches, which were the sine qua non of international programmes in the late 1990s and 2000s. The complexity of drug production, trade and consumption in the Americas and the different contexts that state institutions are faced with can also be argued to undermine such universalist understandings of 'good government'. For many of the states concerned, the focus on law enforcement and drug prohibition 'produces more damage than the drugs themselves'.[88] It is understood that enforcement efforts not only fail to sufficiently reduce the supply and the demand for drugs but that they also have the unintended consequence of providing illegal criminal gangs with huge profit margins, while risking the security of their citizens and the integrity of their democracies.[89]

The 'bottom-up' neoliberal or new institutionalist approach of cultural pluralism holds that there is no such thing as a universal solution to the drug problem, particularly at the level of formal framings of law, good government and institutional capacity. While drugs might be a problem, using the law to prohibit drug production, transportation and use is also a problem where the sociocultural context militates against its effective operation, or produces even more problematic unintended consequences in the increase of police and paramilitary power. It seems that the paradox of universal liberal approaches is that the unintended consequences of their adoption appear to be just as problematic as the problems they are intended to resolve. The 'paradoxes' or 'contradictions' of interventionist approaches based on universalist assumptions have of course been well rehearsed in the international peacebuilding and statebuilding literatures.[90]

Pluralist approaches attempt to escape this paradox by either working to adapt local cultures to the rule of law or (using the same ontological framing, but privileging 'local' rather than 'international' voices) adapting law to the social context. The pluralist approach as portrayed in the OAS report appears to adopt the latter perspective, advocated by the more pluralist critics of liberal peace,[91] and outlined in the 'Pathways' scenario, which rearticulates the drug problem in less universalist terms.[92] The reason for a pluralist approach, it is argued, is that the drug problem and the use of law enforcement to address it cannot be properly grasped outside of the specific cultural-socio-political context:

> [T]he international drug control framework may operate well enough for some countries but generates serious problems for others. For example, harms and costs related to drug consumption in the region (loss of productivity, dependency, treatment costs, stress on families) and those related to drug control enforcement are unevenly distributed and do not affect every country in the hemisphere in the same way or to the same extent. Political leaders in some Central and South American countries where there is drug crop cultivation believe that problems of drug-related violence, high homicide rates, insecurity, overcrowded prisons, and human rights violations are made worse or are even largely caused by efforts to prevent the illicit production and trafficking of drugs.[93]

This argument to a certain extent reflects the discussion in the United States where the war on drugs has been seen to be a war on the poor and marginalised (both inside and outside America). It is argued that the balance needs to be refocused in a more 'emancipatory' way to concerns of human rights, health provision and the development and protection of cultural and indigenous rights.[94]

The cultural pluralist understanding focuses much less on the institutional frameworks and more on the specific cultural context in which the law operates, and in this way seeks to mitigate the unintended consequences of universalist approaches. The location of the solution is shifted downwards to experiment with alternative legal and regulatory frameworks. The most consensual regulatory shift in this regard is experimentation with the decriminalisation of softer drugs such as cannabis and focusing more resources on major criminal networks than on small-scale production and consumption. In this way, resources can be better distributed, lifting the burden on police, prisons and courts as well as reducing the drug market and enabling drugs, which are decriminalised, to be better regulated.

Of course, in this framing, law is being adapted to the sociocultural reality rather than making a 'culture of lawfulness' attempt to adapt sociocultural reality to the law. However, the problems of privileging local culture and values and of adapting law to the reality of the 'local' – the paradox discussed above – become clear. In relation to the discussion in the US, regarding the decriminalisation of cannabis, the contradictions have been highlighted by critics, such as *Wire* creator David Simon, who have argued that such changes would be just as 'artificial', merely benefiting privileged middle class white kids while intensifying the criminalisation of poor African-Americans in crack-infested communities.[95] There are clear limits to the capacity of adapting law to local reality, as removing the universal 'detachment' of law from reality leaves the law open to accusations of arbitrariness and cultural relativism. If law really was 'culture,' then these accusations would be hard to avoid.

The 'Resilience' approach is notable in that the focus is no longer on law and its enforcement nor on how law may be pluralised but instead is placed on states' 'improved social capital to build community-based approaches, in which the underlying emphasis shifts from treating drug use and related violence as primarily a legal or security matter to responding to the drug problem by strengthening community resilience'.[96] The resilience approach locates the problem of drugs as an outcome of complex societal practices, not as something which can be dealt with as a discrete problem to be tackled by law. Rather, 'the drug problem is a manifestation and magnifier of underlying social and economic dysfunctions that lead to violence and addiction'.[97]

It should be clear that not only is the drug problem not a discrete problem to be solved in isolation, but resilience approaches, of necessity, construct the drug problem as a matter of community practices and amenable to community solutions. In resilience approaches, communities imbricated within the production and trade of illegal drugs are less likely to be seen as criminal objects of the law and more likely to be understood as in need of facilitating intervention to enable them to be the leading agents of transformation. The individuals most likely to be involved in the production, trafficking and consumption of drugs, and the communities in which they live, would be subject to enabling interventions designed to use cultural, communal and informal networks to produce less problematic practices. Rather than intervene coercively to enforce the law or adapt law to the differentiated level of the 'local', resilience approaches seek to use the 'really existing' power of the local community as a transformative mechanism.[98] It is this element of internalisation of the problem and focus on local transformative agency that distinguishes resilience approaches from those of the external subject positions of liberal peace, both the liberal top-down approaches – which see individuals as objects of law and subject to social engineering – and those of cultural pluralism, which understand local cultural-sociopolitical milieus as barriers to universal frameworks of law and thereby seek to adapt the law to the circumstances.

As the OAS scenarios report suggests, the resilience approach works directly with – and not over or against – individuals and communities caught up in the drug problem:

The significantly expanded drug and alcohol treatment, harm reduction, screening and early intervention programs, and alternatives to incarceration, decriminalization of possession for personal use in most regions, drug treatment courts, probation services, monitoring, and counselling, health services within prisons for drug-dependent users, and restorative justice initiatives involving victims and offenders – all lead to an increased number of people who benefit to such an extent that many of them manage to rebuild their families and work lives. These successes, in turn, impact levels of crime, family cohesion, and community health in a number of areas.[99]

Rather than a cultural pluralist or new institutionalist approach, which emphasises the hold of the past, in terms of path dependencies and deep cultural values, resilience approaches argue that everyday settings can be enabling and transformative. As well as focusing on the 'roots' of the problem in terms of those directly involved in the practices of producing, trafficking and consuming drugs, there is also a great deal of attention to the community networks and relationships seen to provide the context for practices; thereby resilience responses

are supported by the flowering of initiatives in other related fields as well: regional Responsible Fatherhood and Motherhood campaigns, values programs for schools, prison education programs, sports and cultural programs for underprivileged communities, vocational training programs, basic skills for a successful life programs for young, uneducated parents, and community-based policing programs for the region.[100]

The emphasis, as stated, moves away from drugs per se to a focus on resilient people and communities. As the OAS report states, in this framing: 'citizens gradually become aware that they are [a] fundamental part of the solution and not just victims of the problem'.[101] With this shift, the focus is no longer on the problem of community understandings and values – the problem is not understood to be 'in the heads' of local people, but in the context shaping the outcomes of their practices. Law is no longer the key framework for measuring success in dealing with the 'drug problem', instead the metrics concern everyday practices from parenting to employment training: 'The paradigm change of focussing on building resilient societies forces people and governments to look inward for solutions and to acknowledge the need for social reforms.'[102]

Conclusion

The transformation of neoliberal governmental understandings, towards the pragmatic philosophy of resilience, moves beyond the 'abstractions' of formal frameworks to focus on the 'reality' of the everyday. In this way, the paradox of neoliberal 'social engineering' is overcome and neoliberalism is transformed from a discourse of limits to liberal universalist understandings into one of the potential of governing through local practices and everyday reasoning. In this way, international intervention is no longer hamstrung by either the 'top-down' understandings of international statebuilding, which sought to change 'local' rationalities through state-level institutional reform, or 'bottom-up' understandings, which sought to transform local culture from below. Both of these approaches depended on highly interventionist practices, which problematically assumed that international interveners possessed superior knowledge of how to instrumentally 'socially engineer' the local to achieve liberal peace and developmental goals (and, of course, could thereby be accountable for policy failure). When neoliberalism became a governing rationality, it revealed that it lacked a positive programme of interventionist policy-making, able to overcome the limits of liberal internationalism, which it had so easily articulated in the past.

As noted in this chapter, neoliberal governmentality was only able to adapt to policy-intervention through assuming liberal frameworks of instrumental knowledge and linear cause-and-effect assumptions of institutional and cultural change. Despite developing an understanding of the epistemological and governing limits of complex life, neoliberal frameworks were not able to adjust to understanding complexity as facilitating governance rather than as being a barrier to it. The transformation of neoliberal governmentality into the framework of resilience required the assimilation of critical sociological thought, which shared its deconstruction of universal liberal assumptions but did not view local practices and understandings as 'hidden' or inaccessible to governance or only 'revealed' through the mediation of market indicators. The 'local' was not the 'local' of universal modernist understandings, replete with epistemological exclusions and reductionist homogenising assumptions, but a different 'local' of plural and situated enactments and practices.[103] For critical analysts, drawing on pragmatist thought, local knowledge was available on the 'surface' and accessible in the form of the 'everyday'. The discursive centrality of the 'everyday' enabled a new regime of international intervention based on uncovering a new sphere of practices, which needed to be facilitated and enhanced without instrumental means-ends assumptions: the 'organic processes', understood as amenable to 'plussing up'.

The limits of neoliberal approaches and the rise of resilience were sharply highlighted in attempts to rethink the governing rationality of international intervention in the 2000s. However, it is very important to note that international intervention as a thematic failed to draw out the full importance of constructions of complexity and resilience-thinking in the international sphere. The shift to the 'local' and the view of enhancing and facilitating local solutions expresses well the retreat from liberal internationalist frameworks of the 1990s but the discourse of intervention itself already presupposes a separation between policy-making subject and the object of intervention. It is precisely this gap that the embedded and relational ontology of resilience-thinking seeks to bridge, in the urge to self-reflexively derive policy from the object of intervention – complex life – rather than imposing policy over or against it. The next chapter concludes this part of the book on 'Resilience and the International' by considering discourses of resilience which shape international policy-making not through intervention but through under-standing that governing power is already and always in an embedded relation-ship with the object of governance: in this case, the international.

Notes

1 According to Hayek: 'The conception of man deliberately building his civilization stems from an erroneous intellectualism that regards human reason as something standing outside nature and possessed of knowledge and reasoning capacity independent of experience' (Hayek, 1960: p.22).
2 North, 2005: p.162. (I am grateful to Jessica Schmidt for emphasising the importance of this passage to me.)
3 Ibid. See further, the discussion on Hayek in the concluding chapter.
4 Ibid.: pp.163–4.
5 See, for example, Paris, 2004; Richmond, 2011a; Mac Ginty, 2011; Newman *et al.*, 2009; Campbell *et al.*, 2011; Tadjbakhsh, 2011; Richmond and Mitchell, 2012.
6 It could be argued that this impasse of binary essentialism is implicit within all liberal sociological approaches to formal institutional frameworks, see, for example, Max Weber's investigation of the cultural roots of the 'irrationality' of law and administration in Confucian China (Weber, 1951).
7 Ricoeur, 1970: p.27.
8 While liberal peace approaches involve the assumption of a universalist subject position, described well by Ole Jacob Sending as an external 'Archimedean' position, resilience approaches remove the external subject position entirely (see Sending, 2009). A good example of the removal of the subject position of the external actor is provided by Louise W. Moe and Maria Vargas Simojoki (2013) in their study of the Danish Refugee Council's work in promoting community development in Somaliland.
9 This discussion has been cohered through the publication of a high-profile report from the General Secretariat of the Organisation of American States, suggesting that international policy interventions have failed in this area (OAS, 2013a).
10 See, for example, Morton, 2011; Cammack *et al.*, 2006; Miraglia *et al.*, 2012; Tokatlián, 2011; Sogge, 2009; see also the Pulitzer centre project 'Fragile States: The Drug War in Central America', information available at: http://pulitzercenter.org/node/10031/all.
11 See, for example, Fukuyama, 1995; Risse *et al.*, 1999; Cortell and Davis, 2000; Chandler, 2013d.
12 OAS, 2013b: p.55.

13 See, for example, North, 1990; Mahoney and Thelen, 2010; Guy Peters, 2005; Scott, 2008.
14 This gap, between *de facto* legal standing and a purely *de jure* one, began to enter the sphere of international legal and political understandings of sovereignty with the end of the Cold War. See, for example, Jackson, 1990.
15 Tamanaha, 2004: p.58.
16 Cesarini and Hite, 2004: p.7.
17 In this context, research projects and even entire research institutes (such as the Käte Hamburger Kolleg, Centre for Advanced Study, Law as Culture) work on the basis of the need to investigate 'law as culture'; see Gephart, 2010.
18 Zimmermann, 2007: p.29.
19 See also the initially pessimistic views of North regarding the difficulties of understanding how exported institutions will interact with 'culturally derived norms of behavior'; North, 1990: p.140.
20 See, for example, Roberts, 2008; Richmond, 2009; Mac Ginty, 2011; Richmond and Mitchell, 2012.
21 Zimmermann, 2007: p.29.
22 Ibid.
23 See Chandler, 2013d.
24 Zimmermann, 2007: p.30.
25 See further, Chandler, 2010.
26 Dobriansky, 2004.
27 Ibid.
28 NSIC, 2011: p.ii.
29 Ibid.
30 Ibid.: p.1.
31 Ibid.: p.iii.
32 Ibid.: p.iii.
33 Ibid.: p.1.
34 For an excellent study of how these approaches can end up in the pathologising of populations subject to intervention, see Pupavac, 2005.
35 NSIC, 2011: p.2.
36 Ibid.: p.9.
37 Ibid.: p.11.
38 Ibid.
39 Ibid.: pp.12, 27.
40 Ibid.: p.13.
41 Ibid.: p.14.
42 Ibid.: p.16.
43 Ibid.: p.18.
44 Ibid.: p.24.
45 Ibid.: p.26.
46 Ibid.: p.20.
47 Local sociocultural understandings and values are usually grounded upon contextual realities, such as structural and socioeconomic frameworks of inequality and exclusion, and thereby are not necessarily amenable to interventions at the level of formal understanding (see further, for example, Acharya, 2000; Belloni, 2008; Chandler, 1998; Paffenholz, 2009).
48 Moe and Simojoki, 2013: p.400.
49 See, for example, Duffield, 2007: 233–4; Richmond, 2009; see also Jabri, 2007: p.177.

50 Brigg and Muller, 2009: 135.
51 Richmond, 2011a.
52 For an excellent critique along these lines, see Shannon, 1995.
53 Richmond, 2009: p.566.
54 See also Sabaratnam, 2013.
55 Richmond, 2009: p.570.
56 Ibid.: p.578.
57 Mitchell, 2011.
58 As Ann Swindler has noted, 'a culture is not a unified system that pushes action in a consistent direction … it is more like a "tool kit" or repertoire' (1986: p.277); see also Sewell, 1999.
59 A useful critique of the neoliberal, constructivist and post-structuralist understandings of culture as constructed meaning is Scott, 2003.
60 See, for example, Brigg, 2010; Mac Ginty, 2008.
61 Richmond, 2009.
62 This is where practice-based understandings become particularly useful. For example, Annemarie Mol's work on the treatment of diabetes draws out how abstract or universal, objective, medical approaches of prescribing treatment also need to account for the context of social practices. They also need to be concretely 'attuned' to these and for interventions to be seen as 'a part of ongoing practices: practices of care as well as practices to do with work, school, family, friends, holidays and everything else that might be important in a person's life' (see Mol, 2008: p.53).
63 Boltanski, 2011: p.44.
64 de Certeau, 1998.
65 Latour, 2007, 2004a; Boltanski, 2011.
66 Latour, 1993.
67 See also the influential work of Nigel Thrift (especially 2008).
68 de Certeau, 1998: p.40.
69 Ibid.
70 Ibid.: p.41.
71 See, for example, Scott, 1990; there is a similar framing in Rancière's work on politics as a rare eruption from below into the 'natural' order of social domination (see Rancière, 1999; Tambakaki, 2009). Similarly, Henri Lefebvre's understanding of the 'everyday' could be seen as one that is under the surface of modernity rather than constituting its appearances (see, for example, Lefebvre, 1987).
72 The extension of non-representational understandings continually sets the bar higher; see, for example, Nigel Thrift's critique of de Certeau's 'weak humanism', seen to lead to the underplaying of the possibilities for embodied, post-rational, forms of knowledge (2008: pp.75–88).
73 Boltanski, 2011; Latour, 2004b; see also de Certeau, 1998: pp.45–60; and for a good overview, Celikates, 2006.
74 Boltanski, 2011: p.23.
75 Ibid.: p.24.
76 Ibid.: p.31.
77 As de Certeau intimates, the 'critical' framing of difference as an ethnological reality remains even with the import of a radical pluralising of identities; these are still understood as either 'enlightened' or as 'problematic' (1998: p.64).
78 Banakar, 2013. The limits of law as an instrument of policy have also been widely discussed in terms of the 'new paternalism' proposed by Richard

Thaler and Cass Sunstein, the authors of *Nudge* (2008), and taken up by the UK Cabinet Office, UK Prime Minister David Cameron's Behavioural Insight Team (the 'nudge unit') and the Royal Society for the Arts' Social Brain project; see further Chandler, 2013b.

79 Banakar, 2013: p.21.
80 See further, Walzer, 1983; Kymlicka, 1995; Tully, 1995; Gutmann, 1994.
81 Stockholm Resilience Centre, *What Is Resilience: An Introduction to Social-Ecological Research*. Available at: http://www.stockholmresilience.org/download/18.5ea7abe0139d0dada521ac/resilience_summary_lowX.pdf.
82 Where Richmond does bring into his analysis de Certeau and the tactics of the everyday this is still seen in terms of flexible and hybrid approaches combining liberal and non-liberal understandings, rather than as a pragmatic or resilience approach based on practical policy consequences (2009: pp.571–2).
83 As Manuel DeLanda notes, the key to non-linear understandings of complexity is that the internal organisation of an entity is more important than the external or extrinsic factors, which 'are efficient solely to the extent to which they take a grip on the proper nature and inner processes of things'. One and the same external set of policies or causal actions 'may produce very different effects' (2006: p.20).
84 Comments at the International Paternalism workshop, George Washington University, 4–5 October 2013 (notes with the author).
85 OAS, 2013a.
86 OAS, 2013b: p.23.
87 Ibid.: p.30.
88 Ibid.: p.41.
89 Ibid.: p.42.
90 See, for example, Paris and Sisk, 2009.
91 However, the challenge to liberal universalist understandings could also be seen as a less emancipatory lowering of expectations, analogous to Merilee S. Grindle's conception of 'good enough governance' (see further Grindle, 2004, 2007).
92 OAS, 2013b: p.43.
93 Ibid.: p.45.
94 Ibid.: p.47.
95 Vulliamy and Ray, 2013.
96 OAS, 2013b: p.20.
97 Ibid.: p.23.
98 As Moe and Simojoki note, key to interventions based on pragmatic rather than liberal peace understandings is the mobilising and organising of 'existing capacities' (2013: p.407).
99 OAS, 2013b: p.58.
100 Ibid.
101 Ibid.: p.61.
102 Ibid.: p.62.
103 This point is clarified by John Law (2004: p.155).

6
A NEW GLOBAL ETHIC
The transformative power of the embedded subject

Introduction

This chapter seeks to analyse the rise of 'resilience ethics' in terms of the shift in ethical approaches, away from the liberal interventionist projects of the 1990s and neoliberal constructions of 'top-down' and 'bottom-up' state-building in the 2000s, towards broader and more inclusive understandings of ethical responsibility for global problems. This shift in ethical attention away from the formal international politics of interstate relations and towards the unintended consequences of both institutional structures and the informal market choices of individuals has diversified understandings of global ethical responsibilities. It is argued that the recasting of ethical responsibility in the increasingly sociological terms of unintended and indirect consequences of socio-material embeddedness constructs new ethical differentials and hierarchies of responsibility. These framings have facilitated new policy practices, recasting interventionist policy-making in terms of the growing self-awareness and reflexivity of Western actors, reframing ethical foreign policy as starting with the choices of individual citizens, and, at the same time, operating to reify the relations of the market.

It is taken as a truism that today we live in a globalised and complex world, but what has been less analysed are the implications that this new reality has for liberal modernist understandings of ethical responsibility. With complexity and the rise of resilience-thinking it is particularly problematic today to make the distinction between public ethics (the guide to the government of others) and personal ethics (the guide to the government of the self). This distinction was essential to Rawlsian and post-Rawlsian analytic political philosophy, enabling a moral distinction between the basic structure of society and individual character and conduct and also making a clear distinction between deontological and instrumentalist understandings of ethics. Modernist framings of ethics depended upon the liberal rationalist construction of the subject which has been challenged by new institutionalist understandings in economics and the social constructivist frameworks of institutionalist sociology and international relations, which have suggested that rather than having pre-given rationalist 'interests', ideas and understandings are shaped by historical experiences and the social contexts in which actors are embedded.[1] In these increasingly dominant post-rationalist framings, the individual is no longer seen as an isolated actor but rather as a socially, environmentally and materially embedded subject. It is also argued that our social and material embeddedness does not just differentiate, limit and constrain our rationality but that, even more problematically, the consequences of our decisions take on greater importance as our actions are inserted into powerful processes of complex global interaction, extending the impact of our individual actions and choices.[2]

In a globalised world, the most important impacts of our choices and decisions are held to be unintentional: or 'side-effects' in the language of Ulrich Beck.[3] In this way, global complexity and interconnectivity are held to pose substantial problems with regard to judging where responsibility lies for the world and for the provision of a satisfactory moral compass for our everyday lives. Global complexity, and the ethical constructions it gives rise to, discursively tends to elide any clear divide between the subject and the external world and between the public and the private. For this reason, Weber's binary ethical ontology that: 'all ethically orientated action can be guided by either of two fundamentally different, irredeemably incompatible maxims … an "ethics of conviction" or an "ethics of responsibility"',[4] seems to be much less tenable today. In a world of complexity, ethical responsibility tends to be reformulated to take account of the fact that the consequences of our actions are dependent upon the socio-material processes into which they are inserted. The field of ethical and political responsibility is therefore defined less by our personal or our public choices and more by our embeddedness in emergent chains of causality.[5] In a global relational ontology, our ethical responsibilities stem from the unintended consequences of our relational embeddedness and our ethical duty to become reflexively aware of this. This very distinct and, I argue, problematic reformulation of ethical responsibility is conceptualised here as 'resilience ethics'.

This chapter seeks to stake out a series of claims with regard to the rise of the relational ethics of resilience, premised upon our ontological embeddedness in complex chains of global interconnection.[6] First, it is concerned with drawing out how understandings of relational responsibility have become increasingly central to mainstream policy and academic thinking, highlighting the conceptual links between the ontological or 'new materialist' turn in social theory and the rise of post-rationalist or post-Rawlsian thinking more broadly. Second, it highlights how the ethics of global relational embeddedness redistribute ethical responsibility in ways which rather than challenging power inequalities appear to affirm or reify them. Resilience ethics rearticulate 'Western responsibility' for global outcomes on the basis of relational embeddedness, rather than superior liberal values or institutions, and rearticulate the outcomes of market relations in terms of the embedded relational choices of individuals. In essence, relational ontologies may provide a new ethical compass of self-reflexivity for a fluid and complex world, but they only do so at the expense of the ethical separation of the self from the world. Without the separation of the ethical subject from the world, it is impossible to engage in transformative political projects based on the critique of structural relations of power and the market. Instead, critique of the world is displaced by reflexive ethico-political work on the self.

The following section considers the rise of these 'ontological', materialist understandings of ethical responsibility as a shift away from the liberal and neoliberal 'top-down' constructions of the 1990s, in which the West assumed traditional political responsibilities for the outcomes of intervention, while assuming that 'criminal' elites and individuals bore sole responsibility for war crimes and human rights abuses. 'Top-down' global ethics worked on the basis of direct responsibilities, assuming direct political and legal authority over subjects denied equal rights.[7] The following sections discuss the evolution of 'resilience ethics', which works on the basis of indirect assumptions of responsibility, not on the basis of legal, moral or political responsibility but on the basis of our relational embeddedness: the understanding of indirect side-effects caused by our associational connectivity in a complex and globalised world. On the international level, powerful Western states take responsibility for the unintended or indirect outcomes of market forces and their institutional frameworks. However, it is important to stress that this 'responsibility' cannot be properly understood in either political or moral terms. Resilience ethics fit with neither Weber's 'ethics of responsibility' nor his 'ethics of conviction'. Instead we see the rise of a relational, material or ontological ethic: a sociological recognition of the side-effects of complex global associational interconnections and their emergent properties.

This chapter seeks to problematise this shift by arguing that at the heart of resilience ethics is the rearticulation of power hierarchies and the reification of market relations and outcomes. The sociological framing of global complexity tends to understand the inequalities and conflicts that exist in the world as products of unintended consequences in a world in which modernist rationalities no longer operate. In other words, they show that the outcomes of liberal frameworks of political and legal freedoms and market exchange, in a world of difference and clashing temporalities, can reproduce inequalities and become a barrier to progress. In this perspective, Marxists are therefore correct that the market is irrational and can reproduce inequality; where they are wrong is in the assumption that we can somehow stand outside the associational interconnections of a globalised world. The sociologisation of the market, as a self-emerging complex and adaptive process of indirect chains of connection and causation, in which we are all embedded at different levels with different consequences, removes the liberal understanding of direct political or ethical responsibility for our choices.

The ethical and political duties emerging from these indirect responsibilities operate on a different register to the traditional liberal framing of law, sovereignty, rights and intervention as, for the sociologically embedded subject, there is no assumption of preexisting autonomy. Two examples of this framing of indirect responsibility are analyzed in the work of Paul Collier and Thomas Pogge. These authors are taken as heuristic examples to demonstrate the ontological framings which enable the construction of indirect understandings of responsibility today. Neither author is known as a complexity or a resilience theorist; rather, both are generally read as liberal-minded policy-reformers. Drawing out the implications of their writings for resilience ethics thereby involves reading their work at a level of ontological structure which they themselves do not explicitly draw out and would probably normatively dispute. In conclusion, I will suggest that the flatter (but not flat) ontology of indirect responsibility replaces a liberal framing of responsibility to the self or to the community, with responsibilities externally imposed upon actors through their embeddedness. In our relational embeddedness, we become responsible for the world but are capable only of working to change the world indirectly through working on our own ethical self-growth. In this sense resilience ethics work beyond the public/instrumental and private/deontological divide.

Resilience ethics

Under discourses of complexity and social relationality, power relations can easily evaporate into complex processes of indirect interconnection, where responsibility for the actions of governments as much as the actions of individuals, are seen to be shared much more equally. This process of dismantling frameworks of individual and collective responsibility often appears as an enlightened, socially rich, actor-networked perspective.[8] These richer social ontological approaches – highlighted in the rise of assemblage theory, new materialism, and post-humanism – tend to work on the basis of 'flat' or 'bottom-up' ontologies of interconnection.[9] Here, as considered in the previous chapter, agency is distributed away from the formal centres of political power (the focus of liberal ontologies) and towards the margins or the 'everyday' where the 'tactics' of ordinary people contest and disrupt the strategies and understandings of the powerful.[10] In these more fluid ontologies, governing or personal intentionality is much less important than the complex ontological reality of social interconnectivity. The more broadly the connections are drawn, the more diverse are the actors and agents that need to be drawn in to provide an adequate explanation of concrete policy outcomes.[11] The focus on the social relational embeddedness that produces concrete realities, rather than on the abstract or metaphysical constructions of human purpose and intention, also enables agency to be redistributed beyond purely human, or anthropomorphic constructions of intentionality.[12]

However, it is important to note that resilience ethics do not merely problematise the understanding of individual responsibility and bring the contingency of assemblages of interconnection into play, but also articulate a new framing of international hierarchy, which builds upon these ontological understandings of associational embeddedness.[13] This is because resilience ethics work through establishing the ontological power of social relational interconnection but then rearticulate the gap between conscious intention and concrete outcomes in terms of the ethical demand for self-reflexivity. Resilience ethics work back from the appearance of the world to enable an embedded ethical reflexivity to guide the subject's own self-transformation.[14] In this framing, the problems of the world can be reinterpreted as ethical lessons for self-growth and self-awareness. The indirect ethical responsibility derived from self-reflexivity can thereby be neither understood as instrumental (it is the self-reflexive responses to outcomes which are important rather than the outcomes per se) nor as deontological (ethics are derived from external consequences). In this way, in a more interconnected world, Western agency can be rearticulated in terms of this distinct form of indirect ethical responsibility. Western powers can claim responsibility for the world, but rather than these claims of responsibility generating moral opprobrium or demands for political accountability, they can be used to produce new, reflexive, forms of ethico-political authority.

To explain how this inversion works, it is worth recalling a point emphasised in the work of Hannah Arendt on how agency works in relation to 'guilt'. As Arendt noted, when we claim that 'we are all guilty' we are actually expressing 'solidarity with the wrong-doers' rather than the wronged.[15] This is the mirror-opposite of direct relations of political solidarity with the wronged, which suggests that we support their challenge to power in righting those wrongs. I wish to draw out, in particular, how this inversion works in relation to capitalism or market relations. In modernist framings, political solidarity was often demonstrated in understanding a common cause of struggle against market relations and its enforcement through the coercive political power of capital. In today's understandings of embedded associational responsibility for the unintended consequences of our actions, we are more likely to see our lifestyle or consumption choices as responsible for inequalities, conflict or environmental problems.[16] In an age of political complexity, when it is 'easier to imagine the end of the world than the end of capitalism',[17] in effect, responsibility is recast or internalised, displacing capitalism as the problem through vicariously seeing ourselves as responsible: understanding capitalism as merely a complex emergent process of exchanges in which we are to differing extents embedded and therefore indirectly responsible. In an age when the overthrow of capitalism seems unimaginable, capitalism is transformed as the sociological vehicle of connection, displacing the conscious and direct chains of politics.

It is precisely in this inversion, in this shift of political responsibility from social structures and political frameworks external to ourselves to the recognition of our own indirect social or societal responsibility, as complicit through our own choices and actions, that resilience ethics operates. Resilience ethics redistributes responsibility and emphasises the indirect, unintended and relational networks of complex causation because problems are reconceived as not political, economic or moral but as societal or ontological. They are the problems of 'side-effects', 'externalities', of 'second-order' consequences, of a lack of knowledge of the emergent causality at play in the complex interconnections of the global world. The more these interconnections are revealed through the work of self-reflexivity and self-reflection, the more responsibility governments, other actors and individuals, acting in the world, have. We learn and learn again that we are responsible for the world, not because of our conscious choices or because our actions lacked the right ethical intention, but because the world's complexity is beyond our capacity to know and understand in advance: the unknowability of the outcomes of our action does not remove our ethical responsibility for our actions; it, in fact, heightens our responsibility for these second-order consequences or side-effects. In a complex and interconnected world, few events or problems evade appropriation within this framing, providing an opportunity for recasting responsibility in these ways.

Resilience ethics and international relations

In the international sphere, the articulation of political and ethical responsibilities has become transformed since the end of the Cold War. In the early 1980s, US President Ronald Reagan controversially described the Soviet Union as the 'Evil Empire', in an attempt to reinvigorate the ideological certainties of the geopolitical divide, but no one in the West assumed that Western governments or citizens were in any way responsible for the acts of the Soviet Union. The concept of Western moral or ethical responsibility for the actions of other governments only began to arise in the 1990s, with the articulation of global moral or ethical understandings underpinning the foreign policies of Western governments and giving content to the doctrines of humanitarian intervention and human rights enforcement.

Discussions of humanitarian atrocities, from Rwanda to Srebrenica, focused on individuals and elites, held to bear individual moral and political responsibility for war crimes and human rights abuses,[18] but they also focused on the West's responsibility to intervene to prevent these atrocities and to protect basic human rights. While the West was not held to be responsible for the crimes of Stalinism, it was held that there was complicity through non-intervening, which was seen as allowing the crimes of human rights abuse in sub-Saharan Africa or the Balkans. It was argued that the globalised world was increasingly becoming one community with shared norms and values and that foreign policy was not merely about national interests but liberal universal concerns of laws and rights.[19]

In the 1990s, the ethical or political responsibility of the West was generally cast in the direct terms of intervention to prevent human rights abuses by 'others'. The articulation of responsibility in a global world was couched in the universal rationalist terms of liberal discourse. Crimes of war or of human rights abuse were held to constitute an ethical and political 'right' of intervention (even if this right was not formally upheld in international law).[20] So, while the West or the 'international community' had a 'responsibility' to intervene, the understanding of responsibility for the crimes themselves was placed squarely with the 'other' criminal, insane or maleficent elites and individuals, held to be responsible for mass humanitarian abuses in the 'new wars',[21] and therefore liable to military intervention, regime change and to judgement through new international courts and tribunals. The liberal discourse of rights and law pitted intervention against sovereignty, with the top-down claim that sovereign rights were lost and replaced by new international sovereign responsibilities, clearly manifested in the 1990s' protectorate powers over Bosnia, Kosovo and Timor-Leste.

This understanding of responsibility maintained a clear dividing line between qualitatively different types of responsibility. 'We' had the responsibility to intervene, to prevent human rights abuses and war crimes, but our responsibility only arose after the fact, in response to these problems; we had no responsibility in terms of causing these problems. We were not, even indirectly, 'guilty' of the crime itself, merely of passivity in the face of such crimes. The liberal internationalist understanding of political and ethical responsibility was sharply bifurcated: responsibility for war crimes and human rights abuses was restricted to individuals or discrete groups of 'others'; responsibility for the outcomes of intervention was restricted to the international 'saviours' bringing peace, development and democracy.[22] After the 1990s, the rise of neoliberal approaches (as noted in the preceding chapters) increasingly hollowed out responsibility, both for crimes and for interventionist outcomes, which became distributed less clearly.

In the sphere of international relations, the sociological logic of indirect responsibility – of resilience ethics – initially emerged in distinction to the rationalist logic of international liberalism, for example, in work in the tradition of the English School. In Robert Jackson's influential study, *Quasi-states: Sovereignty, International Relations and the Third World*, published in 1990, the discursive logic of societal interrelations is clear. It is the conceptualisation of indirect responsibility that I wish to heuristically focus on here. Jackson did not argue for the return of colonial paternalism, but for what might be seen as a new type of informal or resilience 'paternalism':[23] a recognition that the problems of post-colonial states were not merely of their own making but a problem of emergent causality – a 'side-effect' of the attempt to instigate an international constitutional order on the basis of equal sovereignty. This constitutional order stacked the deck against domestic development and democratisation and is argued to have encouraged despotism.

Jackson did not suggest that the West took formal 'moral or legal responsibility' for post-colonial states on the basis of their incapacity.[24] Instead, the new problematic emerging was one of recognising the unintended consequences of institutionalist frameworks, held to be a barrier to development and democracy in these states. The key point about the emergence of what I am calling 'resilience ethics' is that in recognising 'responsibility' for the problems caused by the 'side-effects' of shared institutional frameworks, there is an understanding of a new type of material ethical responsibility. This is neither moral nor political – the institutions were established for the best of reasons (for example, in the case of the United Nations and the UN Charter's enshrining of non-intervention, the prevention of war) – but an associational, networked, or indirect and unintentional 'ontological' responsibility.

With this new type of 'responsibility' came an imperative to ethically reconsider these institutions in the knowledge that the institutional framework shaped the possibilities and actions of others (in this case, 'quasi-states'). Once the associational link is established, through the connective framework of effects, then the West has the ethical/political responsibility to reflexively consider a different set of institutional practices which may more positively affect the outcomes in post-colonial states. Resilience ethics argues that, like it or not, powerful states shape international institutions and therefore bear responsibility for their unintended consequences. The argument then follows that if international institutional frameworks have a deleterious effect on 'quasi-states' then others should be considered which could have a positive effect. While not assuming political responsibility for post-colonial states, as in the top-down paternalism of colonialism or of 1990s' liberal internationalism, the associational responsibility confers upon the West the right to intervene *indirectly*, through the institutional framework, to positively affect the outcomes at the level of the post-colonial state. This is neither the old paternalism of colonialism nor the equal sovereignty of the post-colonial period but the recognition that inequality (the fact that powerful states shape the international institutional framework) gives Western states responsibility because they shape indirectly the outcomes for other weaker states.

In the framework of the rise of resilience ethics, there is therefore no such thing as non-intervention. Intervention is no longer understood as the formal undermining of sovereignty, as in colonialism. Intervention is seen to take place indirectly through the institutional frameworks and agreements of the international arena, and therefore the West is understood to be always indirectly intervening in the domestic politics of the post-colonial world through the institutional shaping of both economic and political relations. It is on the basis of this understanding that Western states then have the ethical/political responsibility to reconsider this international institutional framework with regard to these outcomes. In passing, it should be noted that there is a similar resilience ethic at play in the argument that states have a duty to reflexively influence the private choices of citizens.[25] Once there is an assumption that in an interconnected world there is no sphere of autonomous choice-making, there is then no barrier to the rise of the resilience ethics of intervention through indirect means.

The resilience ethics of Paul Collier and Thomas Pogge

It is important to observe that the consequences of a more sociological approach, which understands responsibility as a product of associational links, actor networks or assemblages, are that discourses of responsibility are neither political nor moral but ontological. Responsibility is ontologised, spread much more thinly but also in context-specific ways, so that responsibility is always a shared but fluid concept. This is very different to modernist understandings of responsibility, which operated to demarcate a sphere of ethical understanding: political responsibility stopped with the sovereign or government, whereas moral responsibility stopped with the private conscience. Ontological responsibility knows no political or private subjects, only subjects always and already embedded in fluid and complex networks of association. It is the networks of association that allocate the ontological responsibilities to actors. Responsibility no longer emerges from the decisions of the subject itself – to be legitimised in instrumental or deontological terms. The ethical responsibility is secondary: to reflexively adapt to the unintended outcomes of interactive and emergent processes in which actors are embedded.

The sociological, institutionalist sensitivity, articulated by Robert Jackson, remained at a fairly abstract level, typical of the English School approach, which was concerned with drawing a sociological 'third way' between the rationalisms of Realism and Liberalism in international relations theory. The sociological approach is heuristically drawn out in more depth below in an analysis of the conceptual frameworks deployed by two influential theorists: Oxford academic and World Bank policy advisor, Paul Collier, and Thomas Pogge, a moral and political philosopher and director of the Global Justice Program at Yale University.

Paul Collier's work is notable in that it removes the liberal rationalist ethics of responsibility from understandings of state collapse and human rights abuses by posing the problems of conflict and lack of development as matters of formal and informal associational connections – in effect, reducing both politics and economics to sociological understandings of embedded context. Collier argues against the direct responsibility approach of liberal internationalism: that we cannot rescue them by telling them what to do or by throwing aid money at them. Change 'must come predominately from within; we cannot impose it on them'.[26] However, we can help in terms of our own reflexivity about the international institutional frameworks which rich Western countries support and have established. Changing them 'from within' can be done if change also comes, reflexively, 'from within', at the international level, rethinking the unintended consequences of trade regulations or of not having international agreements on extractive industries or the arms trade. This indirect approach of intervention works on the basis of Western states and international institutions reflexively working to address the unintended consequences of their actions rather than directly intervening or claiming the right of intervention in other states (the cause of the neoliberal paradox, considered in the previous chapter).

Collier, together with his Oxford colleagues, developed the 'greed and grievance' model of conflict in the mid-2000s.[27] This model could be seen as a clear step back from the bifurcated framework of responsibility justifying liberal internationalist interventions in the 1990s. Collier's indirect framing of responsibility has a much richer model of social interaction, developing an understanding of post-colonial or post-conflict societies as shaped by the choice-making context in which actors are embedded. In their critique of theorists who sought to understand conflict in the rational terms of political rights (struggles over grievances), Collier and his team sought to analyse conflict in terms of the institutional constraints upon individual choice-making. In this framing, political causation no longer becomes an explanatory or a legitimating factor; rather, it is the opportunity for rebellion that has explanatory value. Essentially, if finance is easily available (for example, due to easy access to primary commodity exports) and there is little opportunity cost (i.e., few other avenues to earn income, if access to secondary education is low and the economy is stagnant) then conflict 'entrepreneurs' will arise who do not necessarily have any stake in furthering the interests or needs of their alleged constituents.[28]

Political or ethical responsibility for conflict and war crimes is radically redistributed in the new institutionalist model put forward. For Collier's project: 'where rebellion is feasible, it will occur without any special inducements in terms of motivation';[29] 'motivation is indeterminate, being supplied by whatever agenda happens to be adopted by the first social entrepreneur to occupy the viable niche'.[30] Once conflict is understood as the product of the interactive social processes, shaping the choices of individuals, the possibility of reshaping the formal and informal processes of interaction, and therefore the outcome of decision-making, arises. This approach of indirectly influencing the conduct of communities and of individuals, on the basis of the international influence upon these frameworks, highlights the indirect consequences of associational connections at the expense of the political responsibility of both local actors and international interveners.

The work of Collier and his team has been highly influential in the policy developments of the World Bank, which has been keen to take up new positions of reflexive responsibility, focusing on unintended consequences of

institutional structures in a world of political complexity, rather than political or ideological concerns.[31] On an international level, Collier's sociological
framing works in a very different register to liberal debates on intervention
and sovereignty, where Western responsibility recalls traditional paternalist
understandings, formalising inequality and a denial of rights, such as the Libe-
rian government's subordination of financial control to a coterie of international donors[32] or the 'Responsibility to Protect' (R2P) doctrine, a 'full-frontal
assault' on the concept of national sovereignty.[33] Here there is not intervention (as legally and politically conceived) but merely 'interference': the reflexive understanding of associational interconnection. Such institutional reforms
of the international order do not directly undermine sovereignty but seek
to 'interfere' in ways that support progressive ends rather than work against
them, for example, in contractual relations to deter coups where there is a
democratic mandate, support for financial probity or in linking aid with military spending.[34] This sociological framing, Collier argues, takes us beyond the
liberal rights framings contra positioning intervention and sovereignty and
enables 'a compromise between positions that are currently deadlocked'.[35]

The importance of Collier's work is in the clarity of articulating indirect
ethical responsibilities and the practices which flow from these in distinction to the direct interventions of liberal and neoliberal internationalism,
for example, as expressed in the politics of conditionality of the World Bank
and the International Monetary Fund, which sought to bend post-colonial
states to their will, in terms of particular policy outcomes.[36] Collier argues
along similar lines to Jackson, that the international institutional framework
unfairly makes reform or development difficult: despite the fact that change
can only come from within, international states, institutions and private economic actors can assist in ensuring that in their associations with these states
they facilitate progress rather than shore up corrupt and failing regimes. In
effect, the self-reflexive ethics of resilience politicises all associational connections between external actors and the states viewed as problematic or failing.
It does this through the ethic of sociological association: that any contact or
connection, no matter how indirect, has unintentional effects. These connections, which previously would not have been understood as political but as
private contractual relations of trade, are then 'politicised' in terms of where
the wealth goes and how it is distributed. From the sociological perspective
of embedded relationality there is no limit to the ethical injunction to reflect
upon how one's assocational connections 'interfere' with others.

Collier's problematic of responsibility insists that 'they' in the failing or
post-colonial states are, therefore, not entirely to blame for conflicts and
underdevelopment, but neither are 'we' in the rich West.[37] However, he goes

on to argue: 'I am now going to pin some blame on citizens of the rich world, who must take responsibility for their own ignorance about trade policy and its consequences'.[38] The blame upon the West is one of a lack of self-reflection upon unintended consequences. Addressing these unintended consequences means, for example, becoming aware of the impact of tariff protections, which prevent less developed countries from diversifying their production[39] and of the refusal to strengthen institutional frameworks, which could diversify state monopolies over wealth and resources or guarantee intervention if a democratic regime is overthrown. From Collier's perspective, the struggle of the poorest bottom billion 'is not a contest between an evil rich world and a noble poor world. It is within the societies of the bottom billion, and to date we have largely been bystanders.'[40] The intimation is that we in the rich West have an indirect responsibility for the outcomes and that our actions and choices at the moment favour the side of corrupt elites, conflict and poverty when we could make other choices which would favour the side of progress and development.

Thomas Pogge goes further than Collier in the sociological or ontological understanding of responsibility through associational connection. For this reason, his work has been used to challenge Collier's view that 'citizens of the rich world are not to blame for most of the problems of the bottom billion'.[41] The irony, of course, is that Pogge's work on the international regimes of property and resource rights, which the international sovereignty regime enforces (and therefore citizens in the West are complicit with), uses a very similar framework to Collier's sociological understanding of indirect causality as the basis for the extension of ethical responsibility, through market relations. What is interesting about Pogge's work is that he is concerned to point out how global institutional frameworks – both formal and informal – institutionalise global inequalities.

Pogge argues that it is ethically desirable that there should be the spread of democracy and human rights in the international sphere. Reflexively understanding the 'side-effects' of both personal and institutional choices could thereby achieve a transformation of international norms, rules and regulations, which at present create a problematic framework of environmental choices for the less developed world. His work is possibly the clearest example of how resilience ethics have developed. This is usefully articulated in his 2011 comment article, 'Are We Violating the Human Rights of the World's Poor?'[42] Pogge goes beyond liberal rationalist or contractual understandings of rights and duties by asserting the importance of the indirect consequences of our actions and inactions. Key is not the rationalist 'interactional' liberal framing, of government duties to protect rights nor our own duties to respect these rights, but the relational understanding of how the indirect consequences of our actions may 'facilitate' the promotion or violation of rights.[43] In his 2002 book, *World Poverty and Human Rights*, Pogge argued that we should reject the liberal interactionalist understanding entirely,[44] but in the second edition of 2008 this argument has been amended to an understanding that there are two varieties of human rights violation.[45] However, the concern is with the distinction between the two and the importance of highlighting the understanding of indirect relational responsibility:

> There is the interactional variety, where individual or collective human agents do things that, as they intend, foresee, or should foresee, will avoidably deprive human beings of secure access to the objects of their human rights. And there is the institutional variety, where human agents design and impose institutional arrangements that, as they intend, foresee, or should foresee, will avoidably deprive human beings of secure access to their human rights.[46]

Once we lose the understanding of the autonomous liberal subject and instead understand the morality of the world on the basis of formal and informal institutional structures, which we are all complicit in the everyday reproduction of, then it is clear that responsibility for human rights infringements has a much broader, flatter or democratic ontological basis. We are all then to differing extents responsible for what might appear – not as the commissions or remissions of others (the concern of Arendt)[47] – but as indirect market outcomes, outside any individual's direct responsibility:

> Duties to facilitate constitute then a crucial addition which highlights the vital importance that the design of institutional arrangements has for the fulfilment of human rights. ... The purely interactional analysis of human rights deficits must then be complemented by an institutional analysis which traces such deficits back not to wrongful conduct of individual and collective human agents, but to injustice in the design of social institutions: in the rules and procedures, roles and agencies that structure and organize societies and other social systems.[48]

The understanding that indirect responsibility lies in the framing of social institutions and social systems – societal interrelations, with their unending chains of complex causal connection – then means that responsibility for human rights abuses is inevitably transformed, minimising the importance of the liberal or modernist understanding of political or ethical responsibility. Take, for example, the undermining of rights to gender equality or education and welfare of impoverished communities: for Pogge, it is clear that impoverished communities 'cannot reasonably be said to be morally required to undertake political action towards realizing their own and each other's human rights when such action would be excessively risky and costly for them'.[49] Or, to take another example of Pogge's, if you were black-mailed for the ransom of your child by a kidnapper, your moral responsibility would not be merely to ensure that you maximise the prospects of the safe return of your child by giving in to extravagant demands: this would clearly encourage further kidnap attempts on your children but more importantly would also affect the kidnap risk to which other children other than your own are exposed as it 'may attract more people to a career in the kidnap-ping business'.[50] There is a clear indirect impact as individual choices and decisions constitute the choice-shaping institutional framework in which others decide whether or not the kidnapping business constitutes a via-ble career alternative. What is particularly important to note is that we are not all equally embedded in these interactive processes. Clearly, the more power, wealth and influence we wield, and the more that this influence is extended by the technological and socio-material context in which we act, the more indirect responsibility we bear and the more self-reflexive we need to become.

We may be pursuing what appear to be entirely rational and morally cor-rect choices but may be producing irrational and potentially immoral out-comes. The more power we wield within these socio-material contexts, the more responsible we are for these outcomes. The irrationality of the world or of the market system is thereby a product of our lack of self-reflectivity upon the unintended consequences of our embeddedness in these relations of interconnection, but this responsibility is unequally distributed. Here, respon-sibility for poverty and welfare problems cannot reasonably be seen to be that of those people living in these benighted states and seemingly lacking the capacities to resist, nor, necessarily, with their cash-strapped and dependent governments: it lies elsewhere, with the extent to which we are embedded in the complex international system which we are all in part responsible for. If the market, and its institutional framing, is to blame, through indirect links of causation, so therefore are we. The reason for this is that we make the market, we reproduce it and in so doing have the capacity to shape it: to expand or contract the profitability of the kidnapping business, for example.

It is these indirect outcomes which constitute our unequal personal contributions to ethical or moral problems either by our commission or omission. For Pogge, the extension of ethical responsibility to indirect and institutional frameworks of social relations provides an avenue for linking personal citizen and consumption choices in the West with the morally problematic role of transnational regulatory institutions. Once the 'interactive' link between individuals or collective actors and rights violations is broken, then it is the institutional context or relational assemblage which increasingly bears the responsibility, as the framework of incentivisation, or of environmental choice-shaping. This approach clearly challenges liberal understandings of both individual and collective responsibility. In Pogge's work, the international level is the centre of attention, and it is the institutional frameworks shaping market exchanges, in an era of globalisation, which are alleged to bear an increasing responsibility for the level of democracy, development and human rights in the non-Western world. Even where there is development, such as in India and China, this is highly unequal and Western-enforced global regimes such as the World Trade Organization (WTO) and the 1994 Trade-Related Aspects of Intellectual Property Rights (TRIPS) Agreement reinforce these inequalities.[51]

Pogge's work does not merely focus on the impact of global market relations as framed by international agreements on trade and property rights but also on the formal regimes of international law, in particular the principle of sovereign equality – the bulwark of international law – seen to make it more difficult for non-Western states to achieve democratic and developmental stability. The reason for this is that:

> the developed countries are the chief upholders of the might–is–right principle. It is they who insist that the mere fact that someone holds effective power over us – regardless of how he came to power, of how he exercises power, and of the extent to which he is opposed by the people he rules – gives him the right to incur legally binding international obligations on our behalf.[52]

The international sovereignty regime of international law is seen to constitute an international institutional framework which makes democracy and human rights much more difficult for non-Western states, leaving them at risk of military coups or violent sectional conflict. Although Pogge shares with Collier the view of the indirect responsibilities of Western states and international actors through institutional frameworks of choice-making, he extends the links of association much more deeply, down to the level of the Western citizen as an individual actor or agent.

Pogge's work, as a moral philosopher, rather than an economist or an international relations theorist, is probably the best articulation of what could be called resilience ethics and marks the clearest distinction from the liberal ethics of cosmopolitan internationalism of the 1990s. In this framework, global complexity means that responsibility is shared but that it is always indirect and it is always unequal. It is the ontology of associative connection, which constitutes the ethical need for self-reflexivity of Western states and citizens who are encouraged to become more ethical in their choice-making. Having established the 'collaboration' or complicity of Western citizens in ethically unfair regimes supported by their governments, he suggests that there is a moral duty to reflect upon the indirect consequences of our embeddedness in Western societies and in global markets. The solution, in terms of resilience-thinking, is not necessarily that of joining a political party to change policies or offer solidarity with the resistance of the poor and oppressed but to consider how we as individuals might 'compensate for our fair share of the avoidable human rights deficit'.[53] One such way is through charitable giving: 'Citizens can compensate for a share of the harm for which their country is responsible by, for example, supporting effective international agencies or non-governmental organizations.'[54]

The new ethics of indirect responsibility for market consequences can be seen clearly in the idea of environmental taxation, both state-enforced through interventions in the market and as taken up by both firms and individuals. The idea that we should pay a carbon tax on air travel is a leading example of this, in terms of governmental intervention, passing the burden of such problems on to 'unethical' consumers who are not self-reflexive enough to consider the impact of package holidays on the environment. At a broader level, the personalised ethico-political understanding that individuals should be responsible for and measure their own 'carbon footprint' shifts the emphasis from an understanding of broader interrelations between modernity, the market and the environment to a much narrower understanding of personal indirect responsibility, linking all aspects of everyday decision-making to the problems of global warming.[55] Increasingly noticeable is this indirect use of market connectivity to facilitate 'real' processes of emergence. For example, the popular *Financial Times* columnist and BBC presenter, Tim Harford, suggests that global warming can only be addressed through carbon taxes, which would encourage experimentations with alternative energy uses, rather than through international or state targets for emissions.[56]

Unlike the liberal internationalists of the 1990s, Pogge's concern is neither directly with the agency of leading Western states and institutions, nor with the ostensible 'victims' in poor or underdeveloped countries. The concern of resilience ethics is not even with the responsibilities of the 'poor or poorly educated citizens' at home in the West. As Pogge states:

I can suspend judgement about such cases because what matters is the judgement each of us reaches about ourselves. I believe that I share responsibility for what my country is doing in the name of its citizens, and I explain what human rights deficits I hold myself co-responsible for, and why. You must judge for yourself whether you find these reasons compelling or whether, on reflection, you find yourself sufficiently immature, uneducated, or impoverished to be exempt from the ordinary responsibilities of citizenship.[57]

In the age of resilience and the politics of complexity, responsible citizenship, for Pogge, does not involve political or public campaigning as much as individual self-reflexivity about the unintended consequences of our social embeddedness: 'Each of us should … do enough toward protecting poor people to be confident that one is fully compensating for one's fair share of the human rights deficit that we together cause.'[58] Pogge makes a similar statement in an Internet magazine interview, when asked how his view of ethical responsibility worked, in terms of a rejection of existing structures or an attempt to change them from within. His answer was very clarifying: 'There is a third way. I call it the "Oskar Schindler solution": You remain within the system and try to compensate for the human rights deficits that are caused by the system because of your contribution to it. If you simply retreat from the system, nobody benefits.'[59]

It is interesting to note the secular trend involved in the extension of the ethical world through the logic of association. It seems that the more responsibility is spread, the less interest there is in the specific problem itself and the more attention there is to the ethical self. In the bifurcated liberal ethics of responsibility in the 1990s, the attention was squarely on the problem of human rights abuse and war crimes, problems which non-Western 'others' were morally and politically responsible for and therefore lost their rights to political and legal equality in the instantiation of paternalist regimes of intervention and the abnegation of sovereign rights. In Collier's work, political responsibility is eroded through being sociologised: they are less responsible for the contexts in which choices are made and external interveners share less responsibility as direct intervention shifts to indirect 'interference' which does not undermine formal legal and political rights. However, the problems of the world, for example, of the 'bottom billion', are still at the forefront of political and ethical concern. With the radical social relationality of Pogge, the outlines of a fully resilient understanding of global complexity emerge, where, in effect, populations in the West (particularly the wealthier and more educated) become increasingly 'responsible' for the crimes and abuses of the world and there is no real need to distinguish specific problems or specific agents of responsibility.

Conclusion

The resilience ethics of both Collier and Pogge emerge clearly in their desire to 'interfere' more reflexively through the indirect mechanisms of international institutions. They both reject the paternalism of direct responsibility as well as the idea that the West does not have the responsibility to intervene. In both of these frameworks, Western wealth and power – the fact that Western states and institutions set the international agenda and shape the possibilities for the progress and development of non-Western states – is used to argue that there is an indirect responsibility for the outcomes in these states. However, it is important to stress that the unequal distribution of responsibility in discourses of global and complex connectivity does not stop with the calls for reflexive 'interference' with the domestic workings of non-Western states. Implicit in the ontological understanding of associational responsibility is also a licence to 'interfere' or to 'enlighten' the private choice-making of Western citizens, often seen to lack the required self-reflexivity in their lack of understanding of their own complicity in, and responsibility for, these problems.

While Pogge's flatter ontology of spreading 'responsibility' to Western citizens – or at least those enlightened and capable of reflecting on their lifestyle choices and actions – seems to be much more noble and radical than Collier's focus on international institutions and Western states. Pogge is, in fact, more 'interfering' and more paternalist. In extending the argument that political responsibility should be further democratised, he shifts the basis much more to the sociological links of the market than merely to the formal agreements of interstate bargaining. Pogge suggests that the key aspect is not so much the impact of individual actions on international institutional frameworks – he is surprisingly downbeat about the possibilities of governments and powerful business interests voluntarily changing these structures – but in terms of the development of the self-reflexivity of citizens in the West. He argues that campaigns to change international institutional frameworks are of benefit because they:

> help change the attitudes of citizens in the more affluent countries toward the plight of the poorer populations. The now prevalent attitude of condescending pity for peoples somehow unable to get their act together, allowing themselves to be ruled by autocrats who ruin their economies, may give way to a realization that the rich democracies

have a causal and moral responsibility for the great difficulty poorer countries have in establishing and maintaining stable democratic regimes. As more persons in the affluent societies recognize their involvement and responsibility, they may change their behaviour as consumers, reducing their use of products that incorporate resources purchased from authoritarian governments.[60]

What starts as a critique of global inequalities, of powerful states and capitalist relations ends up – as all sociological understandings of resilience and complexity must – as a problem of the need for ethical work on the Western self (at the level of both institutions and individuals). Once there is no separation between capitalism as a structure of social relations and the individual choice-making of consumers, the critique of capitalism operates essentially at the level of self-reflexivity and lifestyle choices. It is thereby through the ethical self-reflexivity of citizens as consumers and as individual choice-makers in their everyday lives that change can happen, not merely in terms of putting economic pressure on regimes but also making it politically difficult for Western governments and firms to collude with repressive regimes. In this way, Pogge argues that democracy in the West is also developed as citizens become more reflexively aware and self-empowered. Developing democracy then becomes a matter of developing self-awareness – rather than of deliberation or formal decision-making – and, essentially, a process of educating and enlightening the masses in their life-style choices, rather than in holding government to account.

This framing also explains how 'anti-capitalist' sentiments sit quite happily with political quiescence. In fact, today 'markets' can easily be blamed for the problems of the world and take responsibility for the choices made by governments and international institutions. This is the beauty of the logic of resilience and associational responsibility in a global complex world. Capitalism or the market then becomes a problem not because of the production relations of exploitation and profitability but because of the individual consumption choices of individual consumers who are not ethically aware or politically reflexive enough to make more enlightened choices. If it is global capitalism that bears the final responsibility and if the dynamic driving the emergent causality of the complex social outcomes is individual decision-making, then there is little that governments can directly do.

Capitalism then becomes a complex system of associative relations which we are all to different extents responsible for because we are all unequally embedded in the global market system wh ich forms a network of interconnectivity stretching from our smallest private choices to the largest global political problems. Rather than understanding capitalism as a social system that can be opposed or struggled against, resilience ethics suggest that we see ourselves as in part responsible for the market and its outcomes (as will be analysed in greater detail in Part Three, 'The Politics of Resilience'). In fact, as Pogge argues, even attempts to exclude ourselves from the embeddedness of the market make no ethical sense as our power to influence the world through our own ethical self-reflexivity depends precisely upon this embeddedness. Power relations are thus inversed, and resilience ethics suggest that enlightened governments may even need to 'interfere' in our own private consumption choices to enable us to recognise our responsibilities. The more we inculcate these ethical reflexivities, called upon by resilience approaches of relational and associational embeddedness, the less we can separate ourselves as subjects capable of acting politically in the world.

It is here that the international politics of resilience works to greatest effect. As noted in the last chapter, in the international sphere, neoliberal framings can be understood in terms of closed systems of complexity, whereby policy-intervention has non-linear consequences and intervening actors increasingly need to reject any external goals or subject positions and instead open themselves to understanding the local practices and rationalities of the 'everyday'. It is clear that resilience understandings in contexts of direct intervention articulate the need for interveners to work on their own self-reflexivity in order to access the 'everyday' and to facilitate 'organic processes', but the division between Western actor and local actors is never fully overcome. In discourses of global responsibility, the division between external actors and the objects of governance is entirely erased. Intervention and non-intervention become irrelevant concepts once it is recognised that Western actors, including individual citizens, are already and always embedded in relational connections with the problematics of global governance. Global problems automatically become literally 'global', shared according to the extent of relational embeddedness. We can all 'interfere' in the outcomes of these problems, not through assuming the external subject position of liberal governance but through recognising our own embedded relational capacities and self-reflexively working on ourselves. It is here that the government of others and the government of the self become indistinguishable: and thus the inner logic of resilience-thinking as a governing rationality is fully articulated.

Notes

1   Exemplified in the rise of new institutionalist understandings, discussed in Chapters 1–5.
2   Beck, 2009; Giddens, 2002; Dewey, 1927; Latour, 2004a.
3   Beck, 1997.

4 Weber, 2004: p.83.
5 Connolly, 2004; Bennett, 2010; Cudworth and Hobden, 2011.
6 As I make clear in Chapter 9, the problem with 'new materialist' social ontologies lies less with the ontological assertions of complex social embeddedness and attention to the contingent nature of our social world, than with the normative philosophical, political and ethical conclusions derived from these understandings.
7 See, for example, Bain, 2003.
8 See, for example, Latour, 2007.
9 DeLanda, 2006: pp.28, 32.
10 See, for example, de Certeau, 1988.
11 See Latour, 2007.
12 For example, Connolly, 2011; Bennett, 2010.
13 This challenges the presumption of some new materialist or actor-network theorists, that the more interconnectivity can be established, the greater the contingency of outcomes and the more even the distribution of agency. Resilience ethics understand connectivity as giving rise to the ethics of governance through self-reflexivity precisely because agency remains unevenly distributed; see, for example, Marres, 2012: p.33.
14 See Connolly, 2011: pp.145–6; see also Chandler, 2013b.
15 Arendt, 2003: p.148.
16 See, for example, Dobson, 2003; Cheah and Robbins, 1998.
17 Jameson, 2003; Zizek, 2011.
18 See further, Ainley, 2008.
19 See, for example, Linklater, 1998; Held, 1995; Falk, 1995.
20 Chesterman, 2001; Welsh, 2004.
21 Kaldor, 1999.
22 Orford, 2003; Mamdani, 2009.
23 Jackson, 1990: p.187.
24 Ibid.
25 Thaler and Sunstein, 2008; see also John et al., 2011.
26 Collier, 2007: p.xi.
27 Collier and Hoeffler, 2004; Collier et al., 2006.
28 Collier and Hoeffler, 2004.
29 Collier et al., 2006: p.19.
30 Ibid.: p.20.
31 De Herdt and Abega, 2007; Fritz et al., 2009; World Bank, 2008.
32 Collier, 2010: p.216.
33 Ibid.: p.218.
34 Ibid.: pp.202–27.
35 Ibid.: p.226.
36 Collier, 2007: p.67.
37 Ibid.: p.157.
38 Ibid.
39 Ibid.: p.160.
40 Ibid.: p.192.
41 Segal, 2008.
42 Pogge, 2011a.
43 Ibid.: p.12.
44 Pogge, 2002: p.65.
45 Pogge, 2008.

46 Pogge, 2011a: p.18.
47 Arendt, 2003: p.147.
48 Pogge, 2011a: p.13.
49 Ibid.: p.17.
50 Pogge, 2007: p.253.
51 Pogge, 2011a: p.26; 2010: p.177.
52 Pogge, 2007: p.266.
53 Pogge, 2011a: p.32.
54 Ibid.
55 See, for example, Marres, 2012.
56 Harford, 2012: p.168.
57 Pogge, 2011a: p.3.
58 Ibid.: p.33.
59 Pogge, 2011b.
60 Pogge, 2007: p.270.

PART III

The politics of resilience

7
REVEALING THE PUBLIC

The reality of the event and the
banality of evil

Introduction

This chapter seeks to analyze how resilience-thinking works to 'reveal' the
public through the emergence of complex life. In liberal frameworks of representation, the public was already constituted through formal representation
and the collective decision-making processes in the public sphere (a subject
given greater consideration in the following chapter). While, for some, the
public could just be taken for granted as an existing fact, for others, this
constitutive process was bolstered and cohered through discourses of collective political and moral understanding separating 'us' from 'them'. Today,
resilience-thinking no longer operates on the basis of the political constitution of a public through the public sphere nor on an assumption that the
public is necessarily bounded by formal representation. Instead, the public
is conceived as a plural and fluid actor which reveals its associational power
through the emergence of issues or 'matters of concern', usually highlighted
by a shocking or surprising event. Once it is assumed that, as embedded subjects, we all have a multitude of relational interconnections (as highlighted in
the previous chapter), publics can be revealed through their implied relation
to the event, which puts the matter of concern on the agenda as a problematic of governance.

Rather than an unexpected or shocking event existing in isolation from
society or having only *post hoc* responsive consequences, resilience-thinking
enables (in fact, requires) any event to be comprehensible as a public product

and therefore as implying lessons with regard to how that public should be facilitated and enabled by governing authority. Events are thus transformed from a 'spectacle' to be passively consumed, and distanced from reality and the everyday, to become the clearest revelation of the reality of complex life.[1] The event thus becomes transformative and creative, revealing the public and enabling governance, having a power and importance well beyond the immediate needs occasioned by responses of community support and assistance. How the event becomes conceived of as a way of accessing the reality of the public, rather than a way of concealing or distancing this reality, is the subject of this chapter.

As will be considered in this chapter, for resilience-thinking, it is not possible to exclude a traumatic or exceptional event from the ongoing process of learning the lessons of governance from complex life. Lessons literally have to be learned from any event so that governance can operate on the basis of the reflexive ethics of continual work on 'good' public modes of being to attempt to prevent their recurrence. This is an ongoing process in which events thus substitute for traditional programme-based policy-making. By way of illustrating this process, this chapter will focus on the way in which events which previously would have been understood as exceptional have become enfolded into the ongoing process of reflexive governance. Of particular interest here is the way that traditional moral frameworks of inclusion and exclusion have become reworked within resilience approaches. Rather than clear lines of good and evil, resilience flattens moral understandings and rather than excluding exceptional – or evil – acts, enfolds them into mechanisms of rule, revealing good or bad governance. 'Evil' is no longer considered to be an exception to public norms but reveals the emergence of particular publics and is transformed into a positive ethical learning resource.

In conditions of complexity, where the world seems much less amenable to any stable ordering, events assume a much larger importance for enabling governance to reflect upon itself. While the public, as officially constituted in frameworks of liberal representation, seems to be passive, disengaged and difficult for power to relate to in traditional ways, events are increasingly understood to be the framework through which the public and its problems are revealed. Events, in fact, produce the public by revealing the nature of its bonds of interconnection and by suggesting ways in which governance can enhance these 'organic' bonds or remove barriers to their operation. In this way, events exceed liberal frameworks of representation, based upon fixed and reductionist understandings, and reveal the organic or 'real' interconnections which constitute the public as a meaningful actor. Events, in this way, can be understood to break through or to destabilise previous understandings of social interconnection, raising new and unexpected relationalities and actualising something unique, which previously was merely an immanent possibility.[2]

Once governance is understood to rule through complexity, then events are to resilience-thinking what election manifestos were to liberal modernity: they are the creative moment when the public and its problems are brought into clear view. The role of the event is then to provide a governing programme, based on the reflexive awareness of the nature of the public and the demands of the public that the event reveals. Of course, the most important events for the resilience problematic are disasters, either 'natural' or 'man-made' – which reveal publics at different levels of relational connection; resilience-thinking would not recognize any ontological distinction between the two because all events are understood to reveal the importance of self-reflexivity for governing. The more surprising the event, the more self-reflexivity is necessary as a response and the more 'reality' is understood to have emerged into view.

It is important to stress that the enfolding of evil into societal understandings of governance is intimately connected with the ontology of the event in discourses of resilience. If the complexity of life is accessible through the everyday appearances of the world, it is the sudden or shocking event which is understood to be the most revealing insight into the emergent causality at play. In order to bring the shocking or disastrous event into the process of governance as self-reflexivity, 'evil' necessarily becomes transformed from an aberration and becomes something which we understand as an unfortunate necessity – one which has a functional role in making us more self-aware.[3] The appearance of evil acts or disastrous events is thereby understood to enable and necessitate a reconsideration of reified understandings of social life and to facilitate self-reflexive forms of government both of others and of the self. The 2011 case of the mass killings by Norwegian Anders Breivik will be highlighted as an example of this process.[4]

The enfolding of 'evil'

As considered in the preceding chapters, the globalised, complex 'runaway' world appears to be out of the conscious control of humanity,[5] operating within the governing framework of liberal modernity. Governance cannot therefore start with government programmes, presupposing the ability to know, direct and implement our phenomenological constructions of the world, as if there was a fundamental separation between government as subject and the world as object. This causes fundamental problems for moral philosophy (as indicated in the previous chapter). It is only possible 'to speak Evil' and to make judgements of good and evil if the capacity exists to link future outcomes with intentions 'to do wrong'.[6] The ontology of complexity thereby removes the 'intent', which is concomitant with the freedom of the subject, replacing moral freedom with the relational ethics of *post hoc* reflexivity.[7]

For resilience-thinking, humans are not so special; we are not somehow subjects separate from or distinct from the world in which we live. For post-Cartesian approaches, increasingly dominant in the disciplines of social science, subjects are embedded and dependent upon their external environment and relational social contexts.[8] The autonomous individual has been increasingly effaced in our discourses of understanding through two interconnected processes which downplay the importance of the subject as an intentional or moral agent but stress the subject's causal agency in the production and reproduction of the world.

The first process is the understanding that individuals are not autonomous actors but are embedded products of their social contexts and relations. Rather than having decision-making autonomy, individuals are understood to have a constricted or bounded rationality, shaped by past experiences and by the institutional cognitive and ideational processes in which they are embedded.[9] In effect, the individual is no longer seen as an isolated actor but as a social product. It is also argued that our social and material embeddedness does not just differentiate, limit and constrain our rationality but that, even more problematically, the consequences of our decisions take on greater importance as our actions are inserted into powerful processes of complex global interaction, extending the impact of our individual actions and choices.[10] The combination of our advances in science and technology and the globalisation of our world makes our social powers the biggest threat both to ourselves and to the planet upon which we live and reveals the modernist myth of the autonomous rational subject to be particularly problematic.[11]

The second shift is the ambiguation introduced into the idea of the moral responsibility of an individual for their actions where intentionality is much less central to the concept of responsibility. The individual is 'responsible' for causing the outcomes of his actions or decisions, but this understanding increasingly escapes traditional liberal groundings of direct responsibility as, in a world governed by complexity, there are no clear relations between actions and outcomes: in other words, less linearity of relation between cause and effect. There is, thereby, a greater level of social determinism prior to the act or decision of the individual and a greater level of contingency or indeterminism subsequent to the action or behaviour. Through both of these shifts in understanding, the autonomous individual becomes increasingly less liable to be judged not only in terms of formal legal framings (with the rise of societal, medical and therapeutic understandings) but also in terms of moral values of good and evil.

The individual, as an embedded subject, becomes much less distinct from his or her socio-environmental relational context, preventing individual actions from being excluded as 'evil'. Evil actions thereby become emergent consequences of a badly governed public, which reflexively needs enabling. For example, the sociologist Frank Furedi notes:

> Today the traditional categories of sinners and the morally inferior have been displaced by jargon drawn from behavioural economics, evolutionary psychology, and neuroscience. The resources of the disciplines have been mobilized effectively to discredit the idea of moral autonomy.[12]

With this discursive shift, it is argued that it is human hubris – our inability to understand our true, interconnected associated nature and its consequences – that explains the gap between the surprising and shocking concrete 'reality' of events and the illusory promise of the liberal modernist vision.[13] Events enable this gap to be bridged through revelation: reflexively bringing our understanding in line with the complex or emergent reality of the public. Acts that were once 'evil' – which we would previously have seen as external or 'other' – now reveal the societalisation of evil: the social, emergent nature of the world. Emergent conceptions of evil enable ethical self-reflection to displace the modernist disavowal of our real social interconnection and its consequences. Rather than exceptions to the norm, 'evil' events reveal a 'truth' or a 'message' about our own modes of existence – one that, beneath the surface expressions of shock or of outrage, seems strangely compelling or reassuring.[14] Evil is therefore increasingly 'all about us', not about 'us and them'. It is important to highlight the implications of this shift: from a liberal understanding of evil as 'other' – as isolatable or containable through discourses of moral responsibility and criminal punishment – to the socialisation of evil as an emergent social product or unintended outcome of complex social interconnection.

As Baudrillard perceptively commented, evil is effectively banished from this world, in which autonomous subjects bleed into social processes, no longer permitting the clear distinctions of Self and Other. The attenuation of the liberal subject means that in the West: 'We can no longer speak Evil.'[15]

As Baudrillard put it, we 'will' the societalisation of evil – and its transformation into good and bad – not as a spur to collective or political action but as a ratification and rationalisation of the need to be more attuned to our own weaknesses and inadequacies.[16] The moral 'ability to speak Evil' was a call to action in the world and the reflection of a cohered and engaged subject. The less we can speak Evil the more actions which once reflected the 'truth' of the distinctive nature of the 'other' are understood to reflect the truth about ourselves. The difference is a marked one: in the past, it was often understood that the crimes of Hitler's Germany or Stalin's Russia were evil, or even perhaps the US dropping of the atomic bombs on Hiroshima and Nagasaki. But in these cases evil stood as a call to action in the external world: a call to politics, to collective, transformative engagement. This is very different from the evils of market inequalities, global warming or social fragmentation today, which, in the framework of resilience-thinking, tend to elicit an inward-looking self-orientated concern with individual and collective ethical self-reflexivity. Evil no longer works to clarify the world of 'friend and enemy' as an external field of policy intervention,[17] but to enable an internalised understanding of *post hoc* ethical self-reflexivity.

The banality of the event: From Eichmann to Breivik

As long as we had liberal ontologies – the social contract understanding of the autonomous subject: the morally autonomous individual – as the basis of modern framings of law and politics, then evil could always exist as a way of framing the 'other' as an exception to the norm. The exhaustion of this perspective, the societalisation of evil to society, through embedding the individual in their material, affective, cultural and ideational contexts, always lurked beneath the liberal surface. This subterranean world – in which evil, along with moral autonomy, could be effaced – and its disruptive effects on liberal framings of the operation of law, was acutely highlighted in Hannah Arendt's powerful examination of the 'banality of evil' in her discussion of the Eichmann trial in Jerusalem.[18]

Comparing the Eichmann trial with that of Breivik throws up some problematic analytical questions about the enfolding of evil into the governance process of resilience-thinking. The striking aspect is the problems that the Breivik case posed for modernist understandings of law, compared to most previous mass murders carried out by isolated and individual fantasists. Escaping the inclusion/exclusion binary of liberal modernist framings of law, Breivik's actions were not discursively framed in terms of those of an 'evil' or insane 'other', nor in terms of a morally responsible autonomous individual. The most compelling aspect of the case was the resistance to any understanding of Breivik as 'other', reflected in the widespread criticism of the original psychiatric report that he was insane and incapable of guilt as a paranoid schizophrenic.[19] In response, the court took the unprecedented step of ordering a second psychiatric report that found that he was perfectly sane, with no signs 'that he suffered from impaired consciousness'.[20] The argument that Breivik was perfectly sane did not, however, reduce his actions to those of a morally responsible criminal individual. Instead, the case developed a set of meanings with similarly disturbing implications for Norwegian society as those of the Eichmann trial, in terms of banalizing or normalizing his acts, which had such shocking and dehumanizing consequences.

The difference, of course, was that Eichmann followed military orders under a Nazi regime, making his crimes difficult to isolate or understand as the 'evil' acts of an isolated individual or as the freely willed choice of a liberal subject. Eichmann's actions did, indeed, fully reveal the degraded 'reality' of the bureaucratised and militarised public under the Nazi regime. Eichmann could not be portrayed as an exception, or 'other' to the norm, and it was his 'normality' that was exactly the morally appalling aspect which Hannah Arendt sought to draw attention to.[21] The key aspect of the Breivik case, which it is important to illustratively highlight, is the social or cultural sensitivities at play which sought to see Breivik in similar terms to Eichmann: as revealing a deeper emergent societal cause. Rather than exceptional – 'evil' – acts of an individual, Breivik's actions have been broadly understood as a 'wake-up call' or urgent lesson for the society in which he lived. The evil of Breivik was societalised and understood as a social and unintended product of emergent causality.[22] Rather than Breivik being interpellated as an 'evil' individual, societal institutional or environmental frameworks were seen as in need of reflexive adaptation in order to prevent such chains of interaction from reproducing more events of this type.

In short, Breivik's actions were understood as revealing the problematic processes through which the public was governed, even in Norway, which is considered one of the most successful liberal orders. These governance frameworks were not understood to be at fault materially, for example, through depriving him of material needs, or to be at fault intentionally or negligently, as if the consequences of institutional arrangements could have been understood in advance, making them amenable to rational or scientific planning. Breivik's institutional and ideational environment was judged to be the unintentional emergent outcome of societal practices and understandings, leading to problematic behavioural outcomes. The event of mass murder was read backwards to indicate what needed to be done in terms of adaptive environmental changes to prevent such actions from recurring. Rather than being isolated as an exceptional event, Breivik's actions were seen as a demand for self-reflection upon society itself, understood as an emergent social process of interaction, which formed the environmental context for his murderous decision-making. It was Breivik's embeddedness that enabled his action (which could otherwise have been seen as an arbitrary act of an individual fantasist) to be societalised.[23] This framework of understanding highlights the consequences of a shift from rationalist approaches to the subject – which maintain moral autonomy – to embedded approaches that enfold the event, or internalise 'evil', as an emergent unintentional social product with no concomitant subject/object separation.

If we can no longer stand apart from the world, then we are left only with immanent understandings of complex chains of emergent causation. Rather than good and evil as metaphysical or normative constructs, good and bad forms of interconnection are revealed through their practical consequences as relational ontologies trace outcomes back through concrete social processes. Gilles Deleuze in his 'practical philosophy' captures this idea well: 'Ethics, which is to say, a typology of immanent modes of existence, Ethics overthrows the system of judgement. The opposition of values (Good–Evil) is supplanted by the qualitative difference of modes of existence (good–bad).'[24] In a globalised world of unintended consequences of interconnection, the appearances of the world enable us to reflect upon the ontological necessity of reflexively learning to adjust modes of social being. Here the appearance of the event seems to enable just such reflexive learning, indeed to impose self-reflexivity as an ethico-political social necessity.

Evil thus provides a framework of experiential learning but only on the basis of understanding evil not as an exception to the norm but by inversing this reasoning to understand evil as revealing an underlying truth or ontological reality through its emergence. The immanent ontology of resilience-thinking continually strives to bring in, to enfold, externalities and in this way reduces (flattens) the world to a process of self-reflexive governance. Even reappropriating events as revelations of good and bad modes of being lessens the distinction between good and bad as the event-governance process becomes a continual one of developing attributes of responsivity and therefore becoming attuned to the continual need to work on bridging the gap between bad and good rather than on clarifying the distinction (as with conceptions of Good–Evil).

This understanding of evil as an emergent causality, a product of the unintended effects of societal interconnection and association, was provided by the Breivik case. The treatment of Breivik provided a snapshot of a world beyond good and evil, where evil is considered as much less the 'other' to the norm than as entirely imbricated within it. Breivik illustrated an 'evil' which was entirely socialised, understood as immanent beneath the social surface, and as generated by a problematic process of societal interaction. The response, therefore, was similar to that of post-Nazi Germany, of engaging in a correcting process of social intervention. The Breivik trial itself was less about proving the guilt or innocence of Breivik – there was no doubt about this – but about 'sending a message', a demonstration of the democratic consensus and its importance to Norwegian society, along with the gory and in-depth descriptions of the horrors that can occur if there is a fault in this process. In order for Breivik's case to perform this ethical work of community self-reflection in the milieus through which the problem was seen to arise, it was vital that Breivik's 'evil' was understood to be not the arbitrary, criminal or insane exception to the norm but rather an emergent social or societal product.

The evil of Breivik, much like that of Eichmann in Arendt's reading, was societalised or banalised precisely because it was no longer possible to understand it as an isolated act of an individual. The individual may still be legally responsible, but is no longer considered to bear the full moral responsibility – the moral responsibility is that of society, not the individual. Evil is a social product – a problem that cannot be 'othered' or excluded. This approach is so dominant that a typical example of the 'lessons of Breivik' goes as follows:

> The onus falls on everyone in society to raise their voice a bit more often to correct that borderline racist in the pub or that colleague spreading bigoted nonsense about Muslims or immigrants at work. Once the terrible grief has eased in Norway, one of the conclusions may well be that the 'it couldn't happen here' complacency of a civilised country that did not prepare properly and was too tolerant of the sentiments of the likes of Breivik was a factor in failing to stop the horror. ... Well, it did happen there. And it could happen here too if we do not take adequate steps to prevent the growth of extremism in all its forms.[25]

The fact that there is no clarity or consensus on exactly how or which milieu-shaping institutional practices are at fault or stand in a causal relationship to Breivik's acts is not a barrier to the perceived necessity of 'learning the lessons'. These lessons are those of reflexive governance: of societal empowerment as a 'milieu-shaping' project understood to be a preventive and precautionary exercise of adapting societal institutions to prevent the repeat of human tragedy. This is a process driven by the lessons of necessity, and therefore to be taken across Norwegian society itself, ensuring the inclusion of every avenue of societal-shaping-influence, from schools and workplaces to places of worship and the media. And, as the above quote illustrates, the societalisation of evil does not stop at the Norwegian border; in a globalised world, Breivik teaches the need for 'everyone in society' to take moral responsibility for the environmental milieu in which social values are inculcated.

Revelation and the event

One of the most insightful presentations of the complex world beyond good and evil was that of the philosophical pragmatist John Dewey, who outlined these ideas clearly in his 1927 classic *The Public and Its Problems*. For Dewey, liberal subject/object understandings made little sense in a world in which associative behavioural interconnections meant that social outcomes were not amenable to individual understanding or fixed frameworks of meaning. Dewey understood this as a 'new era of human relationships' where 'indirect consequences of conjoint activity outweigh, beyond the possibility of reckoning, the results directly contemplated'.[26] In a world of rich social effects, it was clear that efforts to improve the world could no longer work in top-down ways – through morals and law – as the public was no longer constituted in fixed communities with shared frameworks of norms and understanding. For Dewey, publics could not be constituted by choice or by fiat but only through the emergence of problems which revealed the shared associational consequences of public interconnection. In a pragmatic framing, hostile to metaphysical constructions, evil was no longer externalised as an exception but internalised as a shared experience, which enabled communities not only to reveal themselves in the absence of formal means of political affiliation and participation but also to give a positive purpose to this associative framework.

Following the logic of Dewey (which will be given further consideration in the next chapter), we could then understand the societalisation of evil as a way of revealing 'real' communities through the continual search for ethical 'lessons' which provide a means of self-reflective governance for both states and individuals. It appears that rather than great 'causes' or political principles, it is the revealed ethics of the event which can bring people together and can reassert relational ties through a new conception of shared 'responsibility'. Societal reflection upon the mechanisms of social existence provides an ethic which seeks to replace the moral certainties of the past. This idea of a reflexive ethic of public responsibility fits with Dewey's idea of democracy as 'the idea of community life itself'.[27] Political community then becomes real, not through its formal constitution in the public sphere but in the reflective considerations of the consequences which emerge from community association and reflexive attempts to adapt to and manage potential consequences. For Dewey, the ontological fact of associative community only emerges with this self-reflexive awareness of the consequences of social affinities and relations.[28] Political community does not emerge merely from social relationality, which is unconscious and unplanned, but only when self-reflection reveals the emergent causality, which indicates the real inner characteristics of the community.[29]

For resilience-thinking, there can be no such thing as an event from which the 'real' is not seen to emerge as a 'surprise'.[30] However, this surprise is very different from the event as unexplainable. The event is never excluded from the possibility of appropriation through the governance discourse and insertion into the ongoing process of ruling through events as the revelations of complexity. Therefore the event is the opposite of an 'act of God', which supposedly could not have been foreseen or predicted and was therefore out of human (governance) control. As Nigel Thrift notes (following Bakhtin), the event 'must have eventness' and thereby not be an 'utterly predictable outcome of earlier events'; surprise is thereby necessary to enable the agency of the actors, preventing them from being seen as 'piano keys or organ stops'.[31] However, the key point for resilience is not the 'surprisingness' of the event but the fact that it cannot be contained in itself as a discrete act or set of facts.[32] It is a surprise which is not mystified or excluded but insightful in that it exceeds its appearances – the event is thereby always part of a process of 'becoming' – it is the flash of revealed 'reality' which illuminates the concrete interactions of its past and enables self-reflexivity and the possible prevention of its future reoccurrence.

No event can therefore be separated from the social-environmental evolutionary process from which it is part. Events are not discrete – and therefore not possible to exclude from society – merely the momentary revelation of the processes through which the public becomes real, as opposed to being passive and fixed objects of representation. Events are fragile moments, which shine a light on the complexity of the world, in which social interconnections are revealed as they really are. While events are necessarily a 'surprise', the surprise is the surprise of revelation of the concrete actuality of the world, which destabilizes the abstractions of representational knowledge: the event is really 'real'. As Alfred North Whitehead suggested, the event is understood to provide knowledge which is more than merely an insight into the general nature of the world and equally is beyond merely presentational immediacy – the event reveals relations and interconnections in a concrete, determinate fashion, linking the immediate with the distant and conceptual thought with the immediacy of feeling.[33]

This may seem slightly abstract at first sight. What would it mean to transform an event from an unreal spectacle or an exception to the norm into an essential part of the governance process? A good example is the disappearance from resilience-understandings of a 'natural disaster'. Natural disasters can no longer be understood as somehow excluded from the governing process: they are no longer separate from the problem of governing complex life, but instead become central to this. As Jessica Schmidt observes, the 2004 United Nations report *Living with Risk*, highlights the end of previous forms of exclusion, which sought to demarcate natural disasters or acts of God from the responsibility of governance.[34] As the report states: 'Disaster reduction strategies will have succeeded when governments and citizens understand that a natural disaster is a failure of foresight and evidence of their neglected responsibility rather than an act of God.'[35] Whereas, previously, governments and societies responded to natural disasters as discrete events, today such events are seen as products of the way society is governed: as indicators of whether the process of governance is good or bad ('responsible' or irresponsible).

Disasters on the other side of the world – as diverse as civil conflict, economic collapse, earthquakes and regime-sponsored genocide - can help construct a global public and reflexively reveal the ethical responsibilities that come with membership of this public (as considered in Chapter 6). Disasters which occur domestically can help in the revelation of a domestic public, not through the immediate collective response or resilience of communities to the danger, but through the event as revealing something deeper about the nature of community interconnection. In order to emphasize the importance of the event, and the drive to include the 'surplus' revealed through it, to reveal and then enable the governance of the public, a striking example is the transformation in the approach (considered above) to what would previously have been understood (and excluded) as the action of an 'evil' individual or grouping.

It is important to emphasize that the event, as the key to self-reflexive governance, does not merely provide a necessary programme for governments. The urge to enfold events into the self-reflexive search for governing applies as much to the governance of the self as the governance of others (as discussed in the previous chapter). This process of enfolding is done through enlarging the possibilities of responsibility through embedded relational interconnection. Perhaps the political theorist most sensitive to this process as it relates to current sensibilities is William Connolly. Connolly has increasingly articulated the importance of the event in terms of revealing the process of emergent causality, not so much for revealing the public, but in terms of enabling a self-reflexive ethic that can act as a guide to a political ethos fitting for engagement with a world of complexity.

For Connolly, the extension of responsibility and interconnection, which the event reveals to us, need not work in terms of calculative relational understandings of our carbon or human rights 'footprints' of the sort undertaken by Thomas Pogge (considered in Chapter 6). The extension of our understanding of the power of the event to reveal the need for self-reflexive approaches is heightened by our capacity for responsiveness:

> The task here is to readjust the Kantian and neo-Kantian balance between attributions of responsibility to self or others for wrongs committed and the cultivation of *presumptive responsiveness* to beings and processes whose ways are not yet discernible to you.[36]

It is this capacity for responsiveness which is the key goal for resilience-thinking, and as Connolly suggests, this capacity is developed not merely through the revelatory power of the event but also through our subjective capacities to magnify and make the most of the stimulus of the event. For subjects of governance equipped with adequate responsiveness, events become much easier to access and the revelation thereby much more powerful. As Connolly argues:

> A world of becoming is replete with multiple forces that sometimes intersect to throw something new into the world [the event]. So strategic events ... periodically arrive when it is pertinent to dwell in an exploratory way in the gap between the disturbance of an emerging situation and those prior investments of habit, passion, faith, identity, progress, and political priority you bring to it. In the Greek tradition those who specialized in similar activities were called seers; in the religions of the Book they are often called mystics or prophets.[37]

The excess or surplus revealed through the moment of event is vital for the responsive subject, trained in using the event to enable self-reflexivity. The reality of the interconnections revealed is such that prior understandings will inevitably be inadequate to grasp the meaningfulness of this glimpse into the 'real'.

It is for this reason that Connolly (along with Nigel Thrift, Brian Massumi[38] and other influential theorists) have turned to 'post-human' or 'non-representational' forms of knowledge, to allegedly enable greater access to the revelatory power of the event. If (as discussed in Chapter 3) the key problematic for resilience-thinking is the barrier of liberal modernist frameworks of representation, fixing our categories of thought and excluding the possibility of accessing the fluidity of emergent and complex life, then the event is urgently required to continually 'destabilise' these limits and enable a greater play of self-reflexivity. In this way, the event itself can become enfolded into the everyday, as responsiveness to our embedded relationality becomes a process of everyday existence: a new mode of being. Equipped with such resilient sensibilities, as Connolly notes, citing Nietzsche:

> [D]uring a protracted present of potential metamorphosis, 'it is important to ignore no signal from the emotions of whatever kind'; you also need to absorb 'the slightest instigation' as you immerse yourself in a *hypersensuous* situation in which new disturbances are absorbed experimentally and some fixed judgements begin to melt away.[39]

Here, despite the abstruse nature of the argument, we can clearly see the logic of resilience-thinking at work in the necessary drive to include more and more aspects of the world, seen to be excluded by liberal modernist frameworks of thought. In this process, the subject's relationship to the world is inversed as resilience encourages a radical opening up to the world in which we learn through our awareness of our relational attachments rather than through a practical engagement with transforming the external world.

Ironically (as will be further analysed in Chapter 9), our increased responsiveness to the event and inculcation of openness to the external world illustrate our alienation from our external environment, rather than our connection to it. The world becomes all about us. Just as Good–Evil becomes flattened to good–bad modes of being and then to the ongoing process of self-reflexivity, so events become essentially indistinguishable from each other and even the event itself becomes unnecessary once we are resilient enough to develop the capacities for self-reflexivity in our everyday interactions – to see the event in the everyday. This process of flattening or of the enfolding of the world into the experience of the everyday is increasingly taken for granted in our understanding of the event.

This is well illustrated in the growing importance, to the ethico-political lexicon of resilience-thinking, of the 'extreme weather event'. In the past, tragedies, such as typhoon Haiyan (in the news as I write) – which swept the Philippines, killing an estimated 10,000 people in November 2013 – would have been seen as a natural disaster and thereby as an exceptional event (a humanitarian emergency). Today, such events have governance lessons for us all. It is our newly gained relational sensibility or 'presumptive responsiveness' which enables this transformation – our assumption that we live in a complex and interconnected world, where we cannot stand outside or separate from the events or the appearances of the world. Although we do not have the scientific capacity to trace the complex interactive links of emergent causality at play in such extreme events, we are nevertheless morally and politically encouraged to infer the lessons for governance, through linking such tragedies to our behavioural choices through the mediation of global warming.[40]

The need for the event (especially the tragic and unexpected disaster), as a governing programme of political and moral guidance, for both governing institutions and individuals, appears to drive the official and critical encouragement of 'hypersensuous' and affective bonds of connection which cannot be established merely through our modernist forms of scientific knowledge. Turning such disasters into 'extreme weather events' may seem like a step forward for a new politics of inclusivity and connectedness, but it can easily end in reducing the appearances of the world to morality lessons and to ignoring the fundamental structural and economic inequalities, which often underlie the catastrophic death tolls in such cases. In effect, resilience-thinking turns problems of social and economic inequality – which were previously seen as amenable to instrumental policy intervention and to necessitate critical political engagement in the external world – into problems of ethical consumption and behaviour, which require responsive work on the self or government intervention to enable and empower citizens unable to take this responsibility upon themselves.

Conclusion

Just as our understanding of the 'everyday' has shifted from an aspect of resistant life, beneath the radar of liberal rationalities, to an accessible surface phenomenon, so the 'event' has become less the exceptional or the spectacular, distracting us from reality, and more a way of making this reality accessible. As considered in Chapter 5, the inaccessible limits to liberal rationalist understandings, state governmentality and representational thought have been reworked in discourses of resilience to become the points of access to the plural and fluid 'reality' that needs to inform the self-reflexivity necessary for the responsive governance of complexity. In this way, the exhaustion of modernist programmes of government becomes positively articulated as an enlightened understanding of the limits of power as traditionally conceived.

As Latour has noted, all the areas that were excluded from modernist frameworks of power and responsibility seemingly reenter 'with a vengeance'.[41] The event, which enables a multitude of publics to be revealed, responsively sharing responsibility for the Breivik mass murder, is no different – ontologically – from the events of global warming or any other 'matters of concern' which make their appearance in the world (as discussed in the previous chapter). Through the light shone by the event, the reality of the public enables responsive individuals and governance agencies to self-reflexively experiment with new approaches to policy-intervention, for example, by enabling the public to raise their voice against 'borderline racism' or extremism in a bar. The revelation of the public thereby constitutes the public not as agents of rule and policy-making but as objects of policy-making – in order to enable them to make responsive changes to prevent acts of racism or extremism, or to save energy or minimise air travel, in order to prevent global warming and extreme weather events.

The process of the responsive work of self-reflection in relation to the event thus enables a new post-liberal or post-modern programme of governance, which does not operate on the basis of standing above society or directing and controlling outcomes. Events, revealing the 'truth' of the public, legitimise reflexive policy-making in the absence of public engagement in electoral politics. In the place of the formally constituted public, the event is held to reveal the 'real' public, and sudden, unexpected or disastrous events are understood to provide particularly valuable materials for governance as self-reflexive understandings of the relational embeddedness of complex life. It is for this reason that 'evil' is necessarily enfolded into the social sphere of associational life and made banal, rather than radically excluded. As will be considered in the following chapter, the processes at work in the event – of revealing the reality of public agency as it operates at the level of everyday interaction – has its conceptual political roots in both pragmatist and neoliberal understandings of complexity. The following chapter analyses how resilience-thinking articulates this hollowing out of the public realm as an act of empowerment and democratisation in the sphere where 'real' power lies: the informal sphere of societal interaction.

Notes

1 Thus inversing the critical understanding of the situationists (see further, Debord, 1983).
2 Much academic work has been done on the nature of the event and its relation to political processes and understandings, mostly stressing the creative possibilities provided by the 'surplus of life' revealed through them (see further, for example, Thrift, 2008: pp.109–50).
3 As William Connolly notes, with regard to the satirical message of Voltaire's *Candide*, that 'every evil is functional': 'I embrace a post-Voltairian cosmology, one that fixes attention on recurrent moments when a shock or event disrupts some of the ingrained habits and assumptions that preceded it' (2013: p.6).
4 On 22 July 2011, Anders Behring Breivik, a right-wing extremist, set off a bomb near the government building in Oslo, killing eight people, then went on a shooting rampage on the nearby Utoeya island, where the ruling Labour Party's youth wing was hosting a summer camp. He killed 69 people on the island, most of them teenagers.
5 Giddens, 2002.
6 Arendt, 1963: p.277.
7 In the 'onto-ethical' understanding of resilience, there is no transcendental divide between the internal and external worlds: the subject is part of the world rather than external to it (see, for example, Cheng, 2011: p.20).

8   For example, Bennett, 2010; Cudworth and Hobden, 2011.
9   Exemplified in the rise of new institutionalist understandings.
10 Beck, 2009; Giddens, 1994, 2002.
11 Dewey, 1927; Latour, 1993, 2007.
12 Furedi, 2011: p.136.
13 Latour, 2004a; Connolly, 2011; Bennett, 2010.
14 See, for example, Baudrillard, 2002.
15 Baudrillard, 2009: p.97.
16 Ibid.
17 Schmitt, 1996: p.26; Mouffe, 2005: p.76.
18 Arendt, 1963.
19 Traufetter, 2012a.
20 Traufetter, 2012b.
21 Arendt, 1963.
22 Of course, this does not mean that there was a consensus on how to understand this emergent process of interaction or on which aspects of this environmental context were more decisive – whether it was the interactive contribution of poor parenting, of Internet chat rooms or gaming, of right-wing political parties or of government-sponsored multiculturalism, or of violent or non-constitutional political protest. Each of these frameworks suggested ways in which societal processes could be better managed or regulated to prevent other individuals from making similar behavioural choices.
23 Fleming, 2012; Orange, 2012; Moore, 2012.
24 Deleuze, 1988: p.23.
25 Knott, 2012.
26 Dewey, 1927: p.107.
27 Ibid.: p.148.
28 Ibid.: p.149.
29 Ibid.: pp.151–2.
30 Aradau, 2013.
31 Thrift, 2008: p.114.
32 Ibid.: pp.114–5.
33 Whitehead, 1978: pp.80–81.
34 Schmidt, 2013: p.190.
35 UN, 2004: p.viii.
36 Connolly, 2013a: p.135 (emphasis in original).
37 Ibid.: p.134.
38 See, for example, Massumi, 2002; Thrift, 2008.
39 Connolly, 2013a: p.134 (emphasis in the original).
40 The 2012 synthesis report from the Intergovernmental Panel on Climate Change noted the difficulty of linking changes in complex events like cyclones to climate change: 'The uncertainties in the historical tropical cyclone records, the incomplete understanding of the physical mechanisms linking tropical cyclone metrics to climate change, and the degree of tropical cyclone variability provide only low confidence for the attribution of any detectable changes in tropical cyclone activity to anthropogenic influences. Attribution of single extreme events to anthropogenic climate change is challenging' (IPCC, 2012: p.7).
41 Latour, 2003: p.37.

8
THE DEMOCRACY
OF PARTICIPATION

Introduction

In liberal modernity, the democratic collective will of society was understood to emerge through the public and deliberative freedoms of associational life. Today, however, democratic discourse (as discussed in the previous chapter) is much more focused on the formation of plural and diverse publics whose participative importance is in the private and social sphere. In these approaches, central to resilience-thinking and the governance of complexity, democracy is no longer seen to operate to constitute a collective will standing above society but as a mechanism to enable the responsive and adaptative capacities already possessed by individuals and communities, as the ultimate decision-makers. Government is brought back 'to the people', and democracy is seen to circulate through the personal decisions made in everyday life. This chapter seeks to analyse the development of resilience-thinking in relation to the political sphere and highlights how these approaches overcome the rationalist assumptions of the public/private divide, paying particular attention to the work of two key liberal political theorists, John Dewey and Friedrich Hayek.

Democracy has been historically linked to the problematic of constituting a collective public will above the plurality of competing private interests within the social sphere. In liberal modernity, this collective democratic will was constituted through the establishment of a public sphere of formal equality before the law and at the ballot box and through civic freedoms – of the press, speech, association and the like. This struggle, between the civic aspiration for the development of the collective good and the threat to the collectivity posed by the corruption of private interests and power, seems to have become much less central to democratic theory. Today, democracy works on a different problematic, not that of manufacturing a single collective will – separate to and distinct from the private wills of groups and individuals – but the problematic of legitimising rule through bringing democracy down to the societal level of plural and individuated 'everyday life'.

It is increasingly held that, in a complex and non-linear world, the public must be understood as self-constituting through everyday decision-making and interaction. The democratic state thereby no longer stands above or separate to society but works to facilitate a more responsible or reflexive operation of plural and differentiated private judgements.[1] This chapter seeks to draw out how both the processes of democracy and the space(s) in which it is held to operate have been transformed and pluralised. In particular, it focuses on the development of the analytical framings of resilience-thinking as a response to the perceived problems of democratic representation in a world of increasing complexity and the breakdown of traditional, linear, state–society relations. In this discussion, the limits of democratic will for- mation no longer constrain the growth of democracy but rather facilitate it, extending democracy into the 'everyday' and the 'politics' of 'life' itself.[2]

The analytical framing of resilience approaches, bringing democracy down to the level of everyday life, will be heuristically drawn out through engaging with the first major treatments of complex life in liberal theorising, in the work of Walter Lippmann, John Dewey and Friedrich Hayek. In doing so, the radical claims made on behalf of current complexity critiques of rationalist assumptions and of the public/private divide will be explicitly challenged. In these frameworks, the personal becomes political, but not in the sense of the early feminist movement understanding that 'personal problems are political problems'.[3] The 'personal is political' was a radical call to see how politics percolated down to shape the everyday experiences (the 'personal problems') of individuals. In representing personal problems as not individual but as col- lective political problems, these feminists aspired to politicise women towards greater public political engagement. However, in resilience-thinking and complex and emergent understandings, which seek to extend the spaces and processes of democracy, the opposite relationship is in play: individuals and communities are to be empowered to reflexively work on their personal choices and practices in order to effect political change. 'Political problems' are thereby 'depoliticised' and represented as 'personal problems' which can be dealt with by empowered individuals and communities.

The democratisation of 'everyday life' understands that political subjects are embedded in differentiated, plural and overlapping social and cognitive communities of interaction. It is important that, in this framing, the social sphere is understood as distinct from both the contractual relations of the market and the formal public sphere. In representing political problems as 'personal' or social products, leading Foucauldian sociologists Peter Miller and Nikolas Rose have noted that individuals are governed 'neither as isolated atoms of classical political economy' – i.e., as interest-bearing subjects – 'nor as citizens of society' – as rights-bearing subjects – 'but as members of heterogeneous communities of allegiance, as community emerges as a new way of conceptualizing and administering moral relations among persons'.[4] In this framing, democracy can be promulgated without the assumptions of universality, rationality and autonomy presumed in the discourses of modern liberalism. Miller and Rose articulate the current problematic, with regard to the 'new specification of the subject of government';[5] thus:

> Within this new regime of the actively responsible self, individuals are to fulfil their national obligations not through their relations of dependency and obligation to one another, but through seeking to fulfil themselves within a variety of micro-moral domains or 'communities' – families, workplaces, schools, leisure associations, neighbourhoods. Hence the problem is to find the means by which individuals may be made responsible through their individual choices for themselves and those to whom they owe allegiance, through the shaping of a lifestyle according to grammars of living that are widely disseminated, yet do not depend upon political calculations and strategies for their rationales or for their techniques.[6]

Governing authority no longer becomes exercised in the old way, as intervention and regulation from above society, in the form of liberal government on behalf of, or over, the social whole. Rather, new forms of governance appear as ways of democratising society itself through 'empowering' or 'capability-building' the citizen, enabling political subjects to take societal responsibility upon themselves and their communities. Miller and Rose are entirely correct in noting that this 'ethical a priori of active citizens in an active society is perhaps the most fundamental, and most generalizable, characteristic of these new rationalities of government'.[7] Mitchell Dean concurs that the task of government today lies precisely in the inculcation of the agency of the governed. The solution to problems of society, whether in the form of welfare, crime or conflict, becomes then not that of liberal forms of state intervention but of the development of societal agency:

> Victims of crime, smokers, abused children, gay men, intravenous drug users, the unemployed, indigenous people and so on are all subject to these technologies of agency, the object being to transform their status,

to make them active citizens capable, as individuals and communities, of managing their own risk.[8]

The modern state does not withdraw from society and leave rational and autonomous subjects to their own devices; rather, it is discursively constructed as an active and facilitating state – acting through the agency generated by societal interaction, rather than from above. The state thereby seeks to address social problems precisely through the strengthening of democracy at the societal level, on the basis that political problems can only be addressed at the personal or community level through harnessing the knowledge and practices of its citizens. As Dean states, once problematised, 'individuals are required to agree to a range of normalizing, therapeutic and training measures designed to empower them, enhance their self-esteem, optimize their skills and entrepreneurship and so on'.[9]

In our complex and globalised world, reflexivity demands that the democratic society is autonomously self-constituting without the guidance or direction of a collective will. Self-rule today is not a matter of a return to understandings of 'direct democracy' at the level of the workplace or the local community. Democracy is increasingly a question of private or individual cognitive and social responsiveness rather than political or public representation. The problematic of individual self-reflexivity is one in which the will of pluralised and fluid publics emerges interactively through the social processes of life itself. In this process, the relationship of the public to the formal political sphere is inversed; rather than deliberative reason and representation constituting the public as a collective body, the plural public of the social sphere is enabled and empowered in their 'everyday' decision-making capacity as democracy devolves down to the level of the private individual.

As the UK Royal Society for the Arts 'Social Brain' project suggests, responding to the problems of the governance of complexity is not a matter for government regulation but a concern of individuals as the key decision-makers. The problems of complexity mean that citizens need to be able to reflexively respond to externalities autonomously and responsibly:

> [L]ife politics is the politics of choice in a deep existential sense – a politics where one is aware of what it is like to live reflexively in a post-traditional and globalised world. … Whether we like it or not, in late modernity citizens need to be able to reflexively chart their way through the choppy waters of a globalised economy. And whether we like it or not, they need to find ways of changing the way they live if they are to counteract problems like entrenched inequality and environmental degradation.[10]

In today's world, governments and international institutions are leading the call for more democracy or for the democratisation of areas of social life. The call for more democracy tends to put the emphasis on society rather than the state, and demands for democracy relate to social responsibilities and responsivities rather than to making the government more accountable to the people. A good example is the UK government's experimentation with 'Big Society' in which social problems are addressed through the extension of democracy, empowering active and responsive citizenship, particularly in addressing environmental, social and health problems. As the government website states: 'We think that the "Big Society" is (or should be) a new approach to social challenges. ... We think that in the context of austerity, the government can no longer solve all the problems we face, and neither should it.'[11]

Democracy, we are continually informed, is much more than voting in elections; it is about the public and individuals and their behaviour and understanding on an 'everyday' level. It is the limited capacity of states to cohere policy-making on the basis of a 'general will' that is reflected in understandings of democracy as an emergent societal process. This support for the extension of democracy into the social and informal sphere marks out the resilience-thinking approach to democracy from the legacy of the linear paradigm of both the premodern and modern world. The non-linear understandings of resilience and complexity do not operate on the basis of constitutional or institutional solutions to the problem of democracy or the problem of collective will formation. Rather than making constitutional distributions of rights or the checks of legislation or judicial frameworks the solution, democracy as societal reflexivity works in a different register, on the problematic of the legitimating power of plural and shifting publics as they reveal themselves in the social or private sphere. Rather than starting with constitutional order and rights subjects, resilience approaches start with the problematic of the social production of reflexive and responsive subjects.

This chapter attempts to demarcate the linear or liberal approach from that of non-linear and resilience approaches: first, through drawing out the centrality of the separation between the public and the private sphere in liberal modernist frameworks. The following sections then consider the development of non-linear analytical framings. Emphasis is placed on the influential role of Walter Lippmann's sceptical problematic of complexity and non-linearity in the 1920s and on the complementary ideas of 'emergence' stemming from the application of Darwinian evolutionary psychology. It is suggested that non-linear approaches and the shift in understanding of the role and location of the public are then formulated in analogous ways both by pragmatist philosopher John Dewey and neoliberal ideologue Friedrich

Hayek. In this framework, democracy no longer operates through the constitution of a formal public sphere but rather through the facilitation of private
choice-making and personal and community modes of self-government.

Democratic reason

Engagement in the collective deliberation of democratic reasoning has been
understood, from the Enlightenment theorists to the present, as the highest
exercise of freedom. From Rousseau onwards, the 'general will' was seen to
be capable of emerging above corrupting private interests on the basis of the
formal constitution of a public as the source of political legitimacy.[12] Social
contract theory established the rational autonomous subject at the heart of
the modern liberal democratic doctrine, and Immanuel Kant provided probably its most articulate defence. For Kant, the democratic space for individual
freedom and autonomy was that of the public realm, where individuals could
act as universal rational subjects in relation to other equally rational beings.
It was only in the public sphere that individuals were held to be freed from
relationships of obedience and authority, which dominated the private sphere
of work (hierarchy of management) or of specialist needs (doctors, financial
advisers etc.). The collective will could only emerge as a product of the exercise of public reasoning, through free and active engagement in discussion
and debate in the public sphere.[13]

The Enlightenment drew heavily upon classical understandings of the
constitution of a democratic collective will through pubic political discourse,
whereby citizens had not just a right but a duty of participation. It was the
public sphere of the assembly 'in which the free existence of a free citizen
manifested itself'.[14] In the pre-Socratic age of Ancient Greece, the key to
the link between democracy and the constitution of a collective will was
the construction of this artificial sphere, separate from the inequalities and
dependencies of economic and social existence. The outcome of deliberation
would only be based on persuasion not on obligation or coercion between
unequals, constructing a 'circular relation' between public reason and democracy.[15] Today, few theorists maintain the importance of such a division,
understanding a formal realm of democratic discourse as artificially separated
from private interests operating in the societal sphere of interaction, although
this legacy can be seen in Habermasian theories of dialogic reasoning and
communicative rationality[16] and in deliberative approaches.[17]

It is important to emphasise that the critique of the formation of a democratic will is today not couched in elitist terms, as a critique of democracy,
but in support of the extension of democracy to the social sphere through
the inculcation of personal reflexivity. The discourse of complex life and

resilience thereby moves beyond the Platonic 'reversal', which forms the basis of traditional conservative thought, suggesting that democracy would merely result in mob-rule and the corruption of power.[18] It also moves beyond the 'Aristotelian hesitation', whereby democracy was defended not on the basis of the constitution of a collective will but on the basis of limiting and altering power and thereby negatively restraining private interests.[19] The legacy of Aristotelian approaches to democracy can be seen today, for example, in John Keane's conception of 'monitory democracy'. Here, the role of citizens is not that of public decision-making but of maintaining checks on executive rule, with the use of new communication technologies enabling citizens 'in big and complex societies' to scrutinise the workings of power.[20] Keane argues that democracy today cannot be based on 'heading backwards' to the Greeks, 'to recapture the (imagined) spirit of assembly-based democracy – "power to the people"'.[21] He criticises contemporary advocates of 'deep' or 'direct' democracy,[22] who argue that what counts is 'the commitment and capacities of ordinary people to make sensible decisions through reasoned deliberation and empowered because they attempt to tie action to discussion'.[23]

As we shall see below, for approaches based on complexity, representation and the control over government is no longer the central concern; rather, it is social processes and interactions that are at the centre of analysis. In the sections which follow, I seek to draw out the development of today's democratic understandings of the need for a resilient and self-reflexive citizenry, locating the power of self-government not in the formal public sphere but in the social sphere. Crucial to this analytical framing is the scepticism of linear reasoning found in both the pragmatic approach of John Dewey and the neoliberal approach of Friedrich Hayek. Both of these understandings challenged the linear and rationalist assumptions of liberal democratic theory, which as Koopman notes, even today, 'is still excessively enamoured of state-based rationality'.[24]

Lippmann and non-linear thinking

The problems of complexity, modernity and democratic reason were firmly articulated by progressive thinkers in the interwar United States, of which Walter Lippmann was probably the most well known and a fundamental influence upon the work of John Dewey. Lippmann was important as a mediating link in the shift of democracy discourses from the public sphere to the social sphere because his critique of the democratic will was neither state-based nor based on differences in capability between elites and masses. His critique was sociological: based on the complexity of social relations. Writing in the 1920s, the problematic he opened up was that of public representation in what we today would call a 'globalised' and complex world. For Lippmann, fixed territorialised communities – or formal publics – with collective interests or purposes were a liberal fiction or partisan self-deception. Instead the public was not static and unified but shifting and plural and could not be understood without being 'put in its place'.[25]

Lippmann's critique of liberal rationalist and linear approaches was not overtly elitist: the problem was not social or educational inequality, which was potentially resolvable through social reform, but rapid change and social complexity. Even the most avid and educated citizen 'cannot know all about everything all the time, and while he is watching one thing a thousand others undergo great changes'.[26] The world was moving too fast with too many interconnections for even the greatest of minds to grasp the consequences of public policy-making.[27] Moreover, change occurred unevenly, through shifting and clashing temporalities, continually altering the interrelations between variables and causing new and unexpected disharmonies.[28] Lippmann was exceptionally clear in the importance of non-linearity for deliberative or rationalist understandings of democratic rule: 'In an absolutely static society there would be no problems. A problem is the result of change. But not of change in any self-contained element. Change is significant only in relation to something else.'[29] As he stated, this meant that problems could not be addressed as singular issues: all issues now were dependent upon 'complex social *relations*'.[30] Interrelationality necessarily threw into question linear forms of knowledge or understanding; responses needed to be determined entirely by time and place and context: 'This may sound like splitting hairs, but unless we insist upon it we never define a problem accurately nor lay it open successfully to solution.'[31]

For Lippmann, linear or deliberative reasoning could not act as a guide to policy-making: even the pretence of collective understanding was an impossible ideal, which could only lead to disillusionment.[32] While the public was a fiction or a founding myth, so was the idea that the business of government could be guided by any coherent or collective reason: 'Modern society is not visible to anybody, nor intelligible continuously and as a whole.'[33] Lippmann argued that no subject stood above the particular interests and limited understandings of individuals and the narrow range of choices they made. Importantly for what follows, he argued that it was these narrow and individual choices that 'in detail are in their cumulative mass the government of society'.[34] The differentiated and plural public only acts as a decision-maker or executive in its immediate choices in the informal social sphere, otherwise it can only indirectly act, by taking sides when issues of controversy enter the public sphere. Popular will, of a shifting and random public of those interested, rarely manifests itself and even then does not itself govern; it merely takes the side of one party or another.[35] The power of the public in relation to formal politics was thereby merely fragmentary, transient, passive, indirect and unformulated.

Lippmann's sceptical critique of democratic representation cohered the non-linear and non-rationalist approach, upon which Dewey developed his much more positive understanding of democratic possibilities. Dewey similarly criticised the way liberal theory 'idealized the state'[36] as somehow a product of collective reason with teleological aims[37], and he agreed with Lippmann's view of the impossibility of government knowing or directing the vast associational connections of modern complex societies. Where Dewey differed was merely on the conclusions to be drawn from this:[38] on the prospects this meant for democracy. If the social and associational sphere was where individuals had executive powers of decision-making, then democracy was alive and well but it was not where democracy theorists had been looking for it: in the formal political sphere of decision-making. For Dewey, the public was not constituted from on high by governments but socially, through these associational links and the concerns elicited by them. Lippmann was right that the public did not rule from the top down through the mechanisms of government representation: 'We shall not, then find the public if we look for it on the side of originators of voluntary actions.'[39] The public didn't rule through a monolithic government of the collective or 'general will'. Instead, the public ruled plurally, through its active executive choice-making in the informal social sphere.

Lippmann's work on the unplanned and organic complexity of the modern polity was also praised by Hayek, who shared the view of the non-linear understanding of democracy in the social sphere as the limit to government. Rather than a linear understanding of democracy as a formal check on power in the public sphere (akin to Aristotelian approaches), Hayek followed Lippmann in arguing that the limits of governmental reasoning needed to be recognised as located in the complex societal sphere of interaction. Hayek's ardent defence of democratic freedoms was therefore not based on classic rationalist understandings of the political subject but on the recognition that only individual freedom enabled reflexive responses to change, by the free subject in society. It is this shift in understanding which was highlighted when Hayek quoted Lippmann's statement that 'in a free society the state does not administer the affairs of men. It administers justice among men who conduct their own affairs.'[40]

While the Platonic 'reversal' and the Aristotelian 'hesitation' established the basis for the linear problematic of democracy and reason in modern liberal thinking – making institutionalist frameworks, through which representation could be channelled, key – the non-linear paradigm of democracy and representation operates on a different basis. Following Lippmann, the Deweyan and Hayekian 'inversion' argued that no coherent democratic will could be formed because the evolutionary nature of society and its interrelational organic complexity meant that social outcomes were emergent and could not be known, predicted or controlled. In this framing, the problem of democratic rule was no longer the formal or constitutional relationship between the elite and the mass but the informal exchanges, affectivities and cognitive understandings of social interaction, which were understood to need to be sufficiently reflexive, open and adaptable.[41]

Dewey and Hayek shared an understanding that reflective or deliberative democratic reasoning in the public sphere could not constitute a collective democratic will but that a different, emergent form of adaptive, reflexive, experiential reasoning could be inculcated in the societal sphere of practical engagement with problems and through individual choice-making, imbricated within spontaneously evolving feedback loops. Democracy could be inculcated in 'everyday life', in families, communities and associative attachments, where local experiential knowledge was always superior to the distant dictates of majoritarian rule. Whereas linear reasoning operated on the fiction that a unitary public will could be constructed in the political sphere, non-linear reasoning sought to enable the empowerment of a plurality of publics in the societal sphere.

Dewey, Hayek and non-linear reasoning

Both Dewey and Hayek are understood to be liberal thinkers, though they are usually construed as being from very different (if not opposite) ends of the liberal spectrum – one a progressive anti-market educationalist, the other a neoliberal free market advocate, until recently neglected by left-leaning democratic theorists.[42] However, more recent work has highlighted shared aspects between the two thinkers[43], and the University of Oregon philosopher Colin Koopman has explicitly argued that now 'the time is ripe for Deweyans to take another look at Hayek'.[44] One of the key distinctions was that Dewey, the 'social reformer', sought to move beyond the public/private divide, while Hayek, the 'neoliberal', was often read as being a staunch defender of the public/private dichotomy, with freedom of the private sphere safeguarded through restrictions on the reach of governmental power. However, their distinct normative stances should not be allowed to obscure their very similar ontological framings of the democracy problematic under conditions of emergence and complexity.

What was key to both of their works was their scepticism with regard to linear, rationalist approaches to the formation of democratic reason and preference for emergent processes of societal interactive reason. For pragmatist theory and for Hayek, liberal rationalist approaches failed to grasp the non-linear nature of human affairs. For both theorists, rationalism was critiqued from two directions: first, they critiqued the Cartesian subject, viewing thought as secondary to and entirely imbricated with being in the world; second, they understood the world of human affairs as complex and transitory, not amenable to central direction or planning. They both thereby shared an evolutionary or emergent understanding of politics, which today resonates well with the political sensitivities of resilience-thinking and complex life, with which traditional frameworks of democracy and representation no longer seem to fit.

As Hodgson points out, both Dewey and Hayek were strongly influenced by Darwinist understandings and were resolute in their hostility to behaviourist approaches.[45] Darwin's theory of evolution through natural selection was understood to fundamentally challenge religious ideas of the uniqueness of man (the human/nature divide) and the Cartesian dualism of thought and being. The application of Darwinism to theories of the mind led to the development of evolutionary or emergent understandings, whereby thought and reason were understood to evolve from inherited and acquired predispositions. William James, the founding father of pragmatist philosophy, distinguished instincts as phylogenetic (inherited) and habits as ontogenetic (acquired or learned), both of which preceded and shaped reason and understanding.[46] In this framing, the unconscious mental processes provided the platform for the more highly developed conscious processes: the past, both genetically and environmentally, therefore heavily weighed upon the present. In this way, both the classical liberal modernist understanding of the autonomous rational subject and the radical social science view that consciousness was determined by underlying structures, with subjects as merely the bearers or intermediaries of their social relations, were rejected.[47]

The removal of both Cartesian rationalism and determining social structures was vital for the shifting articulation of democracy away from the emphasis on the public political realm. How subjects responded to changes or crises was therefore neither a matter of autonomous rationalist reflection nor a matter of government engineering (ensuring that the right stimulus or incentive would elicit the desired behaviour). Subjects were innately 'political' in the sense of being self-directed decision-makers; however, the frameworks, through which those decisions were made owed much to both evolutionary psychology and to societal habits and norms.[48] For both Hayek and Dewey, reasoning was not something separate from experience and social practice: reasoning was not a rationalist reflection upon the world but a response to the world based upon associational norms and experiences.

Dewey was particularly forward-looking in his critique of the liberal 'individualistic' mythology of the human as an autonomous rational subject, which he saw as a contingent and *post hoc* justification for the American and French Revolutions, dependent on Newtonian metaphysics and its import into economic *laissez-faire* understandings.[49] As Dewey wrote:

> [S]ingular beings in their singularity think, want and decide, *what* they think and strive for, the content of their beliefs and intentions is a subject-matter provided by association. Thus man is not merely *de facto* associated, but he *becomes* a social animal in the make-up of his ideas, sentiments and deliberate behaviour. *What* he believes, hopes for and aims at is the outcome of association and intercourse.[50]

Although Hayek was often mistakenly understood to be an advocate of rationalist individualism, his advocacy of the free market was not based upon the reasoning autonomy of the subject but, in fact, upon a critique of the classical rationalist assumptions of *homo economicus*. For Hayek, like Dewey, human reasoning was merely a phenomenological product of 'interpretations' based upon inherited and learned experiences that mediated between the experience and the response. For Hayek: 'we cannot hope to account for observed behaviour without reconstructing the "intervening processes in the brain"'.[51] Hayek turned to psychology to explain how internal differentiations facilitated varying responses to events or crises, particularly to those that were unfamiliar or unexpected. According to Hayek, brains were complex, integrated networks but they were also malleable and capable of adaptive change, depending upon the extent to which 'phylogenetic', inherited patterns and connections, and 'ontogenetic' aspects, acquired by the individual during the course of their lifetime, interacted.[52] Hayek's work on the psychology of the brain focused on how human responses were shaped through resilience and adaption, in ways that were little different to any other living organism:

> The continued existence of those complex structures which we call organisms is made possible by their capacity of responding to certain external influences by such changes in their structure or activity as are required to maintain or restore the balance necessary for their persistence.[53]

Individuals, especially more complex organisms like humans, would respond differently to external stimuli in ways that enabled them to react differently. Often these reflexive differences would not be intentional but arbitrary or accidental. The key point for Hayek was that differential

experiences and reactions necessarily resulted from the innate practical experiential differences of individuals and the complex interaction between their
'milieu intérieur' (internal, mental environment) and their external, societal
environments.[54] This evolutionary or emergent understanding of reflexive
subjectivity was, of course, to map well onto current understandings of the
problem of governing complexity.

Hayekian and Deweyan perspectives understood reasoning and intentionality as neither existing independently of, nor prior to, social engagement but
as emerging through inherited and social structures: reason thereby developed adaptively. Instead of understanding reason as a reflection or representation of reality in thought, Dewey argued that reasoning was a product of the
ongoing practical interaction of subjects with their environment.[55] Reasoning was therefore not 'deliberative' or 'rationalist' but an acquired capacity
to respond and to adapt to the world. For Hayek, too, it was implicit or
tacit knowledge, which was key to reflexivity and to the construction of
decentralised and efficient complex orders.[56] For both authors, there were no
dualist understandings of subject–object relations at either the individual or
state level. Neither individuals nor states were seen to be autonomous goal or
target-setters, engaged in means-ends instrumentalism. Both therefore argued
against foundationalist understandings and understood democracy as a process of societal experimentation and adaptive learning.

The two key aspects of this anti-rationalist understanding are those of process and plurality.[57] There was no single universal or rational order: neither
that constituted by the objective structures of the world (which we can only
partially perceive through our limited practical experiences and desires) nor
that imposed by some Cartesian rationality (as our subjective understandings and desires are similarly shaped by our societal associations, customs and
habits). Reason was thereby an evolutionary process of plural experiences
and understandings: reason, like society, was a self-organising and emergent
social product. There was no possibility of going beyond this to some monis-
tic view of knowledge, somehow standing outside and independently of our
social attachments. The human world was one of complex social interactions
with contingent and emergent outcomes beyond human reasoning or control from above.

For Hayek, the most adapted and complex social, legal and political institutions resulted from human action, not from human design: they were
self-organised or emergent. These societal institutions therefore were not
established on the basis of instrumental rationalism and lacked any ultimate
end or purpose, evolving through social practice as a framework of often tacit
rules and customary norms and shaping the citizen's habitual and unreflec-
tive practices. Of course, for Hayek, the most important of these institutions

was the market, which, following Adam Smith's 'invisible hand', was held to regulate the complex transactions of society much more efficiently than any government could do through planning. The operation of the market – as allocator of goods and services and the provider of symbolic guides (prices) for decision-making – was seen to be the key institution through which individuals were able to make executive decisions and choices and through this to constitute an emergent institutional order.

Of course, when it comes to resilience-thinking today, it is clear that Hayek is understood to have overstated the divide between the rationality of the market and the irrational 'fatal conceit' of government regulation (discussed further in the concluding chapter).[58] However, the alternative to the failings of market rationality from the Deweyan pragmatist perspective would not be that of state intervention, but the highlighting that market rationality is itself determined by society's democratic ethical commitments. As Koopman argues,[59] through democratic ethical reasoning, society could ensure that markets worked more efficiently, for example, through ethical consumption raising the demand for organic, locally sourced, labour-friendly, fair-trade products. The critique of market rationality did not necessarily lead to a state-based solution but, logically, to a society-based solution. For Dewey, as for Hayek, states with their means-ends considerations and limited knowledge were powerless before the real sphere of democratic reason: society. It is increasingly from within this framework of social, interactive, moral and ethical development that democracy is understood to be furthered today, in the language of enablement, capacity- and capability-building.

After representation

Dewey and Hayek both prefigured the 'life politics' of the world of complexity and resilience-thinking through their emphasis on societal interaction and the process of reflexive decision-making in the 'everyday'. It is important to emphasise that the critique of political rationalism inevitably meant that the political subject was embodied in social and environmental attachments and that it was at this level that democratic reflexivity needed to operate: upon democracy as an ethic or way of life. Democracy cannot be a product of rationalist deliberation as if thought was somehow distinct from practice. If it is to mean anything, it has to enable society to be responsive to contingencies arising from and revealed through human association. Both Dewey and Hayek speak to us today because of the different register of their sensitivity to the problems of politics. These are not those of individual or collective rights or of needs and desires, as in rationalist discourses, but the unintended problems of association (which differ according to the complexity of each society across time and space).[60] This associational power is self-generated, emergent, unintended, and unknown except for its consequences, which can be traced back but only after the 'event' (as we saw in the last chapter) or the appearance of the problem in the world.[61]

The problems for both thinkers did not involve the formal politics of representation but the social understandings and reflexivity elicited from the contingent and unintentional effects of association. The problem was one of emergent social reasoning, not rationalist 'political' reasoning. Politics was therefore a process of responding to concerns regarding these externalities, which revealed pluralist publics with a stake in reflexively responding to facilitate their resolution.[62] This complexity, driven by technological change, was described well by Dewey:

> Indirect, extensive, enduring and serious consequences of conjoint and interacting behaviour call a public into existence having a common interest in controlling these consequences. But the machine age has so enormously expanded, multiplied, intensified and complicated the scope of the indirect consequences, have formed such immense and consolidated unions in action, on an impersonal rather than a community basis, that the resultant public cannot identify and distinguish itself.[63]

For Dewey, like Giddens,[64] it was a 'runaway world' whereby 'man has suffered the impact of an enormously enlarged control of physical energies without any corresponding ability to control himself and his own affairs'.[65] Once this control could no longer be regained through the construction of a state-based deliberative public the only solution was that of complex life revealing a pluralised public, reflexive about its associative connections and 'responsive to the complex and world-wide scene in which it is enmeshed'.[66] This public was not formally politically constituted, and thus it operated on both local and global levels – 'while local, it will not be isolated'.[67] The solution to the runaway world of extended associational powers was not that of state regulation or formal representation, but that of developing interactive social responsibilities. If anything, Dewey could be read as arguing that the separation of the public sphere from the social one was the key barrier to unleashing social reasoning – the real intelligence which was already embedded in social interaction and could not be articulated as long as it was forced to take artificial political forms. Social interactive ties made conscious and reflective could then provide real democratic reasoning.[68] It is here that the 'life politics' of Giddens and Beck or the actor-network theorising of Latour can be seen to provide models for resilience as a framework for governing in a non-linear world.[69]

For both Dewey and Hayek, the sphere of reason was not located in the artificial public realm of government and representation but in the private and informal realm of societal interaction. Yet neither of these thinkers advocated the freedom of the private and informal realm on the basis of reason as rationalist knowledge but rather on the basis of the contingency of understanding and the need to inculcate adaptive learning. Both considered how adaptive learning could be facilitated by governing institutions, rather than considering the state as an executive, decision-making actor. For Dewey, 'the regulations and laws of the state are … misconceived when they are viewed as commands' as if the state directly represented the Rousseauian 'general will';[70] there was no politically constituted subject capable of directing and controlling society:

> Rules of law are in fact the institutions of conditions under which persons make their arrangements with one another. They are the structures which canalize action; they are active forces only as are the banks which confine the flow of a stream, and are commands only in the sense in which banks command the current.[71]

Dewey and Hayek[72] both understood the modern state to be a self-reflexive, enabling state rather than a directing or decision-making state, through the preference for constitutive rules rather than regulatory ones.[73] What the state reflexively was able to enable was the emergence of social reasoning: the true democratic reason. In this emergent and evolutionary understanding, states played a role analogous to that of custom or habit, providing the framework for decision-making in the informal, private, sphere but not dictating it, enabling social experimentation and adaptation to take place in the social sphere. The meaning of democracy was thus transformed from the representation and contestation of views and preferences in the deliberative public sphere to democracy as a mode of being or a mode of life: democracy as responsive capacities for adaptive learning in the societal sphere.

Conclusion

The work of Dewey and Hayek prefigured the post-1990 resilience understandings of how politics and democracy needed to be reworked in order to govern a world of complexity, after the perceived decline of the linear politics of Left and Right, which had shaped liberal modernity since the French Revolution. What is particularly important to note (and has been emphasised in each chapter in this book) is that, in resilience understandings, 'real' power is located not at the level of the state but at the level of society itself. It is this shift that enables a new type of political solution to problems; not addressed to the question of institutional mechanisms of representation at the state level but to problems as they are democratically reframed at the societal level.

In traditional liberal rationalist frameworks, the problem of state policy-making was understood to be the limited capacity of the public to understand (or to be interested in) the complexity of government policy-making and therefore to hold government properly to account as representing the public will. This is the traditional Aristotelian view, replicated at some points (more negatively) by Walter Lippmann in the *Phantom Public* and engaged with anew (more positively) in John Keane's advocacy of 'monitory democracy'. In Aristotelian framings of the problem, the solution was that of reworking public accountability at a smaller community level of decentralized power, making mechanisms of accountability more simplified or transparent or increasing the educational or informational knowledge of the public. All these responses presupposed traditional state-based rationalist understandings and operated around the problematic of representation with the growth of political communities and the complexity of government. Institutional changes were envisaged, or the public was to be educated or empowered, in order for the mechanisms of representation to work more efficiently and for the liberal promise of government as representing the 'will of the people' to be reaffirmed.

As long as we lived in the world of political contestation – of Left and Right – with state power at the centre of political life and contested by (at least two) rival ideological understandings, given shape and coherence by political party organisation and social contestation, the problem of representation was at the centre of democratic theorising. Today, we no longer live in such a world, and with the decline of state-based understandings of politics, we have seen a revival of evolutionary, emergent, and resilience-understandings, which no longer have the problematic of representation at their heart. When government authorities and policy think tanks talk of giving 'power to the people' today, they do not necessarily discuss ways of developing more efficient mechanisms of representation.

Democratic politics in a world conceived as complex is less concerned with representation than with the development of social responsiveness. The 'power' which 'the people' are seen to require today is social empowerment: the removal of barriers to their power to take reasoned and responsive decisions in their everyday lives. This capacity to think autonomously and responsively in a world of change and of complexity is the power of resilience. In this framing, there is no limit to the extension of democracy through social capacity-building, the 'powering' of communities or the empowerment of decision-making individuals. Once the problematic of constituting the public will is seen to be the responsibility of the pluralised public itself, in its continual emergence (as we saw in the previous two chapters), we are all enjoined to the democratic task of working on ourselves and reflecting upon our own attachments and responsibilities to those around us. The personal is indeed then the political. This reduction of political understandings to reflexive work on the self, rather than work on transformation of the external world, is not merely the prerogative of resilience-thinking at the level of governing power. The dominance of this inversion of liberal modernist understandings of the subject, the public sphere and of power is perhaps even more clearly demonstrated in the work of political theorists who are generally seen to be radical critics of dominant frameworks of rule and their frameworks of legitimation. It is to these that we turn to in the final chapter of this part of the book.

Notes

1 See for example: Lash, 2002; Latour, 2004; Dallmayr, 2010; Connolly, 2011; Giddens, 1994; Beck, 1997; Beck and Beck-Gernsheim, 2002.
2 See further, Michel Foucault's juxtaposition of sovereign power vis-à-vis biopower, Foucault, 1981: pp.135–45; 2003: pp.239–63; 2008.
3 Hanisch, 1969.
4 Miller and Rose, 2008: p.25.
5 Ibid.: p.213.
6 Ibid.: p.214.
7 Ibid.: p.215.
8 Dean, 2010: pp.196–7.
9 Ibid: p.197.
10 Grist, 2009: p.16.
11 Big Society, 2012.
12 Rousseau, 1998.
13 Kant, 1991.
14 Foucault, 2011: p.34.
15 Foucault, 2010: p.155; see also Arendt, 1998; Samons, 2004.
16 Habermas, 1986; see also Disch, 1997: p.152.
17 Elster, 1998; Gutmann and Thompson, 2004; Dryzek, 2012; Fishkin, 2011.
18 Plato, 2007; see also Foucault, 2010: p.224; 2011: p.61.
19 Aristotle, 1992; Foucault, 2011: p.46.
20 Keane, 2011: p.214; see also Keane, 2009.
21 Ibid.: p.219.
22 For example, Fung and Wright, 2003.
23 Keane, 2011: p.219.
24 Koopman, 2009.
25 Lippmann, 1993: p.145.
26 Ibid.: p.15.
27 Ibid.: p.17.
28 Ibid.: pp.72–74.
29 Ibid.: p.78.
30 Ibid.: p.146.

31 Ibid.: p.80.
32 Ibid.: p.29.
33 Ibid.: p.32.
34 Ibid.: p.35.
35 Ibid.: pp.51–52.
36 Dewey, 1927: p.5.
37 Ibid.: p.20.
38 As he himself stated, see ibid.: p.116, n.1.
39 Ibid.: p.18.
40 Hayek, 2006: p.388.
41 This approach was further developed in the new institutionalist economic understanding of the evolutionary paths of 'open' and 'closed' societies; see, for example, North et al., 2009.
42 See Gamble, 1996.
43 For example, Ralston, 2012; Mulligan, 2006.
44 Koopman, 2009.
45 Hodgson, 2006.
46 James, 1957.
47 See further, for contrasting views, Althusser and Balibar, 2009; Latour, 2007.
48 In a similar phenomenological framework to that of Edmund Husserl (see Husserl, 1970).
49 Dewey, 1927: pp.84–92.
50 Ibid.: p.25 (emphasis in the original).
51 Hayek, 1952: p.44.
52 Ibid.: pp.80–81.
53 Ibid.: p.82.
54 Ibid.: p.109.
55 Dewey, 2007: p.21.
56 Ralston, 2012.
57 Drawn out well in Koopman, 2009.
58 Hayek, 1991.
59 Koopman, 2009.
60 Dewey, 1927: p.33.
61 Ibid.: pp.32, 106.
62 Ibid.: p.73.
63 Ibid.: p.126.
64 Giddens, 2002.
65 Dewey, 1927: p.175.
66 Ibid.: p.216.
67 Ibid.
68 Ibid.: p.219.
69 See, for example, Giddens, 1994; Beck, 1997; Latour, 2007.
70 Dewey, 1927: pp.54–55.
71 Ibid.: p.54.
72 Hayek, 1960.
73 Dewey, 1927: p.54; Hayek, 1982: pp.169–95; see also Rawls, 1955; Searle, 1969.

9
THE POVERTY OF
POST-HUMANISM

Introduction

In the 'human' world of liberal modernity, we believed that we could transform our external world, through our own creativity and agency: understanding the laws of the external world and mastering them through the
development of culture, science, and technology. In the 'post-human' world
of complexity and resilience-thinking, we are told by new materialists, actor
network theorists and post-humanists that creativity and agency still exist,
but that they are not the property of humans alone, but rather a product of
our embedded relations – the complex life of assemblages, associations and
relationships – through which we are attached to the world. Rather than
attempting to understand and act in the world on the basis of our separation
from it – articulated in the constraining, alienating and resentment-filled
modernist divides of human/nature, subject/object, culture/environment –
we should become more aware of our embedded 'attachment' to the world. It is
in developing these attachments that we can govern ourselves as self-reflexive,
and thereby responsive and resilient, subjects. This chapter critically
examines these claims and suggests that, on the contrary, we become less
'attached' and that the external word becomes increasingly alien and mys-
terious to us. In doing so, it mounts a defence of subject/object understandings and social constructions of a divide between humanity and the
world external to us.

New materialist, actor network theory (ANT) and post-human approaches
all claim to have a liberating and emancipatory ethic of freedom, democracy,

inclusion and progress through paying a renewed attention to emergent agency as a result of our relational embeddedness in the world.[1] The key understanding at stake is that of the new materialist deployment of a much broader, more connected, more social, understanding of causal 'agency' which involves the appreciation of complexity and emergent causality as opposed to the fixity of structures in either the social or natural world. This radicalised, more agential, materialism derives traction from its critique of liberal modernist conceptions of a binary world in which agency is seen to lie solely in the human subject, invested with 'free will' and subjectivity. Outside and external to this constructed world of the subject lay 'nature', the external or non-human world. This was conceived as a world of purely passive objects, mechanically destined to merely exist as causal intermediaries, with no agency of their own. This external world was contrasted to the world of human 'freedom' as a world of necessity; bound by law, regularity and repetition, waiting for the human subject to appropriate it as its object. In this binary understanding of Enlightenment or modernist frameworks, familiar in all the works of complexity theory, humans constituted themselves as ends and everything else – nature – as merely a means.[2]

For the French sociologist of science, Bruno Latour, we were imprisoned between Scylla and Charybdis – between a mythical 'world of transcendence', based on anthropocentric hubris, with all the dangers of conflict, exclusion and environmental destruction implied – and the 'world of immanence' – the inevitable working out of the natural laws of regularity and cause and effect of Newtonian mechanical materialism.[3] Discourses of two separate worlds, of 'human' freedom and of 'natural' necessity, operated to stabilise the liberal order of power: 'the Old Regime enjoyed the advantages of a double transcendence: it could extricate itself from simple matters of fact by appealing to values, and it could always appeal against the outdated requirements of values and law, to the harsh reality of facts'.[4]

The leading conceptual frameworks of critical complexity theorising – new materialist, ANT, non-representational theory, and post-human approaches – promise us another type of freedom and emancipation as an alternative to the enslavement of modernist promises of human 'freedom'. In this chapter, I wish to draw out that this new freedom also has a price: that we should govern on the basis of what in the modernist frameworks of Enlightenment understanding was called 'blind necessity' – merely responding to the world rather than progressing through acquiring greater knowledge and control over it. In fact, far from simple binaries of separate worlds of (human) freedom and (natural) necessity, the modernist understanding of progress was based on the dialectic of transforming necessity into freedom,

transforming the unknown (blind necessity) into causal regularities amenable to understanding (necessity) and thus 'humanising' the world, making
it amenable to human understanding.[5] Latour, in fact, captures this process
well in his understanding that 'facts' are not just 'out there' to be discovered
but, in fact, take a huge amount of work to produce or to be 'manufactured'
in laboratories.[6] Latour's empirical studies of the development of science are
fascinating; the problems only start when conclusions are drawn for political
philosophy. We are freed from the structures and laws of necessity (constitutive of human freedom) but only to be subordinated to the arbitrary and
unknowable whims of emergent causality (to which only enslavement is
possible).

Radical advocates of complex life set up the constructed binary of fixed
(rather than dialectical) understandings of freedom and necessity as a straw
man, to be rapidly knocked down. They argue that the advances in our
understanding of the work of the natural sciences mean that the external
world of objects/non-humans/nature is not, in fact, mechanically bound by
fixed and timeless laws and regularities open to the discovery and control
of humankind. Therefore, the external world is not passive or objective and
lacking in creative agency. Ergo, humans are not the only agents or subjects
in the world and – in a world where agency is spread more widely or thinly –
humans now have the possibility of recognising, rejoining and re-embedding
themselves in the world. The historic struggle for human mastery of necessity in the name of collective human freedom (as a 'war' against nature) is
thereby declared over. There is no longer an 'outside' to be conquered, there
is 'no more environment', 'no more nature': 'Political philosophy abruptly
finds itself confronted with the obligation to internalize the environment that
it had viewed up to now as another world'.[7]

This chapter seeks to draw out the consequences of our perception of
the end of the outside – the end of the artificial subject/object and society/
nature binaries constituted by liberal modernity – and suggests that rather
than enabling us to become more connected or 'at home' in the world, these
understandings reflect and rationalise our growing alienation and estrange-
ment from the world. The argument is straightforward: if there are no longer
causal regularities to be discovered – operating both in 'nature' and through
social relations – then we would be entirely subject to what appear to us
as our own alienated social products (the event, for example, as discussed
in Chapter 7). Our own social products would appear to take on a life of
their own and literally appear to rule over us, in a parallel fetish to that critiqued by Marx in *Capital: Volume One*, with regard to the fetishism of commodities, which in reality appear to dictate prices, wages and employment

possibilities under capitalist social relations.[8] Without the modernist constructions of subject/object, we could no longer aspire or strive to learn and develop as part of a goal-orientated process of engagement in the external world. Rather than necessity becoming the precondition for freedom, the critique of our hubristic belief in human freedom would lead us merely to humble ourselves before the altar of life as complexity.

Governance, adaptation and 'blind necessity'

Liberal discourses of government centred upon the conception of sovereign power, its constitution, its legitimisation, and its limits; current discourses of governance work differently.[9] Discourses of governance recognise a different set of limits to rule. These limits are not constituted in the frameworks of liberal binaries, which previously operated to fix the boundaries of sovereign power: the limits of the inside and outside (of law and anarchy) or the limits of the public and the private or the modernist divide between the formal sphere of politics and law and the informal sphere of the social and economic. Nor are these limits articulated in the liberal terms of natural rights and freedoms or of rationality, universalism and autonomy.

A new rationality of governing has been derived from a new understanding of limits, based upon understandings of the need to adapt to a complex, interconnected and globalised world of emergent causality: to inculcate resilience.[10] The discursive rise of resilience-thinking as a dominant cultural outlook in the West, and the crisis or decline of liberal framings of representation, can be understood as a product of the end of the Cold War or the end of the politics of 'Left and Right'.[11] Of course, ever since the Enlightenment, modernist ideas of human 'exceptionalism' and of the freedoms of the political and the certainties of the sciences have been critiqued and the 'hubris of reason' expounded upon.[12] However, as long as the social struggle was at the forefront of ideologically contested understandings of politics and progress, from the French Revolution onwards, government and sovereign power were subject to liberal discourses of limits. However, in the post-political world, it appears that human concerns, contestations and interests are not enough to fill the political world and to give coherence to government programmes or legitimacy to elected regimes. Politics, without the clarifying frameworks of ideological social contestation, seems to confront a world of complexity and to call forth or elicit the ethico-political concerns so well articulated in the post-human extension of politics and understandings of democracy, agency and rights to assemblages of complex human and non-human life – to the new 'cosmopolitics' of the cosmos, or the 'political ecology' of the earth.[13]

Without the social struggle and the social understandings it gave rise to, the modernist edifice is rapidly disappearing. The world appears to lack the imprint of human construction and therefore to be 'post-human'. We are reborn or born-again in a world in which we appear to be without the signposts of modernity. Today's sensibilities mean that we are much more likely to be drawn towards globalised understandings of complexity, captured well in physicist Ilya Prigogine's view of complexity as 'the irreversible succession of events' where 'the arrow of time' ensures that circumstances are never stable for repeatable cause-and-effect relations, destabilising any possibility of acting on the basis of knowable eternal or fixed 'natural' laws.[14]

Currently, one of the most influential theorists of complexity appears to be Bruno Latour. Latour's key attribute could well be that he finds himself in the right place and at the right time,[15] in order to reintroduce the sceptical products of the philosophy of science into the social sciences, arguing that there is nothing to be 'discovered' under the surface of appearances:

> To assert that underneath legitimate relationships there are forces invisible to the actors, forces that could be discerned only by specialists in the social sciences, amounts to using the same method [as] for the metaphysics of nature ... it amounts to claiming that there exist primary qualities – society and its power relations – that form the essential furnishings of the social world, and secondary qualities, as deceitful as they are intensely experienced, that cover with their mantle the invisible forces one cannot see ... If the natural sciences have to be rejected when they employ that dichotomy, then we have to reject the social sciences all the more vigorously.[16]

If there are no laws or regularities to be discovered by social science, then there can be no freedom either. Latour in his removal of structures, laws and regularities consciously goes beyond the freedom/necessity problematic essential to the progressive thought of modernity. The foremost radical thinkers, such as Lenin, argued that humankind 'must necessarily and inevitably adapt themselves to' the necessity of natural laws.[17] Lenin also understood the importance of 'blind necessity', of the operation of the external world unknown to us: of 'unknown necessity'.[18] The difference between this understanding of the world and that of today's dominant framings is in the way in which freedom was understood in relation to necessity. For radical thought, human freedom depended upon a dialectical understanding of the relationship between freedom and necessity. The external world thereby constituted an ongoing and unlimited realm of possibilities for human freedom precisely because the external world could never be fully known or understood:'the recognition of the objective reality of the external world and of the laws of external nature, and of the fact that this world and these laws are fully knowable to man but can never be known to him with finality'.[19]

The recognition of the attenuated subject/object distinction in an age of complexity radically alters or inverses modernist understandings of the relationship between freedom and necessity. The declaration of the end of the struggle to emancipate the human from external necessity is declared as genuine, post-human, emancipation. Emancipation in this case is a project of work on the human itself, rather than the external world, once we accept that the previous understanding of the linear liberal telos – of the ongoing war for domination, understanding and control – was in fact dehumanising and divisive. New materialism argues that we can emancipate ourselves once we throw off the shackles of humankind being endowed with divine purpose, reason or capacities for mastery. In recognising the limits of human capacities and appreciating the agency and effects of non-human others, we can then allegedly unleash our 'inner' human and become what we 'are', no longer alienated from each other and the world we inhabit.[20]

The newfound appreciation of complex life and the ethos of self-reflexivity is therefore about the transformation of the human subject rather than the world. It is a message of a new politics and a new ethics: for some it is the ethics of ecopolitics, for others, of post-humanism, and for others, of vital materialism. This new ethics of the radical work on the self and of a greater sensitivity to others is often articulated as a radical break with previous theorising in politics and international relations. However, the new ethical politics of the post-human could also be understood as a radical extension of the cosmopolitanism critiques of the 1990s. The driver behind cosmopolitan discourses was also the critique of the limited and constrained subjectivity of political thinking, trapped inside the modernist politics of the nation state.

For theorists, such as Andrew Linklater, the demand for cosmopolitan thinking was about transforming and radicalising political and ethical sensitivities through 'expanding the realm of dialogic commitments'.[21] In this way, the growing call for 'cosmopolitics' highlights the ethical imperatives uniting 1990s' cosmopolitan theorising and the new materialism of those, like Isabelle Stengers and Bruno Latour, who also proffer a 'cosmo-politics' of greater ethical sensitivities (with William Connolly's work straddling both worlds).[22] The ethical inclusiveness expands further, extending from the human to the non-human as our ethical sensitivities see any exclusion as problematic, until we understand that even 'the image of dead or thoroughly instrumentalized matter feeds human hubris and our earth-destroying fantasies of conquest and consumption'.[23]

Distributive agency: The kingdom of 'no ends'

Connolly, Bennett and Latour all make the argument that, on both onto-logical and ethico-political grounds, we need to reject the modernist sub-ject/object divide of freely willed human agency on the one hand and the 'world of objects governed by efficient causality or simple probability, on the other'.[24] This is done through developing a distributive theory of agency, whereby 'proto-agency' – the capacity to create in ways that differ from mere 'mechanical causation' – is possessed by non-human and even non-organic forms of life.[25] As Bennett argues, we need to take seriously 'the capacity of things – edibles, commodities, storms, metals – not only to impede or block the will and designs of humans but also to act as quasi-agents or forces with trajectories, propensities, or tendencies of their own'.[26]

Connolly and Bennett consciously seek to extend the realm of agency and to challenge the anthropocentric link between consciousness and agency that is held to be problematic in its tendency 'to reduce *political* agency to *human* agency'.[27] Bennett argues that effective agency, the role an actant may play in an outcome, needs to be separated from moral understandings of agency, which imply some will or intention. In fact, theories of distributive agency do not start with subjects as the cause of an effect; actants merely influence outcomes but do not necessarily have intentions and purposes.[28]

Human agency is thereby continually limited by the 'proto-agency of other systems', in an understanding of the world as a complex web 'of nodes and levels of agency': it is this complex, multi-agential world of becoming which serves to 'curtail the hubris expressed in the "anthropic exception" allocating agency purely to humans and blind causality to the non-human world'.[29] Bennett seeks to strategically elide 'what is commonly taken as distinctive or even unique about humans'.[30] To the extent that she is willing to:

> emphasize, even overemphasize, the agentic contributions of nonhu-man forces (operating in nature, in the human body, and in human arti-facts) in an attempt to counter the narcissistic reflex of human language and thought. We need to cultivate a bit of anthromorphism – the idea that human agency has some echoes in nonhuman nature – to counter the narcissism of humans in charge of the world.[31]

It seems that for Bennett there is an ethico-political imperative driving attempts to distribute agency. She argues that the understanding of emergent causality of assemblages, rather than more modest understandings of efficient causality, is necessary 'because the rubric of material agency is likely to be a stronger counter to human exceptionalism ... An assemblage owes its agentic capacity to the vitality of the materialities that constitute it.'[32]

This ethico-political imperative is also clear in Latour's assertion of the 'kingdom of ends':

> The ecological crisis, as we have often noted, presents itself above all as a generalized revolt of means. Nothing and no one is willing any longer to agree to serve as a simple means to the exercise of any will whatsoever taken as an ultimate end. The tiniest maggot, the smallest rodent, the scantest river, the farthest star, the most humble of automatic machines – each demands to be taken also as an end.[33]

The strength of the ethico-political argument of distributive agency is that it appears ontologically grounded in the complex and globalised world increasingly dominating our subjective experiences of 'crisis'. It increasingly appears to us that we are, in fact, living in a 'runaway world':[34] that science and technology are out of human control in a world of 'manufactured risk' and uncertainties, so clearly described in the work of Ulrich Beck.[35] It is in this world, a world where science appears to have failed in its attempt to construct a knowable external world and where politics appears to have failed in its attempts to simulate communities of meaning on the basis of acting in this world, that Latour seems justified in asking 'for just a tiny concession: that the question of democracy be extended to nonhumans'.[36]

In focusing on the need to redistribute understandings of agency, posthumanist or ANT approaches have been criticised for removing power relations and reinforcing liberal understandings of individual responsibility.[37] However, as Latour responds, ANT and new materialist approaches do not argue that actors have substantive equality or that they can shoulder the responsibilities of moral autonomy. In fact, this understanding of distributive agency is a far cry from classical liberal framings of strong, capable and autonomous subjects. It could, in fact, be argued that the focus on the subject – as embedded in multiple assemblages, relations and associations – inverses liberal understandings. 'Quasi-subjects' or 'actants' with the power of shared agency cannot be understood or determined by analysis of the isolated or autonomous rational subject.[38] While it is true that there are no hidden 'structures' and no fixed or hierarchical power relations, this is a far cry from traditional liberal interpellations of the subject as a natural, rational or autonomous individual, which served to naturalise the social relations of the market.[39] Here, the subject is transformed or inversed, lacking any natural, rational or autonomous existence and forever negotiating, experimenting and reflecting upon its imbrication within complex, fluid and overlapping networks and assemblages.

Rather than subjects themselves, it is these associations, assemblages and networks which are held to explain the contingencies and unknowability of the world, enabling asymmetries of power when they are least expected: 'An infinitesimal cause can have vast effects; an insignificant actor becomes central; an immense cataclysm disappears as if by magic'.[40] The point is not so much that of the equality of responsibility but of the limits of reason and, with this, the limits of power. These limits can be understood only by expanding our understandings of the connectedness, embeddedness and attachment of human actors to the world – the attachments alleged to be missed by modernist social theorising. It is these 'missing actors' (human and non-human) that are held to explain the superficiality of critical social theorising focused on social explanation of hidden structures. The post-humanist focus on the 'missing masses' brings to the fore the new ethics of awareness of attachment.[41]

However, the price to be paid for our attachments is that we can never constitute our own ends. If we imagined that we could never possibly know in advance, or at the time of our actions or decisions, however minor, what their final or ultimate ends or outcomes would be, we would become incapacitated or paralysed. We could not make free choices because we lacked the meaningful structures through which we could aspire to create our own ends. In a new materialist world, we no longer have the sense of a capacity to choose our own ends – a sense of freedom. Instead we have merely a world of complexity and emergent causality, which appears to dictate to us how we should act in order to self-reflexively respond and adapt to our external environment. Politics then becomes merely a question of responsiveness – of ethical responsibility – not of freedom.

Time's arrow and 'retro-politics'

In this framework of complexity, contingency, agency and creativity, the causal relations can only be established and 'known after rather than before the fact'.[42] Instead, the world of becoming is 'emergent' through the complex actions and interactions of numerous agential assemblages. This, in effect, closes off the future as something that can be grasped as either a calculative probability, a random chance or the hidden outcome of objective causal relations. There is agency everywhere but no fixed structures or necessary regularities, the world is continually 'becoming', with all the risks and potential benefits of creative potential immanent to this process.

The potential outcomes always far exceed the final outcomes because the key to explanation is that of the processes of interaction between different agents or agencies. These outcomes cannot be determined by existing forms of knowledge, which apply to the constituent parts or the individual actors or agents themselves. We have a process of understanding and reasoning that can only work backwards from the complex contingent outcomes, whether these concern natural processes of evolution or social processes of human interaction or the human and non-human assemblages of events. Because understanding only follows the event (as considered in Chapter 7), it appears that subject/object relations are inversed and, this reversal is precisely what enables complex life to reveal itself, to enable a programme of self-reflexive governance. Rather than experimenting on the world to learn and develop our own understanding as conscious agents, the world of complex life appears to be continually testing and experimenting on the human subject to assess its level of responsive self-reflexivity.

Time's arrow can only ever go backwards, never forwards, because the separation of subject and object, which creates the condition of possibility for forward-looking intentional or instrumental actions, is exactly the target of critique. Rather than separating temporally the subject and object, new materialism argues that process overcomes and sublimates both sides of the liberal linear equation. As Bennett states: 'an actant never really acts alone. Its efficacy or agency always depends on the collaboration, cooperation, or interactive interference of many bodies and forces'.[43] There is no separation of subject and object from the process of interaction, or in Bennett's terms the 'agentic assemblage'.[44] It is this assemblage that, through self-organising emergence, distributes agency across an 'ontologically heterogeneous field'.[45] For Bennett:

> The event illuminates its own past, but it can never be deduced from it ... its sources can only be revealed retroactively. These sources are necessarily multiple, made up of elements unaffiliated before the "crystallization" process began. In fact, what makes the event happen is precisely the contingent coming together of a set of elements.[46]

The formative drive of material vitality, for Bennett, 'can be known only indirectly, only by examining its effects'.[47] She argues: 'My vital materialism posits the causality of *both* inorganic and organic matter to be, to some extent, inscrutable to us'.[48] While mechanical materialism is understood to constrain the future, making it a rerun of the past, the new materialism asserts that the future is open. But the future can only be 'freed' on the basis of removing structures of law and regularity, which held the promise of transcendence. Without the possibility of transcending our circumstances, we instead have to adapt: we have to become 'authentic' in the Heideggerian sense, taking ethico-political responsibility for our 'being-in-the-world'. In Latour's language we will be forced to create reflective and responsible communities in which 'agreement is going to have to be reached'.[49]

The fact that the future is closed off to us forces us to build political consensus on the basis of our ethical openness to the world. Nothing can be taken for granted or assumed once the modernist foundations of scientific and political representation have been removed. While there may not be agential hierarchies, there is no assumption of equality either, merely interactions and associations of humans and non-humans within the complex assemblages of the world of becoming. As Latour argues:

> The actors do not know what they are doing, still less the sociologists. What manipulates the actors is unknown to everyone, including researchers in the social sciences. This is even the reason there is a Republic, a common world still to come: we are unaware of the collective consequences of our actions.[50]

The future is closed to us, but the processes of complex or emergent causality can be at least partially grasped to enable a programme of reflexive self-governance, but only after the fact (or the event) and only through the slow, laborious and complex work of tracing the associations of actors, or the assemblages at play in the production or emergence of a particular event. Latour suggests that the baggage of the social scientist needs to be removed to enable the actors to speak for themselves and for the mediating, transforming agency of the full range of human and non-human actants in the network or assemblage to be revealed.[51] Explanation without subjects and without structures can have no analytical framework and by definition can only be descriptive. As Latour argues, there can be no analytical short-cuts of 'explanation' which assume fixed, causal relations, when the object of science is always the particular:

> The danger is all the greater because this is the moment most often chosen by critical sociology, always lurking in the background, to take over social explanations and replace the objects to be accounted for with irrelevant, all-purpose 'social forces' [that actors] are too dumb to see or can't stand to be revealed.[52]

For ANT, in theory, with enough work and effort to trace the associations and connections, every given situation can be explained *post hoc* with the benefit of a concrete, uniquely adequate, account. Rather than theorising beneath the surface, Latour argues that 'the name of the game is to get back to empiricism.[53] For actors to make a difference, for causality to emerge rather than be preexistent, for the political-ethics of post-humanism, every event is necessarily unique. In Latour's words, the alternative to the hierarchies of critical sociology, with structures which turn actors into dopes or puppets, is the liberatory project of critical self-awareness, of reflectivity upon the embedded connections, relations and affinities which enable the construction of humans finally increasingly attached to the world.[54] The better attached and bonded we are, the more reflexive and reflective humans will be.

I beg to differ: the price we pay for our new bonds and attachments is far too high. And the prize on offer is a false one. These new 'attachments' are not with real, struggling, contesting people, colleagues or comrades involved in a forward-looking project over which we have conscious control, but with unknowable, unseen, complex, overlapping and interlinking processes which have already dissipated after the event. These processes create contingent and fleeting chains of *causation* that are not in themselves traceable as causal relations, that is, that precisely do not work through fixed structures of meaning. Our new attachments therefore mean that we can no longer act as subjects in the world. We can speak, have understandings and views – we can be taken, of course, very, very seriously as research subjects in ANT perspectives (as any laboratory subject would be; see, for example, Latour's 'dialogue' with a student)[55] – but we can never be *human* subjects, collectively understanding, constituting and transforming our world.

Being is everything

While William Connolly argues that we live in a 'world of becoming', the key factor or agency in the frameworks of new materialism or post-humanism is *being* itself. For Connolly, the contingencies of becoming are translated into clashes or a coming together of 'multiple zones of temporality' or 'temporal force-fields' that intersect.[56] In this framework, it is the connections or relations between different, distinct forms of 'being' which matter. The process of 'becoming' is a non-intentional, unplanned product of the clashes of 'being'. In this way, the use of 'becoming' is rather misleading for the reader as it is not as if there was an *ex nihilo* cause, tendency or shift which can be traced in terms of transformation from one source to the next. The notion of 'becoming' suggests a certain development with a limited set of causal factors. In fact, the creativity of new material or post-human approaches stems from the attention to a greater range of 'being', enlarging the number of actors and actants and their traces, connections and mediations.[57]

The world of becoming is a world in which being – construed in terms of differing temporalities, actants, actors, agents, proto-subjects and proto-objects – is determinant through the medium of connecting and interconnected zones of temporality, assemblages, associations and relations. Beings (both organic and non-organic) are creative and differential in the accidental and contingent relations between differing modes of existence. It is the clash of being that creates contingent outcomes: the coming together of multiple different actants. Connolly shows us that it is the agency of 'being' which is at work beneath the world of 'becoming'. Each form of being, he states, has its own temporality:

> The bumpiness of time in an open universe is accentuated by the fact that several force-fields or tiers of chrono-time subsist – time measured by a clock. There is geological time, evolutionary time, neuronal time, civilizational time, the time of a specific state regime, the time of a human life, the time of a type of economic organization, and so on almost endlessly.[58]

These differing modes of being – differing time trajectories – clash in unpredictable ways: 'A flock of geese, following one trajectory, might collide with a plane set on another, creating havoc for both birds and humans.'[59] However, what is key to the understanding of being that is at stake here is that it is not determinable beforehand; it is not isolatable as an inner essence; it is being that is determinate only in that particular assemblage or at the particular moment of intersection.

Connolly here relies on Whitehead and Prigogine to reinforce his argument regarding 'the vitality of nonorganic elements whose modes of behaviour change as they become parts of larger assemblages even as they *also* continue to express a vitality or excessiveness that is not entirely governed by the assemblage'.[60] In the example of the collision of the geese and the plane, the exact outcome will depend on the exact constellation of forces generated by the interaction, the directions involved, velocity, types of engine, and so on. Merely knowing about the two distinct 'force-fields' of the plane and the flock of geese is not adequate to understand the contingent consequences of such a collision considering the multiple agencies involved.

Even though Connolly presents the problematic of contingency in terms of agency and of clashing temporalities, the underlying ontology is that of distinct and unknowable forms of being. There is a revival of a Kantian existential 'unknowability', except there is no assumption that it is the inner essence of 'things-in-themselves' which evades us; rather, the contingent assemblage of emergent causality lacks an inner essence which can be determined in advance. It is the contingent clash of separate beings which creates the contingent outcome, through the transformation of being itself:

> The idea of emergent causality does not apply well to micro or macroprocesses in contexts of relative stability. Efficient causality, or more richly, multi-causal intersections work rather well under those circumstances. Emergent causality is most pertinent when a previously stabilized force-field enters a period of heightened instability. Emergent causality is *causal* – rather than reducible to a mere web of definitional relations – in that a movement in one force-field helps to induce changes in others. But it is also *emergent* in that … some of the turbulence introduced into the second field is not always knowable in detail in itself before it arrives darkly through the effects that emerge.[61]

Emergent causality alleges that its ontological focus is being changing being – objects transforming objects – rather than subjects transforming objects. In relations of emergent causality, there are therefore no subject–object relations as this positional divide is overcome through the understanding of process relations: 'If efficient causality seeks to rank the actants involved, treating some as external causes and others as dependent effects, emergent causality places the focus on the process as itself an actant.'[62] It is the assemblage that has agency rather than the specific actors per se. As Bennett argues, worms may be small, but humans would not exist without their constant labour on the soil enabling the 'inauguration of human culture'.[63] Small agents in complex assemblages can have very large accumulated effects. Worms may not have intended to enable human culture, but nevertheless they are actants in the human–non-human assemblage they are crucial to creating.[64]

Here, it is *being* which does all the work with no need for subjects at all. In fact, the world of becoming is a subject-less world – a world of complexity, of being, alone. The fact that it is being which does all the work in 'becoming' is clear once we understand that the 'becoming' of 'emergent causality' can only ever be based upon the world of appearances, a world which confronts the human only in terms of being itself. It is easy to read traces of Heidegger's similar understanding of the human as 'thrown' into the world, where humanity is 'delivered over' to a total, all-encompassing 'thereness' and Dasein must occupy this presentness and take it up into its own existence.[65] For Heidegger, the modernist form of knowing missed out on precisely the deeper ethico-political understandings raised by the post-humanist theorists:

But no sooner was the 'phenomenon of knowing the world' grasped than it got interpreted in a 'superficial', formal manner. The evidence for this is the procedure (still customary today) of setting up knowing as a 'relation between subject and Object' – a procedure in which there lurks as much 'truth' as vacuity. But subject and Object do not coincide with Dasein and the world.[66]

In this mode of understanding, ethical self-reflectivity, community, authenticity, and post-human care or 'concern' can only take place on the basis of reconstructing a philosophy of being, which overcomes the subject/object division so central to modernity.[67]

Interpellating the post-human

The world of the post-human liberates us from the relativist competition over 'truth'. Without modernist certainties there are no hierarchies of knowledge or, indeed, of power. There can be neither fixed understandings of 'insides' and 'outsides' or of 'causes' and 'effects', nor of 'friends' and 'enemies'. Without our modernist understandings of the subject, it appears that the problems and conflicts of our world could be resolved. Problems do not disappear but they do open themselves or 'appeal' through the making of 'propositions', in the words of Latour,[68] to different understandings and different responses. Problems thus (re)presented enable the new rationalities of governance, rather than government. These rationalities – of self-reflexive work on socially interactive outcomes – are the rationalities of resilience. The rationalities of distributive agency, of Prigogine's time's arrow, of being and becoming through 'emergent causality' are not the rationalities of liberal democratic or electoral representation or of the management of contesting collectivities in plural systems of power. These rationalities do not presuppose the circulatory freedoms of the subject, describing the liberal limits and binaries of the artificial sphere of state-based public law and politics, theorised so well by Michel Foucault.[69] Instead, they articulate the shift towards resilience–thinking as a dominant mode of governance, based on complex and emergent life, which can only operate, after the fact, on the world as it appears.

The rise of the rule of self-reflexive governance (especially in contrast to Foucault's understanding of the promotion of circulatory freedoms) has been recognised by many diverse thinkers and articulated well by authors such as Giorgio Agamben. Agamben's work is particularly adroit in flagging up the overcoming of the private/public divide and the reduction of the subject to 'bare life'.[70] Unfortunately, this has been articulated in terms of sovereign power *in extremis*,[71] rather than taking the route which would seem much more explicit in Foucault's later work, on biopolitical governance through working with, rather than against, 'life itself' in *The History of Sexuality, Volume 1*.[72]

The world of becoming thereby is an ontologically flat world without the traditional hierarchies of existence and a more shared conception of agency. For Bennett, therefore, 'to begin to experience the relationship between persons and other materialities more horizontally, is to take a step toward a more ecological sensibility'.[73] Here there is room for human agency, but this agency involves a deeper understanding of and receptivity to the world of complex emergent effects. Rather than the hubristic focus on transforming the external world, the ethico-political tasks are those of work on the self to erase hubristic liberal traces of subject-centric understandings, understood to merely create the dangers of existential resentment.[74] Work on the self is the only route to changing the world. As Connolly states: 'To embrace without deep resentment a world of becoming is to work to "become who you are", so that the word "become" now modifies "are" more than the other way around.'[75] Becoming who you are involves the 'microtactics of the self', and work on the self can then extend into the 'micropolitics' of more conscious and reflective choices and decisions and life-style choices leading to potentially higher levels of ethical self-reflectivity and responsibility.[76]

Bennett argues that, against the 'narcissism' of anthropomorphic understandings of domination of the external world, we need 'some tactics for cultivating the experience of our *selves* as vibrant matter'.[77] Rather than hubristically imagining that we can shape the world we live in, Bennett argues that: 'Perhaps the ethical responsibility of an individual human now resides in one's response to the assemblages in which one finds oneself participating.'[78] Such ethical tactics include reflecting more on our relationship to what we eat and considering the agentic powers of what we consume and enter into an assemblage with. In doing so, if 'an image of inert matter helps animate our current practice of aggressively wasteful and planet-endangering consumption, then a materiality experienced as a lively force with agentic capacity could animate a more ecologically sustainable public'.[79] For new materialists, the object to be changed or transformed is the human – the human mind-set. By changing the way we think about the world and the way we relate to it by including broader, more non-human or inorganic matter in our considerations, we will have overcome our modernist 'attachment disorders' and have more ethically aware approaches to our planet.[80] In cultivating these new ethical sensibilities, the human can be remade with a new self and a 'new self-interest'.[81]

Conclusion

Bennett is right to argue that humans construct the external world in ways which enable them to live in it: 'to live, humans need to interpret the world reductively as a series of fixed objects, a need reflected in the rhetorical role assigned to the word material ... some stable or rock-bottom reality'.[82] To argue that the world is full of flows and that assumptions of fixity are false neglects the important role that human constructions play. As Bennett notes, even Henri Bergson recognised the necessity of fixed understandings in order for humans to act instrumentally and to survive in the world.[83]

We could, of course, choose to understand the human/nature divide as entirely fictional: from a biological perspective, we are made up of materials, and their form and content continually change and pass through us. We could also choose to dismiss Kant's problematic attempts to draw thick dividing lines between organic and non-organic matter or between humans and other organisms.[84] Apparently we share 50 per cent of our DNA with bananas, 70 per cent with slugs and 90 per cent with pigs.[85] Bennett questions: 'Why are we so keen to distinguish the human self from the field? Is it because the assumption of a uniquely human agency is, to use Kantian language, a "necessary presupposition" of assertion as such?'[86] Bennett wages against its progressive necessity. Setting the human on a pedestal is merely in the interests of religious mysticism or of mechanical materialist hubris: 'I believe that encounters with lively matter can chasten my fantasies of human mastery, highlight the common materiality of all that is, expose a wider distribution of agency, and reshape the self and its interests.'[87]

This wager of new materialists, post-humanists and ANT theorists is that the construction of complex and emergent life – an unknowable world where self-reflexivity displaces striving for human goals – would be a better ethico-political bet than the contestation of the world of truths and power. The world where conflicts are based on real contradictions implies a political struggle for 'truth' and knowledge on the basis of the universal telos of the human (now seen as a dangerous transcendental and totalising illusion – with the implication being that the consequences of this illusion can only be the terror of Nazism or Stalinism).[88] They assert that humans will be more attached and better able to adapt to the world once the modernist belief in universal knowledge, and the belief in its development towards certainty, are removed. In fact, the opposite is the case: the world becomes entirely alien to us. Probably the theorist with the richest appreciation of the need to understand freedom within the social construction of meaningful structures of mediation, i.e., of scientific, social, political, religious or natural laws, was

Hannah Arendt. She insightfully appreciated that the world extended only in so far as fixed chains of cause-and-effect were open to us to facilitate our understanding and development. The world which cannot be comprehended meaningfully by us; the world of complex life and emergent causality, which offers the promise of post-human 'freedom', constitutes the end of our world, precisely because it is not amenable to our appropriation as a meaningful structure within which we can consciously engage (and, in the process, expand our understanding). As she stated:

> All laws first create a space in which they are valid, and this space is the world in which we can move about in freedom. What lies outside this space is without law, and even more precisely, without world; as far as human community is concerned, it is a desert.[89]

Today, in Arendtian terms, 'the desert' is understood to be expanding as we place much more importance on the limits to our knowledge and understanding. In fact, it is the relations, associations and assemblages of the unknown and the unseen that are held to have real agency, rather than knowledgeable human subjects.[90] While contingency, of course, need not be underrated, the post-human project needs to be understood as not just removing the centrality of the human but also the meaningfulness of the world itself.

Notes

1 See, for example, Connolly, 2011; Bennett, 2010; Cudworth and Hobden, 2011; Coole and Frost, 2010; Latour, 2007.
2 As Latour vividly captures, in his analogy with the Platonic cave, there is held to be no interconnection between the world of subjects (in the cave of ignorance, values and subjective representations) and the world of objects (outside the cave, and only visible to experts and scientists, who reenter the cave armed with 'proofs') (see further, Latour, 2004a: pp.10–18).
3 Latour, 2004a: p.219.
4 Ibid.: p.187.
5 As Friedrich Engels wrote in *Anti-Dühring*:

> Hegel was the first to state correctly the relation between freedom and necessity. To him, freedom is the insight into necessity (die Einsicht in die Notwendigheit). 'Necessity is blind only in so far as it is not understood [begriffen].' Freedom does not consist in any dreamt-of independence from natural laws, but in the knowledge of these laws, and in the possibility this gives of systematically making them work towards definite ends. This holds good in relation both to the laws of external nature and to those which govern the bodily and mental existence of men themselves.
>
> (Engels, 1947: 1,XI: 6)

6   Latour, 1993: p.21.
7   Latour, 2004a: p.58.
8   Marx, 1954: pp.76–87.
9   These discourses can be understood to be post-liberal; see, for example, Chandler, 2010.
10 See, for example, Edwards, 2009; Grist, 2009; Walker and Cooper, 2011; O'Malley, 2010; Chandler, 2013b.
11 The appreciation of necessity was articulated clearly in the work of Anthony Giddens (for example, 1994, 1998). He advocated 'Third Way' approaches, which presupposed the end of the liberal modernist belief that developments in science and technology might enable the extension of humanity's control over the external world (1994: p.3). The human/nature divide was dismissed, with modern risks and insecurities conceived in terms of 'manufactured uncertainties', which could not be dealt with through Enlightenment prescriptions of 'more knowledge, more control' (ibid.: p.4):

> Today we must break with providentialism, in whatever guise it might present itself. Not for us the idea that capitalism is pregnant with socialism. Not for us the idea that there is a historical agent – whether proletariat or any other – that will more or less automatically come to our rescue. Not for us the idea that 'history' has any necessary direction at all. We must accept risk as risk, up to and including the most potentially cataclysmic of high-consequence risks; we must accept that there can be no way back to external risk from manufactured risk.
> (Giddens, 1994: p.249)

12 See Cassier, 2009; Gay, 1996; Israel, 2008.
13 See, for example, Stengers, 2010, 2011; Latour, 2004a.
14 Prigogine, 2003: p.56; see also Stengers, 2011: pp.105–22; Connolly, 2004.
15 There is little that is new in the attempts to question the hubris of reason through drawing on 'developments' in the philosophy of science to question the certainties of 'mechanical' materialism. From Darwin's theory of evolution onwards, narrow mechanistic understandings have been subject to devastating critique. The early twentieth century, in particular, saw discussions of the 'crisis of the European sciences' and the development of the phenomenological critiques of Edmund Husserl and others, which were to have such an influence on Heidegger and also on Friedrich Hayek (see, for example, Husserl, 1970; Hayek, 1952). One hundred years before Latour, Connolly and other new materialists, 'discovered' the limits of mechanical materialism; the Bolshevik party was riven by debates on the philosophy of science and the response to the crisis of Newtonian 'mechanical' understandings (see Lenin, 1956; Ilyenkov, 1982).
16 Latour, 2004a: p.225.
17 Lenin, 1956: p.190.
18 Ibid.
19 Ibid.: p.192. The essential relation between the social construction of a linear or law-bound external world and the modern human subject as capable of goal-determining freedom has been highlighted in some new materialist work, although, of course, they are keen to debunk or deconstruct this type of 'ontological dualism', precisely for this 'specifically modern attitude or ethos of subjectivist potency' (see, for example, Coole and Frost, 2010b: p.8; Frost, 2010: p.171).

20 Connolly, 2011: p.114.
21 Linklater, 1988: p.109.
22 Compare Connolly, 1991 with 2011 or 2013a.
23 Bennett, 2010: p.ix.
24 Connolly, 2011: p.173.
25 Ibid.: pp.24–25.
26 Bennett, 2010: p.viii.
27 Ibid.: p.xv; Connolly, 2011: p.25.
28 Bennett, 2010: pp.31–32.
29 Connolly, 2011: p.25.
30 Bennett, 2010: pp.viii–ix.
31 Ibid.: p.xvi.
32 Ibid.: p.34.
33 Latour, 2004a: p.216; see also pp.155–6.
34 Giddens, 2002.
35 Beck, 1992, 2009.
36 Latour, 2004a: p.223.
37 Boltanski and Chiapello, 2007; Mirowski and Nik-Khah, 2007.
38 Latour, 2007: p.65.
39 See, for example, Marx, 1954: p.81.
40 Latour, 2004a: p.25.
41 Latour, 2007: pp.244–5. It should be noted that the focus on the power of agency, through relational attachments, was powerfully outlined earlier by the American pragmatist philosopher John Dewey (as considered in the previous chapters).
42 Connolly, 2011: p.18.
43 Bennett, 2010: p.21.
44 Ibid.
45 Ibid.: p.23.
46 Ibid.: p.34.
47 Ibid.: p.67
48 Ibid.
49 Latour, 2004a: p.224.
50 Ibid.: p.225.
51 Latour, 2007.
52 Ibid.: p.137.
53 Ibid.: p.146.
54 Ibid.: p.217.
55 Ibid.: pp.141–56.
56 Connolly, 2011: pp.7-9.
57 Latour, 2007: p.61.
58 Connolly, 2011: p.149.
59 Ibid.
60 Ibid.: p.25.
61 Ibid.: p.171.
62 Bennett, 2010: p.33.
63 Ibid.: p.96.
64 Ibid.
65 Heidegger, 1978; see also Richardson, 2012: pp.106ff.
66 Heidegger, 1978: pp.86–87.
67 See, for example, Latour, 2007: p.114.

68 Latour, 2004a: p.83.
69 For example, Foucault, 2003, 2007, 2008.
70 Agamben, 1998.
71 Agamben, 2005.
72 Foucault, 1981: pp.135–45; see also Foucault, 2003: pp.239–63.
73 Bennett, 2010: p.10.
74 Connolly, 2011: p.66.
75 Ibid.: p.114.
76 Ibid.: pp.113–4.
77 Bennett, 2010: p.xix.
78 Ibid.: p.37.
79 Ibid.: p.51.
80 Ibid.: pp.108–9.
81 Ibid.: p.113.
82 Ibid.: p.58.
83 Ibid.: p.77.
84 Ibid.: p.68.
85 I cannot vouch for the accuracy of this information, obtained from Wiki-Answers.com. Available at: http://wiki.answers.com/Q/How_much_dna_do_humans_share_with_a_earthworm.
86 Bennett, 2010: p.121.
87 Ibid.: p.122.
88 In this sense, post-humanism continues the struggle for 'freedom' – articulated in the idealist displacement of real contradictions with the problem of phenomonological constructions – which reached its high point with the development of postmodernism (see, for example, Lyotard, 1984: 81).
89 Arendt, 2005: p.190.
90 See Latour, 2007: pp.244–5; and the parallels in critical approaches, such as Richmond, 2011b.

10
CONCLUSION

Resilience, the promise of complexity

Introduction

Resilience as a form of governance cannot be grasped in the modernist binary understandings of politics, where there is a clear division between the private ethical sphere – the government of the self – and the public political sphere – the government of others. With regard to the ethics of complexity and resilience-thinking, the fact that there are no a priori or transcendental truths means that personal ethics must be considered as an ongoing process of self-reflexivity. As Paul Cilliers noted, the rejection of transcendental modernist rule-based ethics 'sets us free, not to do as we like, but to behave ethically'.[1] To fall back on universal principles would be to deny the complexity of the social system we live in, but to allow everything would be to evade our responsibility. The ethical problematic is therefore how to 'take responsibility for the future effects of our decisions' despite not knowing these effects or being able to wait to see what these effects are.[2] Behaving ethically in a complex world is to live one's life as a resilient subject, understanding ethical self-reflection as an ongoing process of work on the self. However, what sets apart this process of the government of the self from the classical assumptions of the inner philosophical will as a path to truth[3] is the fact that this process is externalised. While the Socratic injunction to 'know thyself' was orientated towards a contemplative existence, the ethical injunction of resilience is externally orientated towards others and the consideration of the multiple consequences of our actions which guide and enable the process of revising our judgements in line with our self-reflection on these outcomes which can never be known fully in advance.

In resilience-thinking, this outward-looking and self-reflexive process of the development of the government of the self is no different from the process-based relational understanding of the government of others. Resilience-thinking promises that the 'real' processes of complex life, as the object of rule, can be enabled through the indirect process of governance, understood as a process of reflexive self-knowledge of the complex embedded nature of power. Once government is no longer understood to operate in a separate sphere from its economic, social and environmental context – from life itself – then government is an ongoing process rather than a series of discrete or separate acts in a separate space of politics or of the public sphere. The process of governing is also an ever more inclusive one, always reflexively seeking to draw in actors and aspects which had previously been excluded. The limits of governance become increasingly seen as precisely these aspects of exclusion, preventing the process of self-reflexivity from harnessing the power of life itself. Resilience-thinking as a way of informing governance seeks to harness the forces of reality, to latch on to and to engage the organic processes at work in society at every level from the local to the global.

The promise of being able to access the 'real' is the promise of life-as-complexity, which tells us that life can be governed through life itself on the basis that order can autonomously emerge from disorder, if only we govern with adequate reflexivity. Resilience-thinking thereby continually works on the basis of the reality of complex life revealing itself to us. Every event – from road accidents to crime, from terrorist outrages to global warming – can be reinterpreted as a sign of emergence; as a sign of social and material interconnections which need to be governed differently to enable more ordered outcomes. All manifestations of disorder then become governable – or problems of governance – on the basis of retracing their interconnections. This backwards process-tracing works very differently from governance through the imposition of human-centred goals of state government or from imposing the need to adapt to the external or transcendental rationalities of the market or morality. Resilience-thinking inculcates a relational, networked, understanding in the place of previous social, moral, political or economic rationalities.

Social relationality is thereby at the centre of both complexity theorising and resilience-thinking as a governance response. This mode of governing goes beyond traditional liberal or neoliberal understandings, unable to fully shake off the binary divides between state and society or subject and object. States do not stand external to society as the object of governing anymore than humans are understood to be separate or external to their environment. States do not govern through imposing goals or targets or through following the alleged dictates of market forces – both state and market rationalities lack the access to the 'real' promised by resilience. Both state and market ratio-nalities fail to access complex reality because of their reductionist and linear frames of reasoning which exclude the relationalities that resilience-thinking considers vital. State-based reasoning works on crude linear cause-and-effect understandings which cannot account for unintended consequences and side-effects, while market reasoning is just as reductionist, excluding all the relational 'externalities' outside the concerns of the contracting parties.[4]

I do not wish to suggest that all policy-understandings start from the perspective of complexity and resilience as a governing response, but merely that this framing is becoming increasingly dominant in both international and domestic policy-making, as liberal modernist approaches appear less and less viable today. It is important to stress that resilience-thinking has been considered conceptually in this book through the focus on how understand-ings of governance have been reframed to deal with the problem of com-plexity. Resilience-thinking has thus not been narrowly confined to a set of empirical practices, developed to work on resilience (as a set of capacities) in the face of crisis or threats. The key aspects that define resilience approaches to policy-making are the post-modern ontological assumptions about the nature of the world as complex and the consequences for governance as a process of self-reflexive policy responses.

It is quite possible to chart a rise in resilience-thinking as a governing rationality without mentioning the word 'resilience' and, equally, to see the word 'resilience' crop up many times in a policy paper (it is seemingly ubiq-uitous across government policy documents) without this being evidence that a resilience or complexity ontology forms the basis of understanding. The following sections of this chapter will highlight how complex life was initially conceived as a limit in neoliberal understandings and then analyse how resilience works as a governing rationality in both policy-making and academic theorising and in doing so, re-emphasise some of the points made in the foregoing chapters to draw out the coherent (and problematic) nature of complexity and resilience as an ontology of governance. The chapter, and book, conclude with some considerations of whether and how it might be possible to move beyond resilience.

Against artifice: The promise of the 'real'

Resilience-thinking is not new in pitting the reality of complex life against the artifice of human social construction. What is new about resilience is that complex life is no longer seen as merely constituting the limit to the world of governmental reason but as constituting the basis of governmental reason itself. The key manifestation of this shift is that the connection between the market and emergent complex life, so central to neoliberal thought, is absent in resilience-thinking. Resilience-thinking naturalises the market, asserting that we cannot step outside or go beyond it (as considered in Chapter 6), but the market is not seen as providing a rationality for governance. The promise of resilience is not the promise of the 'hidden hand' of the market. In fact, the promise of resilience, that of access to the reality of complex life as a means of governance, is a process of constant work on the self, through reflexive understandings of relational embeddedness. Resilience thereby operates outside of the state/market binary of instrumental Left/Right political understandings and seeks to reflexively bring this 'reality' to the surface of policy-making, governing through complexity on the basis of the unknowability of the world.

Neoliberal discourses operate largely on the epistemological level of reasoning, suggesting that market relations enable and facilitate the governance of complex life, whereas top-down state intervention can only operate in narrow and reductionist ways which limit creative adaptation and can have dangerous unintended consequences and side-effects in a non-linear world. For Friedrich Hayek, often considered the archetypal neoliberal theorist, emergent or evolved life constituted an epistemological problem for human reason, removing the foundational basis of the liberal autonomous subject. Social constructivism, for Hayek, posed an epistemological problem, not a solution: we were forever prevented from having real access to the world beyond our phenomenological constructions. Rather than understanding human subjects as relationally embedded – as evolved products of their environment, whereby human social reasoning could be understood as a 'gradual adaptation to the "nature of things"' – the social constructivism of the modern social sciences was held to inverse the relationship between the subject and the socio-environment, understanding man as being able to understand and shape the external world. The world became comprehended as amenable to human reason rather than human reason being understood to be the evolved product of the world.[5]

This inversion was crucial to neoliberalism's decentring of the subject. While the socio-environmental context, both inherited and experienced, could be understood to be the basis of evolved human subjectivity and the capacity to reason – explaining why different people at different times reasoned in the way that they did – this was very different from the assertion that human reasoning could explain how the world worked: this was a constructivist illusion. The 'real' world remained essentially unknowable through means of immediate reflection. Despite the technical gains of science and technology, Newtonian, or any other 'natural laws' were merely social constructions. For Hayek, knowledge of reality was not that of scientific and technological laws but other forms of adaptive knowledge learnt by imitation and cultural transmission:

> Rules for his [man's, the individual's] conduct which made him adapt what he did to his environment were certainly more important to him than 'knowledge' about how other things behaved. In other words: man has certainly more often learnt to do the right thing without comprehending why it was the right thing, and he still is often served better by custom than understanding.[6]

For Hayek – as for Walter Lippmann, John Dewey and today's philosophical pragmatists, new materialists, non-representational theorists, actor-network theorists and post-humanists – there was no relationship between technical and scientific progress and liberal modernist assumptions of governmental reason, which assumed that technical and scientific knowledge provided government with a greater ability to control or direct policy outcomes. Society was not the product of conscious planning or direction, and neither were social values, cultural norms or even political and constitutional frameworks. While Cartesian or Newtonian constructivism might work for the development of abstract technical and scientific 'laws' with some (although limited) application in the natural sciences, the human world was not amenable to understanding through such conceptual fabrications and crude tools of reasoning.

In the face of 'real' complex life, modernist frameworks thus vastly overrated the power of human reasoning. Social science seemed to operate under the illusion of a rationalist telos: that if the human world was one of progress this meant that it was a product of human reasoning and direction, rather than seeing the market and civilisation as emergent products of 'cultural evolution' – neither 'natural' nor 'planned'. For neoliberal thought, progress and rapid change could neither be stopped nor controlled and directed by techniques of governmental reason:

> All we can do is to create conditions favourable to it and hope for the best. It may be stimulated or damped by policy, but nobody can predict the precise effects of such measures; to pretend to know the desirable direction of progress seems to me to be the extreme of hubris. Guided progress would not be progress. But civilization has fortunately outstripped the possibility of collective control, otherwise we would probably smother it.[7]

For Hayek, governmental reason could not access the reality of complex life from above, from a position external to the knowledges and modes of being of everyday life. The crude abstractions of the natural sciences could work on a reductive basis of cause-and-effect on the basis that the objects of analysis were passive and inert in a world empty of time and space, but this type of 'scientific' knowledge lacked a way of accessing the reality of emergent and evolving human existence with its adaptive and immanent dynamics. Hayek therefore argued that complex life could not be understood and assimilated into liberal ways of 'knowing' based upon Newtonian parallels:

> Today it is almost heresy to suggest that scientific knowledge is not the sum of all knowledge. But a little reflection will show that there is beyond question a body of very important but unorganised knowledge which cannot possibly be called scientific in the sense of knowledge of general rules: the knowledge of particular circumstances of time and place. It is in this respect that practically every individual has some advantage over all others in that he possesses unique information of which beneficial use might be made, but of which use can be made only if the decisions depending on it are left to him or are made with his active cooperation.[8]

Hayek argued that this local and specific knowledge might not be very important if economic and social processes could just be repeated or directed according to technical and scientific rules and measured by centralised statistical methods and if these processes were the same across time and space. As we have seen in the preceding chapters, these assumptions are not held to be true in the 'real' world of complexity. In such a world, as Hayek suggested, governmental reason called for a different kind of knowledge, knowledge which liberal modernist approaches excluded from consideration:

> knowledge of the kind which by its nature cannot enter into statistics and therefore cannot be conveyed to any central authority in statistical form. The statistics which such a central authority would have to use would have to be arrived at precisely by abstracting from minor differences between the things, by lumping together, as resources of one kind, items which differ as regards location, quality, and other particulars, in a way which may be very significant for the specific decision.[9]

For Hayek and neoliberal thought, while governments were denied access to knowledge of complex reality, the market was able to access and use the localised, differentiated, pluralised knowledges of complex life without excluding or judging them on the basis of external criteria. The market was idealised as merely an intermediary connecting local and specific knowledges, through prices as indicators. Prices here played a fundamental role of revealing or giving access to the plural reality of complex life and also acting as a guide to future behaviour – how one should adapt to and learn through this reality. Here, complex reality was revealed through embedded relationality – not through abstraction and the artifice of social construction – in fact, it was revealed so clearly that no theory or thinking or self-reflexivity was required to learn the 'truths' revealed by the price mechanism.

The lessons that complex life revealed, once these were understood in neoliberal frameworks, were that governmental reason should not seek to control and direct the external world and instead should focus on more effective forms of evolutionary adaptation through properly reading market signals. For Hayek, 'the unavoidable imperfection of man's knowledge and the consequent need for a process by which knowledge is constantly communicated and acquired' depended upon the solution of market connections which demonstrated 'how a solution is produced by interactions of people each of whom possesses only partial knowledge'.[10] No new knowledge was required other than what already existed, but the market did all the work of organising this knowledge. Hayek drew upon Alfred North Whitehead (whose work is receiving much wider recognition today), citing his view that:

> It is a profoundly erroneous truism, repeated by all copy-books and by eminent people when they are making speeches, that we should cultivate the habit of thinking what we are doing. The precise opposite is the case. Civilization advances by extending the number of important operations which we can perform without thinking about them.[11]

In Hayek's neoliberal resistance to state socialist views of governmental reason, complex life provided a basis for opposing the hubris of liberal reason, based on Cartesian rationalism and Newtonian linearity, and also suggested alternative or non-liberal forms of reasoning which could access this complex reality. These were pluralist, evolved, mostly subconscious and non-representative forms of reasoning, acquired mainly through cultural evolution, adaptive mimicry or imitation.

The problem for Hayek was an epistemological one of human reason itself. Human subjectivity, the need to impose meaning upon the world, constituted a paradox in which access to emergent, evolving, complex reality was prevented. It was the artifice – the phenomenological constructions – of human reasoning itself that prevented access to the 'real'. The more reason was imposed upon the world the less the real revealed itself; this worked as much at the level of the state as at the level of the individual. The market here worked as the *deus ex machina*, resolving the problems of the limits of governmental and individual reasoning and providing indirect access to the reality of complex life, without the need for conscious reflection. Hayek thus provided a very resilience-friendly understanding of the limits of governing without modernist assumptions, but he provided no way forward beyond these assumptions, other than reliance on the 'hidden hand' of the market.

It is not difficult to see how the constructions of complex life, in today's discourses of resilience, build on and transform neoliberal attempts to derive lessons for governance from life itself. Resilience as a governing rationality seeks to displace both top-down direction and attempts to instrumentalise market rationalities by self-reflexive constructions of bottom-up solutions. The 'real processes' are not directly accessible, undermining the hubristic dreams of state planners, but neither are they accessible to the 'hidden hand' of market price information systems. They are manifested indirectly, in the concrete and emergent relational outcomes of social interaction. This emergent relationality is the basis for market outcomes but also is held to explain the limits of these outcomes and the emergent processes through which these outcomes can be transformed. Market outcomes are therefore no more 'real' than any other reified or fixed attributes given to our phenomenological social constructions.

Thus, the area where resilience-thinking has gone furthest is in the attributes of self-reflexivity and responsiveness necessary for governance in a society which is changing fast and where neither the market nor the state seems capable of directing or addressing the changes required. Hayek's ontology is thereby not quite the same as that of resilience-thinking. Resilience can therefore be understood as an adaptation of a neoliberal ontology to the problematic of governing per se, rather than merely to an understanding of its limits. More specifically, resilience-thinking demarcates itself from neoliberalism as the governing rationality of the 1980s to the 2010s, which attempted to use states and markets to govern complexity in instrumental ways. As noted in Chapter 5, neoliberal governmentality sought to govern complexity through the top down, seeking to intervene in interactive social processes to adjust or transform them from the position of the knowing liberal subject, able to balance the levers of the market and the state in order to direct and set goals. In contradistinction to Hayek, resilience-thinking suggests that governance is necessary and that the market can no longer be seen as the mechanism of knowing and governing complexity. However, in contradistinction to the active interventionist governance project of neoliberalism, after the end of the modernist framework of Left and Right, resilience-thinking asserts that governance is only possible in non-instrumental ways, in ways which do not assume an external subject position and therefore reject the hubristic assumptions involved in using market and state levers to attain policy-goals.

Resilience-thinking therefore brings governance as a set of policy-understandings of intervention into neoliberal constructions of limits. Neoliberalism, which in an age of liberal interventionism articulated the need to respect complex life as the limit to governance, has therefore undergone a transformation, rearticulating complex life as the positive promise of transformative possibilities. It is particularly important to note that neoliberal rationalities of directing market and state levers are discursively framed to be the problem for resilience-thinking, not the neoliberal assumptions of complex life per se. Resilience-thinking thereby intensifies neoliberal understandings of complexity and suggests that neoliberalism still bears the traits of liberal 'hubris' in its contradictory or paradoxical assertions that complex life can be simplified and potentially known by governing power. Neoliberalism as a governing rationality of the last three decades is therefore criticised on the basis of its 'humanist legacies' and its inability to rethink governance on the basis of unknowability. Where neoliberalism failed to properly work through the consequences of post-modernity for governance, resilience-thinking claims to have the solution to the apparent conundrum of governing without assumptions of Cartesian certainty or Newtonian necessity.

UK government examples of life-centred policy-thinking

The increasing centrality of complexity to thinking about governance can be clearly illustrated from examples taken from British policy-making practice and from government elites, both in government and in opposition. A recent example of the centrality of complexity and resilience-thinking can be seen in the UK government's July 2013 document, *The National Adaptation Programme: Making the Country Resilient to a Changing Climate.*[12] While it is important to note the centrality given to resilience and adaptation, it is the methodological assumptions for the governance of complexity that will be highlighted here. From 1994 to 2011, the UK government operated a national programme for sustainable development; in 2011 that programme was replaced by the National Adaptation Programme. The final report from the Sustainable Development Commission makes sobering reading, as attempts to cohere government around the balances of sustainability and progress became increasingly seen to be problematic for their reductive understandings and the assumption that government planning was the answer. As Andrew Lee, the Chief Executive Officer of the Commission, stated in his Introduction:

> [T]here seems to be something buried deep in human nature which finds it hard to treat the future as if it really is as important as the present, and seeks to tackle each problem separately from the others. Yet a great deal

of evidence shows that attempts to solve issues in isolation all too often result in perverse consequences elsewhere. For example, the interaction between decades of policies on food, out-of-town planning, and mobility/ transport has had unforeseen consequences in terms of obesity, carbon emissions and loss of biodiversity. … Increasingly, we face new types of problems – 'wicked issues' – which will require new types of response – flexible, adaptive, using systems thinking, seeing the whole picture not just a part of it. One of the watchwords will be creating 'resilience'.[13]

The National Adaptation Programme (NAP) involves a lot of government intervention and coordination at both national and local levels, even extending new powers to the Secretary of State to direct certain organisations, such as those with responsibilities for critical national infrastructure, to prepare reports on the steps they are taking and will take to deal with the risks from a changing climate: the so-called Adaptation Reporting Power (ARP).[14] The point is not that resilience-thinking is against government intervention but rather how policy-intervention is perceived to operate – not as directing or controlling processes of adaptation but as enabling or facilitating natural or existing capacities by removing institutional blockages understood as the unintended outcomes of markets and state policy-making.[15]

The analytic annex accompanying the NAP programme report expands on the barriers to natural adaptation and 'identifies market failures, behavioural constraints, policy failures and governance failures as the most important'.[16] Market failures are understood to be inevitable and to stem from the limits to adequate information under conditions of complexity and emergent causality, including failures to act on such information, in the belief that others will, and the exclusion of vital public goods (especially those connected with the environment) from market considerations. Even more interesting is the understanding of policy failure:

> Policy failures occur when the framework of regulation and policy incentives creates barriers to effective adaptation. This can happen in the presence of competing policy objectives. Similar to the concept of market failure, which as discussed above is a situation that prevents an efficient market solution, this concept must not be interpreted as a failure of policy, but as a systemic characteristic which prevents an efficient policy solution.[17]

Resilience-thinking tells us that policy failure is, in fact, 'not a failure of policy' but a learning opportunity with regard to the systemic process of unintended consequences and side-effects in a complex world, where failure enables policy-makers to learn from the revelation of these concrete and emergent interconnections.[18] Thus policy failure is construed as distinct from governance failure, which is the failure to reflexively learn from complex life the need to overcome reductionist understandings. Governance failure is the failure of reflexive adaptation, defined as: 'when institutional decision-making processes' create barriers to effective learning.[19] The barriers to governing complexity are thus given full consideration, in terms of the dangers of unintentional outcomes and side-effects:

> The presence of uncertainty risks 'maladaptation'. These are unintended side-effects of implementing adaptation actions. Uncertainty also means it is unlikely to predict the correct future scenario and fully adapt to it. The risks of maladaptation and committing to adapt to a wrong scenario need careful consideration.[20]

Given the barriers to both policy-based and market-based decision-making, under conditions of complexity and uncertainty, the National Adaptation Programme is based upon the assumption that policy-making necessarily becomes an ongoing process of relational understanding, binding the policy-makers with the problem which they seek to govern, rather than one of discrete decisions which are then implemented: 'Uncertainty does not mean that action should be delayed. It means that decision-making should be an iterative process and incorporate regular reassessment to consider the latest available information.'[21]

As UK government policy-making becomes increasingly attuned to the mechanisms of governance informed by resilience-thinking – those of understanding policy-failure as part of the policy-process and the need for a constantly iterative policy-process of feedback and data gathering – the gap between government and the governed is seen to be constantly narrowing, as complex life itself comes to constitute the rationality of governance. Governance is therefore no longer seen to be based upon 'supply-side' policy-making but rather on the understanding of the processes and capacities that already exist and how these can be enhanced. In this way, resilience-thinking should not be understood narrowly, as merely building the capacities of individuals and societies, but more broadly, as a rationality of governing which removes the modernist understanding of government as a directing or controlling actor, capable of understanding, planning and implementing as if it had perfect knowledge in a fixed and stable world amenable to Newtonian cause-and-effect understandings.[22]

The influence of this thinking across the UK government can be seen in the work of both the coalition government and opposition policy-advisors. Education Secretary Michael Gove's key policy advisor Dominic Cummings made UK media headlines in October 2013 with the *Guardian* newspaper's publication of his 'private thesis' on the future of education in a world of complexity, entitled 'Some Thoughts on Education and Political Priorities'.[23] Cummings' key concern in his 250-page document was that, in a world where understanding how complex systems work is vital,[24] there was practically no cross-disciplinary academic instruction concerning complex systems and no specific academic training for powerful decision-makers. For Cummings, the crisis of the political class stemmed not so much from public cynicism about politics as from their total lack of training in how to deal with the 'real' world in which non-linear outcomes are to be expected:

> Most politicians, officials, and advisers operate with fragments of philosophy, little knowledge of maths or science (few MPs can answer even simple probability questions yet most are confident in their judgement), and little experience in well-managed complex organisations. The skills, and approach to problems, of our best mathematicians, scientists, and entrepreneurs are almost totally shut out of vital decisions. We do not have a problem with 'too much cynicism' – we have a problem with too much trust in people and institutions that are not fit to control so much.[25]

According to Cummings, it was not only that policy-makers had no training or knowledge in the complexity sciences but that the knowledge that they did have about state/society relations was seen to be worse than useless: 'Existing political philosophies are inadequate to serve as heuristics for decision-makers.'[26] This was because: 'Established political philosophies including traditional conservatism, liberalism and socialism, which form the basis of background heuristics for political leaders, cannot cope with evolutionary epistemology, either in biology or economics.'[27] For Cummings, the political philosophies of both Left and Right clung to a universal understanding of human nature: for the Right, in order to establish a universal moral grounding in individual responsibility; for the Left, in order to argue for social equality against the workings of the market. These political framings, along with 'the modern "social sciences"' – Marx (in economics), Freud (in psychology), Durkheim (in sociology), Boas (in anthropology) and Rawls (in law) – 'profoundly shaped the "the standard social science model" (SSSM)', which Cummings found to be 'no longer tenable'.[28] Instead of standard social science training, suitable for modern liberal understandings, Cummings advised a synthesis of classical, premodern philosophical training and a trans-disciplinary understanding of the complexity sciences to equip a future generation of political elites:

Such an education and training might develop synthesisers who have 1) a crude but useful grasp of connections between the biggest challenges based on trans-disciplinary thinking about complex systems; 2) a cool Thucydidean courage to face reality including their own errors and motives; 3) the ability to take better decisions and adapt fast to failures; 4) an evolutionary perspective on complex systems and institutional design (rather than the typical Cartesian [top-down] 'chief of the tribe' perspective); and 5) an ability to shape new institutions operating like an immune system that will bring better chances to avoid, survive, and limit damage done by inevitable disasters.[29]

While Cummings has laid out a challenge to rethink the traditional academic training, considered necessary to develop policy-making elites, able to grasp a world of complexity, a key policy advisor to opposition leader Ed Miliband,[30] Oxford Political Theory Professor Marc Stears, a fellow at the Institute for Public Policy Research (IPPR), has cogently put forward the case for rethinking state/society relations on the basis of resilience-understandings in his frameworks for 'everyday democracy' and critical approach to the 'relational state'. Stears is responding to the key problematic driving resilience-thinking in government circles, the limitations of neoliberal frameworks, which have sought to bring state and market rationalities together to impose governing agendas. As IPPR research directors Graeme Cooke and Rick Muir argue:

New public management (NPM) has been the guiding intellectual paradigm for the reform and governance of public services over the last three decades. Emerging as a response to the failings of traditional public administration, it can be characterised by the use of two forms of management technique: targets and markets. Under this model of statecraft, attempts to improve the performance of the state have relied on command and control from above and choice and competition from outside.[31]

Cooke and Muir are worth quoting at length to understand the demand from government for the emergence of complex-life and resilience-thinking:

The proliferation of command and control management techniques has promoted a tick-the-box compliance culture across the public services. Such strategies helped some very poor services to achieve a minimum standard, but they have also demoralised staff and undermined professional status. A 'targets and terror' approach can be effective in addressing terrible performance, but it is poorly suited to supporting excellence, because it hampers flexible responses to local demand and constrains innovation and creativity. Command and control techniques have also led to the growth of expansive monitoring, inspection and auditing processes, which are a drain on time and money.[32]

Command and control techniques, which locate responsibility for performance clearly with government, have led to a proliferation of 'top-down' measures of 'compliance'. These measures are seen to have imposed reductionist, one-size-fits-all understandings, limited creative responses and left government looking incapable and discredited (repeating the problematic understandings of 'compliance' articulated in the liberal peace discussions in the international sphere, considered in Chapter 4). The response to these perceived limitations has been that of complexity and the facilitation of the natural capacities of self-governance understood to be held back by both market and state attempts to regulate. As Cooke and Muir state:

> The theoretical foundations of NPM have been challenged by a wave of new thinking across the social sciences. For example, drawing on complexity economics, network thinking suggests that social problems are situated within complex systems that are unsuited to mechanistic interventions. Rather than attempting to engineer outcomes through 'command and control', governments should focus on crafting the conditions for a variety of agents involved in a given problem to solve it themselves. This suggests a greater priority for experimentation, decentralisation and institution-building.[33]

In his IPPR book *Everyday Democracy: Taking Centre-Left Politics Beyond State and Market* and in debate with previous key New Labour advisor Geoff Mulgan[34] on the understanding of how the state should operate,[35] Stears argues that rather than focusing on traditional Left/Right concerns of how to govern through the state or through the market, governance should be done through the revival of 'everyday democracy'. Stears stresses, of course (as considered in Chapter 8), that 'everyday democracy' should not be confused with old-fashioned liberal representative democracy:

> I do not mean we should learn to celebrate the democracy of old. The democracy of Westminster and Whitehall, of centralised political parties and ritualised election campaigns, no longer possesses the resources to respond to our nation's needs. Many people do not vote, after all, and even fewer join political parties. Nor do I mean, though, that we should engage in the detailed theorising about constitutional change or voting reform.[36]

'Everyday democracy' involves strengthening social relationships and has little to do with representative democracy, which presupposes that governments are responsible for delivering and imposing 'outcomes', while society merely passively holds them to account every few years. 'Everyday democracy' is not about governing from the top-down but about social resilience, understood as the embedded and relational capacities of ordinary people. It is these capacities that are understood to be bypassed or muted by top-down mechanisms of 'compliance' under the dictate of government or of market imperatives.

According to Stears (and as noted earlier in this book), market rationalities are increasingly understood to be no better at dealing with complexity than state rationalities. This is where resilience-thinking marks an important shift away from neoliberal uses of complexity theory as a critique of state/socialist intervention in social and economic policy:

> Put simply, a society that celebrates the free market above almost anything else is a society that encourages people to see each other as tradable objects rather than as people with feelings, commitments, dependents and dependencies. That is why big corporations are able to talk of 'human resources' and why economists sometimes talk of 'human capital'. People are rendered as items on a spreadsheet, on this view, to be moved around at the whim of the powerful in the cause of economic efficiency or success.[37]

Market rationalities are understood to work on the cold metrics of profitability, understanding humans as objects to be manipulated and used. Most importantly, markets are ignorant of the complexity of relational connections, in the reductionist search for profits and exclusion of externalities such as community well-being and the environment.

While a critique of market rationality might be expected for a left-leaning New Labour policy-advisor, the critique of an alternative state-based governing rationality is perhaps more revealing in terms of the centrality of resilience-thinking as a post-liberal mode of governing complexity. Here, Stears turns to James C. Scott's critique of liberal modes of understanding and governing:

> As the anthropologist, James Scott, puts it, people who work within states always see the world in a very distinctive way, and always seem to end up striving for a more easily managed, controlled, and centrally directed society as a result. He explains: "… the modern state, through its officials, attempts with varying success to create a terrain and a population with precisely those standardized characteristics

that will be easiest to monitor, count, assess and manage. The ... continually frustrated goal of the modern state is to reduce the chaotic, disorderly, constantly changing social reality beneath it to something more closely resembling the administrative grid of its observation.[38]

For Stears, the problem with states is that of governing rationality; they 'make things the same.'[39] This may work well when there is the need for a 'technical, mechanical solution which can be employed everywhere', but it doesn't work in an age of complexity when they need 'flexibly to respond to local particularities, when they need to act nimbly or with nuance'.[40] 'Most crucially', for Stears, following the radical critic Scott (although he could equally have used the rather less radical views of Hayek), 'states' drive to standardise is not an option, not one way of being, but is an unavoidable element of what states are. It is built into the very notion of stateness.'[41] Thus:

> Governments and states are not simply ever-morphing agents, acting above, beyond and in some sense in control of the citizens. Rather, they are particular kinds of things, with a capacity to do some things well and others not. They are constrained and enabled, that is, by what they are. ... Things are controlled. There are agents of coercion. But something else appears to happen too, or at least something more specific. There appears to be some force that standardises the otherwise complex pattern of social interconnections. This is a force that is interested in reshaping social life so that it can be more effectively regulated and controlled.'[42]

Stears argues that rather than governing for or governing over society, the state needs to govern through society: through enabling the capacities and capabilities that already exist and could be encouraged if states rejected the Left/Right debates around state and market rationalities. Our natural abilities to cooperate with each other, to innovate and to construct communities of shared interest, have apparently been hampered by the modernist rationalities of both Left and Right. For Stears, the public already have the potential capabilities, but these are excluded and ignored by state-based conceptions, which can only see the public as passive objects of governance:

> Citizens in this story [previous New Labour views, as argued by Geoff Mulgan] generally seem to be passive players, until they are dragooned into behaving in a particular way. Often described as a unitary 'public', Mulgan's citizens always have things done to them by governments – they

just have different things done to them by governments behaving as different kinds of states. In their coercive mode, governments control and direct the public. In their delivery mode, governments give things to passive citizens. In their relational mode, governments somehow elicit new patterns of social interaction, acting together to 'achieve common goals, sharing knowledge, resources and power'. [43]

To justify his critique, Stears draws on arguments from genetic science, 'neuroscientific studies of reward circuits in the brain that trigger when we cooperate effectively', human geography and premodern philosophy to argue that 'everyday democracy', focusing on enabling the practices and understandings of the public themselves, can help to reconstitute an engaged and caring public.[44]

The disagreement between Stears and Mulgan, as senior Labour Party advisors, is an important one for highlighting the difference between instrumental approaches (which rely on both markets and state direction) and resilience approaches. As Stears notes:

> The state can facilitate the creation of relationships if it conducts itself in the *right way*. That, I believe, should be the primary ambition for the kind of state to which we aspire. Our policy agenda should focus not on somehow making the state itself relate more effectively to its citizens, but instead on what it can do to enable citizens to relate more effectively with each other ... this is no small disagreement: if the state always (or at least almost always) acts as an agent of standardisation then its *direct efforts are never likely to promote a fully relational culture*. Its efforts will be too scarred by the monitoring, control, oversight and ... the 'audit culture' which are the essential modern accompaniments to a standardising agenda. What this means is that those services which we wish to provide in a relational way must enjoy some level of *protection from the direct involvement of the state itself.*[45]

Whereas Mulgan argues that the state should act in a neoliberal way, to effectively intervene in and shape markets to enable them to produce social outcomes and to build direct relationships with communities, Stears views state interference from above as contaminating or corrupting the natural capacities for adaptation and resilience which already exist and need to be 'facilitated' rather than instrumentally 'directed' to required ends. As Cooke and Muir recognise, Stears reflects a growing shift in policy-thinking, away from 'outcomes' and towards 'processes':

This critique suggests a politics that does not aim towards a known, identifiable end state. It rejects utopianism and embraces uncertainty. Taken to its logical conclusion, such an approach would be a radical departure for the centre-left, which has long defined itself in terms of a 'vision' for how society should be (in words such as 'equality'). In its purest form, Stears' argument is a call to abandon the pursuit of objective outcomes with politics coming instead to focus on the design of processes – especially ones that enable relationships. The specific 'ends' that people make of these 'means' – both individually and collectively – is then a matter for their own determination. This offers citizens, he argues, the prospect of both liberty and responsibility.[46]

Stears's articulation of what in this book has been called 'resilience-thinking' seeks to abandon liberal modernist views of democracy as existing in the separate space of the public sphere, somehow informing the decision-making of a government tasked with implementing means–ends programmes which can then be judged in periodic elections. In a world of complexity, governments cannot be expected to know what policies work and which do not, and certainly they cannot impose these policies on the world, as if it was a blank slate and policy-making worked in a direct reductionist cause-and-effect way where unintended consequences and the side-effects of social relationality did not need to be taken into account. In a complex, relational world, life is understood to be literally self-governing, as Stears concludes:

> What this leads me to believe is that the most important agents of a relational culture are to be found among those who do not allow their lives to be entirely determined by the market or the state. They are those among us who are not prepared to have their lives reduced to the metrics that appeal to those who prioritise either narrow economics or narrow governability. They are those who know that meaning and purpose is found and sustained in the everyday interactions that escape that control, cannot be quantified, and are often impossible even properly to describe. These people are to be found in every walk of life. We all have neighbours, colleagues, relatives who display these qualities. Taking relationship-building seriously as a political project means doing all we can to enhance their political power.

As we have seen in the discussion of the political genealogy of resilience-thinking (in Chapter 3), the market and the state are considered to be limits to the power of complex social, relational life, reducing the complexity and creativity of life to suit the narrow and reductionist needs of either the market or of government. Rather than a neoliberal understanding of complex life – as the limit to the power of the state and as reflected in market outcomes – resilience-thinking, as articulated by Stears (and as manifested in the variety of policy and academic analysis considered in the previous chapters), argues that governance needs to be reframed in order to enhance the creative power of life itself.

Is there a 'beyond' to resilience?

As noted earlier in this book, it has been argued that the governing ontology of resilience and complexity appears to either silence or assimilate critical opposition through its ability to 'internalize and neutralize all external challenges … to metabolize all countervailing forces and inoculate itself against critique'.[47] The major assumption made here, by Jeremy Walker and Melinda Cooper, is that critical thinking poses an 'external challenge' to resilience-thinking. However, it has been the argument of this book, given particular emphasis in Chapter 3, that critical thought has been central to the transformation of neoliberal thinking into a discourse of governance. Rather than crediting resilience-thinking with the magical powers of assimilating radical critique, if we wish to go beyond resilience it is important to at least question whether resilience-thinking and critical thinking are indeed in an external relationship to one another. From the analysis laid out in the chapters of this book, not only do Walker and Cooper exaggerate the power of resilience-thinking but they also ignore the need to question whether critical thinking needs to be re-evaluated in light of this major shift away from liberal modernist frameworks of government and understandings of the political subject.

A start could be made by assuming that there is no relationship of externality and instead resilience-thinking could be considered as a key driver, cohering so-called critical approaches today. The dominance of critical thinking across the social sciences, in fact, reflects the dominance of resilience-thinking and the ontological assumptions of complexity. This makes intuitive sense, considering that the social sciences have traditionally served as handmaiden to the needs of power and that the rise of critical thought in the academy does not appear to be a reflection of any broader societal radicalisation. Therefore any attempt to go beyond resilience-thinking would first need to problematise the ontological assumptions given the status of a 'critical consensus' in the academic mainstream.

A typical example comes from an email which landed in my inbox while I was drafting this chapter: an information flyer for a course on 'Research Methods in Critical Security Studies', organised by Mark Salter and

Peter Burgess, two leading critical theorists in the field of international security, and hosted by the Peace Research Institute, Oslo (PRIO). Below is their statement of what it means to be critical:

> Critical security studies can be understood as a scholarly approach that is attentive to the workings of power and exclusion inherent in social phenomena. Though objects of research can vary considerably, four basic principles shape the field of critical analysis:
>
> 1. Social and political life are interwoven without any one unifying principle or logic;
> 2. Agency – the capacity to act – is not reserved to individual human beings, but rather is everywhere;
> 3. Causality is emergent. In other words, critical analysis does not identify what necessarily happens, but rather what the conditions of possibility of something happening are;
> 4. Research, writing and public engagement are inherently political.[48]

Critical theorists are held to adhere to these four basic principles, all of which give conceptual support to the ontology of complexity and the governing practices of resilience: that the social and the political are indistinct; that agency is everywhere; that causality is emergent; and that there is therefore an ethical need for self-reflection in 'research, writing and public engagement' because these actions are 'inherently political'.

Let us pause to consider the political implications of such a 'critical' consensus. First, once the ontological claims of complexity are accepted, critique is no longer a matter of challenging what exists – there are no unifying principles, hierarchies of agency or determinate chains of causality – any alleged critique of what exists would thereby only reinforce the essentialised understandings of liberal modernity. If critique is not to reinforce reified categories of thought – of, what are in reality, fluid social constructs – then the consensus is that critique can no longer operate on the basis of revealing 'unifying principles' such as the inner-workings of power or the supposed structures of domination.

Second, if it is no longer possible to critique power from the outside, critique cannot involve theorising an external world (with this in mind, the 'objects of research' we are told are less important and 'can vary considerably') and cannot go beyond surface appearances. What distinguishes the critical scholar from the uncritical one is therefore not a matter of conceptual acumen but an ethos of self-reflexivity. As Salter and Burgess assert, what the researcher does, no matter how minor, 'is inherently political' in having effects in the world for which they are responsible; the critical act is one of political self-awareness regarding these consequences. We become critical as a mode of being, as a process of self-reflection ('as a scholarly approach'), not through our starting intention of undertaking a critique of the world as it appears.

The critical ontology of Salter and Burgess is exactly the same as the governance ontology of resilience-thinking. Critique, like governance, does not start with the human subject confronting the world as its object, but as always and already relationally embedded in processes of emergent causality. What separates good academic work (and makes it 'critical') or good governance (and makes it 'adaptive') is the ability to self-reflexively adjust our thoughts and actions on the basis of their revealed consequences. While complexity assumptions close off the possibility of traditional forms of political critique, they open up a new sphere of critical understanding, that of work on the self at every level, from the individual and the collective up to governing institutions.

Slavoj Zizek provides another insightful example of how resilience-thinking is able to inform radical critique, in his argument that we lack the ability to resist because we lack a language in which we can make sense of power relations and resistance to power today:

> It is here that Marx's key insight remains valid, today perhaps more than ever: for Marx, the question of freedom should not be located primarily in the political sphere proper. The key to actual freedom rather resides in the 'apolitical' network of social relations, from the market to the family, where the change needed if we want an actual improvement is not a political reform, but a change in the 'apolitical' social relations of production. We do not vote about who owns what, about relations in a factory, etc – all this is left to processes outside the sphere of the political. It is illusory to expect that one can effectively change things by 'extending' democracy into this sphere, say, by organizing 'democratic' banks under people's control. In such 'democratic' procedures (which, of course, can have a positive role to play), no matter how radical our anti-capitalism is, the solution is sought in applying the democratic mechanisms – which, one should never forget, are part of the state apparatuses of the 'bourgeois' state that guarantees undisturbed functioning of the capitalist reproduction.[49]

Once formal state powers of governance appear to be inadequate – once we accept that we live in a complex world that is not amenable to instrumental cause-and-effect understandings – politics, of necessity, shifts to the 'apolitical' private and social sphere: our networks of social relations, from the workplace to the family to the material embeddedness of market interconnections. However, once politics has shifted to this social and relational realm, the language of politics – of power, of rights and of freedoms – is no longer meaningful, and use of this language could only further extend the reach of liberal forms of representation, rather than challenging them. For Zizek, it seems that: 'we feel free because we lack the very language to articulate our unfreedom ... today, all the main terms we use to designate the [political world] are false terms, mystifying our perception of the situation instead of allowing us to think it'.[50]

Rather than a crisis of liberal forms of representation, Zizek sees the danger of their extension into the real realm of power, the social relational realm, which is 'the key to actual freedom'. For Zizek, it is this realm that needs to be politicised through use of a different set of political understandings, which can facilitate social and networked relational power without assimilating it to the formal political sphere and enabling this power to be captured by capital and the state. Zizek does not offer much of an alternative but suggests that there is an inner, therapeutic, solution to the political crisis, whose symptoms are manifested in the 'emergence of an international protest movement without out a coherent program':

> The situation is like that of psychoanalysis, where the patient knows the answer (his symptoms are such answers) but doesn't know to what they are answers, and the analyst has to formulate a question. Only through such patient work a program will emerge.[51]

It appears that Zizek's radical critique shares the same ontological understanding as Stears's view of the solution to the political crisis of governance. 'Real' social relational power needs to be worked upon through non-instrumentalised intervention (either that of the ongoing process of facilitation of the therapeutic state or, for Zizek, the lengthy process of intervention by the class-conscious critical theorist as stand-in psychoanalyst). This intervention is necessarily non-instrumental to prevent this 'real' creative and problem-solving power from being contaminated by liberal forms of representation (or knowability) seen as constraining and limiting the potential of life for adaptation or, for Zizek, autonomous political creativity. The development of autonomous capacities, through self-activity – through collective and individual work on developing our self-reflexivity and becoming more aware of our affective and material attachments – is now the dominant framework for both governance and the critique of governance. It seems that the twin movement, the pincer assault upon liberal modernist political assumptions, of post-Marxism and neoliberalism,[52] has filled the gap left by the end of Left/Right political contestation. Complexity ontologies and resilience-thinking have enabled both governance and critique to shift from the sphere of formal politics to the sphere of autonomous emergent life itself.

Conclusion

If there is a beyond to resilience, it seems to be one that is difficult to imagine without the reconstitution of collective forms of struggle and meaning, on the basis that the world is amenable to human projects of transformation. The dominance of resilience-thinking represents our disillusionment with the modernist project and the collapse of the frameworks of meaning and representation which were associated with it. The world without the collective struggle for transformation, and the competing political constructions of meaning associated with it, is a post-human or a post-modern world. The world without the human at the centre was, of course, imaginable to the most prescient thinkers of the last century. They were only too aware of the fragility of liberal modernist constructions of meaning, in the face of attempts to rein in the hubris of liberal reason and displace the rational subject of science and rights with the relational subject of evolutionary emergence. For Foucault, man was 'an invention of recent date'[53] – a social construct of both political struggle and of the regimes of knowledge which shaped and reflected this contestation – and just as he was 'made' he could be as easily 'unmade'.[54] Arendt, too (as noted in the previous chapter), worried about the fragility of the world conceived as amenable to human understanding and human progress, and its potential displacement by the world as an unknowable 'desert' for human meaning. Her greatest fear was that it might be possible for humanity to become 'true inhabitants of the desert' and 'to feel at home in it'.[55]

Resilience-thinking can be understood as representing our 'feeling at home' with the end of the human project of transformative change. In the 1970s, post-modernity was strange and alien to us and could not be clearly grasped, even by its leading advocates. Today it seems that the tables have turned and that we are so attuned to the 'resonances' of post-modernity that modernist assumptions of knowledge and government appear somehow out of time and unreal (maybe something only a Continental philosopher could come up with). As noted above (and in the preceding chapters), it seems that we are so at home in the post-human world that even critical scholars can easily express their concerns through the framework of complexity and resilience-thinking.

Thus, critique increasingly tends to be less concerned with understanding the external world than with deconstructing phenomenological constructions of it. If it is true that there is nothing beyond the world as we experience it, *post hoc* – through the event and the problematic appearances of complex life – then the problems are of our own phenomenological social construction. These problems, reduced to those of thought and understanding, can then be addressed through the analysis of govern-mentality and through the struggle for self-realisation and responsive capacity – rather than through confronting the material contradictions of our social relations. Concepts which previously had meaning for us – space, time, value, capital, states, democracy, rights, oppression, and so on – then become unfit for purpose: understood as fetishised (fixed) forms of representation and as barriers to the technical and pragmatic (already existing) solutions to problems.

Rather than being concerned with the fragility of human constructions of meaning, which bind collectives together and encourage creativity and experimentation, critical approaches today increasingly seek to problematise causal understandings, to 'destabilise meanings', and to liberate us from the reified forms of reductionist, linear, representational thinking. Instead of giving meaning to the constantly creative powers of humanity, and encouragement to the unending and unlimited possibilities of human interaction, we are encouraged to be more humble and attempt to limit or constrain the unintended consequences and side-effects of our being in the world. There is only one winner in the world of complexity, where human-centred assumptions of government are replaced by the promise of governance as resilience: that is government itself.

Government, after the end of the political contestation of Left and Right, had lost its framework of representative legitimacy and the programmatic coherence necessary for meaningful policy-making. As a discourse of power, resilience-thinking removes both the importance of the formal sphere of representation and the need for policy-programmes, while maintaining the importance of governance and, in fact, extending the reach of power. Resilience-thinking, in its assertion that governments do not have power and that policy failure should be reassessed on the basis of how lessons are learned, fills the vacuum where politics used to be. Not only can government forever be merely reactive, never the instigator of policy, but policy-making is increasingly understood as facilitating or enabling the real source of power: the pluralised and diverse public itself.

In the absence of any understanding of an external relationship between the subject and the world – conceptualised in terms of representation – the problems of the world become the problem of the human subject itself. Critique is therefore the mode of understanding of resilience-thinking: it is critical of states (all forms of state power are seen to be a barrier to accessing the reality of complex life), it is critical of the market (its reductionist focus on profit and exclusion of 'externalities' – the relational consequences of putting profits before life itself); it is critical of universal, fixed and reductionist forms of thought (real complex life is fluid and ever changing). The free rein given to critique presupposes the consensus that critique cannot exist externally to its object: thereby criticism (of neoliberal and liberal governmentality, of market outcomes and of reified forms of thought) becomes inverted – from a transformative project of changing the world – to become an elitist project of empowering and enabling the public to realise its responsibilities.

For resilience-thinking, governance has to be consequential to the appearances of the world; the public has already unintentionally 'acted' in the world and revealed the programme of reflexive governance. The conscious agency of the liberal subject becomes bifurcated into the unconscious agency of the human and non-human assemblages of emergent causality and the conscious self-reflexivity of the governance of the self. In this way, resilience-thinking provides a new role for government and justifies new levels of societal intervention and the development of the professional and ethical expertise necessary for this task. The demand of 'power to the people' then becomes a never-ending process of accessing the 'reality' of complex life and enabling existing capacities. Radical critique, framed by the ontology of resilience-thinking, thus becomes the dominant discourse of power, legitimising and reproducing governing authority on the basis of the unknowability of the world.

Notes

1 Cilliers, 1998: p.138.
2 Ibid.: p.139.
3 Given an excellent treatment in Foucault, 2010.
4 As Bruno Latour astutely notes, the world of complexity and relationality can be well described as the world of liberal modernity 'plus its externalities: everything that had been externalized as irrelevant or impossible to calculate is back in – with a vengeance' (Latour, 2003: p.37).
5 Hayek, 1978a: p.131.
6 Hayek, 1978b: p.8.
7 Ibid.: p.22
8 Hayek, 1945: pp.521–2.
9 Ibid.: p.524.
10 Ibid.: p.530.
11 Ibid.: p.528.
12 DEFRA, 2013a.
13 Lee, 2011: p.5.
14 DEFRA, 2013a: p.9; see also DEFRA, 2013b.

15 DEFRA, 2013a: p.7. As the accompanying analytic report (DEFRA, 2013c: p.10, n.20) adds: 'It is important to note that short-term responses to adaptation are a continuous process. Human adaptation has occurred throughout history in response to changing stimuli such as climate. From this perspective one might conclude that humans are already well adapted to the current climates which they inhabit and are not starting from a point of zero adaptation.'
16 DEFRA, 2013c: 6.
17 Ibid.; p.7.
18 As the analytical annex adds: '"Policy failure" is a well established economic concept ... but no value judgment is intended on specific policies. Just as a market failure is a problem which prevents the market from operating efficiently, the economic concept of policy failure must not be interpreted as a failure of the policy to bring about a particular solution, but is rather a systemic problem which prevents an efficient policy solution to a problem' (DEFRA, 2013: p.10, n.21).
19 Ibid.: p.7.
20 Ibid.: p.6.
21 Ibid.: p.2.
22 As the 2013 updated UK Department for International Development, Growth and Resilience Operational Plan states: 'We will produce less "supply-driven" development of product, guidelines and policy papers, and foster peer-to-peer, horizontal learning and knowledge exchange, exploiting new technologies such as wiki/huddles to promote the widest interaction between stakeholders' (DfID, 2013: p.8).
23 Cummings, 2013.
24 '... most interesting systems – whether physical, mental, cultural, or virtual – are complex, nonlinear, and have properties that emerge from feedback between many interactions. Exhaustive searches of all possibilities are impossible. Unfathomable and unintended consequences dominate. Problems cascade. Complex systems are hard to understand, predict and control' (ibid.: p.1).
25 Ibid.
26 Ibid.: p.130.
27 Ibid.
28 Ibid.: p.131.
29 Ibid.: p.2. The elitist implications of complexity understandings were already presciently drawn out by Lyotard, who argued that the end of the modernist meta-narrative meant that knowledge training provided by the University would be reduced to the transmission of technical and professional skills for the masses while elites would require the imaginative skills of 'connecting together series of data that were previously held to be independent' (Lyotard, 1984: pp.52–53).
30 Pierce, 2012; Wintour, 2012.
31 Cooke and Muir, 2012: p.5.
32 Ibid.: p.6.
33 Ibid.: p.6.
34 The former head of the Number 10 Policy Unit.
35 Stears, 2011, 2012.
36 Stears, 2011: p.5.

37 Ibid,: p.12.
38 Ibid.: p.20 (citing Scott, 1998: pp.81–82).
39 Ibid.
40 Ibid.: pp.20–21.
41 Stears, 2012: p.39.
42 Ibid.: pp.36–37.
43 Ibid.
44 Stears, 2011: p.31.
45 Stears, 2012: p.42.
46 Cooke and Muir, 2012: p.9.
47 Walker and Cooper, 2011: p.157.
48 Email communication from PRIO, 15 August 2013. The statement is essentially a repeat of the 'four postures of critical enquiry' as laid out at Salter, 2013: p.2.
49 Zizek, 2012.
50 Ibid.
51 Ibid.
52 Or of the 'curious closeness and parallels' between the Freiburg School of neoliberalism and the Frankfurt School of post-Marxist critique, as Foucault put it (2008: p.105).
53 Foucault, 2002: p.422.
54 Ibid.: p.414. The fragility of the liberal construction of man was such that, for Foucault, he could 'be erased, like a face drawn in the sand at the edge of the sea' (ibid.: p.422).
55 Arendt, 2005: p.201.

REFERENCES

Acharya, A. (2000) 'How Ideas Spread: Whose Norms Matter? Norm Localization and Institutional Change in Asian Regionalism', *International Organization*, 2(1): 65–87.

Agamben, G. (1998) *Homo Sacer: Sovereign Power and Bare Life* (Stanford, CA: Stanford University Press).

Agamben, G. (2005) *State of Exception* (Chicago: University of Chicago Press).

Ainley, K. (2008) 'Individual Agency and Responsibility for Atrocity', in R. Jeffery (ed.) *Confronting Evil in International Relations: Ethical Responses to Problems of Moral Agency* (Basingstoke: Palgrave Macmillan), 37–60.

All-Party Parliamentary Group (2012) *7 Key Truths about Social Mobility: The Interim Report of the All-Party Parliamentary Group on Social Mobility*, 1 May. Available at: http://www.appg-socialmobility.org/.

Althusser, L. (2008) 'Ideology and Ideological State Apparatuses', in L. Althusser, *On Ideology* (London: Verso), 1–60.

Althusser, L. and Balibar, E. (2009) *Reading Capital* (London: Verso).

Aradau, C. (2013) 'The Transformation of Security', Paper presented at the workshop 'Resilience, Security and Law after Liberalism', King's College, London, 4–5 July.

Aradau, C. and Van Munster, R. (2011) *Politics of Catastrophe: Genealogies of the Unknown* (London: Routledge).

Arendt, H. (1963) *Eichmann in Jerusalem: A Report on the Banality of Evil* (Harmondsworth: Penguin Books).

Arendt, H. (1998) *The Human Condition* (Chicago: University of Chicago Press).

Arendt, H. (2003) *Responsibility and Judgement* (New York: Schocken Books).

Arendt, H. (2005) *The Promise of Politics* (New York: Schocken Books).

Aristotle (1992) *The Politics* (London: Penguin).

Bain, W. (2003) *Between Anarchy and Society: Trusteeship and the Obligations of Power* (Oxford: Oxford University Press).

Banakar, R. (2013) 'Law and Regulation in Late Modernity', in R. Banakar and M. Travers (eds) *Law and Social Theory* (Oxford: Hart Publishing). Draft available at: http://papers.ssrn.com/sol3/papers.cfm?abstract_id=2229247.

Bang, H. P. (2004) 'Culture Governance: Governing Self-Reflexive Modernity', *Public Administration*, 82(1): 157–90.

Baudrillard, J. (2002) *The Spirit of Terrorism* (London: Verso).

Baudrillard, J. (2009) *The Transparency of Evil: Essays on Extreme Phenomena* (London: Verso).

Baylis, J. and Smith, S. (eds) (2006) *The Globalization of World Politics: An Introduction to International Relations* (Oxford: Oxford University Press).

Beck, U. (1992) *Risk Society: Towards a New Modernity* (London: Sage).

Beck, U. (1997) *The Reinvention of Politics: Rethinking Modernity in the Global Social Order* (Cambridge: Polity).

Beck, U. (2002) 'Freedom's Children', in U. Beck and E. Beck-Gernsheim, *Individualization: Institutionalized Individualism and Its Social and Political Consequences* (London: Sage), 156–71.

Beck, U. (2009) *World at Risk* (Cambridge: Polity).

Beck, U. and Beck-Gernsheim, E. (2002) *Individualization: Institutionalized Individualism and Its Social and Political Consequences* (London: Sage).

Belloni, R. (2008) 'Civil Society in War-to-Democracy Transitions', in A. K. Jarstad and T. D. Sisk (eds) *From War to Democracy: Dilemmas of Peacebuilding* (Cambridge: Cambridge University Press), 182–210.

Bennett, J. (2010) *Vibrant Matter: A Political Ecology of Things* (London: Duke University Press).

Berger, P. and Luckmann, T. (1979) *The Social Construction of Reality: A Treatise in the Sociology of Knowledge* (London: Penguin).

Big Society (2012) 'Powering' (Big Society). Available at: http://www.thebigsociety.co.uk/projects/powering/.

Boltanski, L. (2011) *On Critique: A Sociology of Emancipation* (Cambridge: Polity).

Boltanski, L. and Chiapello, E. (2007) *The New Spirit of Capitalism* (London: Verso).

Brigg, M. (2010) 'Culture: Challenges and Possibilities', in O. P. Richmond (ed.) *Palgrave Advances in Peacebuilding: Critical Developments and Approaches* (Basingstoke: Palgrave), 329–46.

Brigg, M. and Muller, K. (2009) 'Conceptualising Culture in Conflict Resolution', *Journal of Intercultural Studies*, 30(2): 121–40.

Brown, C. (1995) *Serpents in the Sand: Essays on the Non-linear Nature of Politics and Human Destiny* (Ann Arbor: University of Michigan Press).

Burg, S. L. (1997) 'Bosnia Herzegovina: A Case of Failed Democratization', in K. Dawisha and B. Parrot (eds) *Politics, Power, and the Struggle for Democracy in South-East Europe* (Cambridge: Cambridge University Press), 122–45.

Byrne, D. and Callaghan, G. (2014) *Complexity Theory and the Social Sciences: The State of the Art* (Abingdon: Routledge).

Cammack, D., McLeod, D., Menocal, A. R. with Christiansen, K. (2006) *Donors and the 'Fragile States' Agenda: A Survey of Current Thinking and Practice* (London: Overseas Development Institute).

Campbell, S., Chandler, D. and Sabaratnam, M. (eds) (2011) *A Liberal Peace? The Problems and Practices of Peacebuilding* (London: Zed Books).

CARE Netherlands (2013) *Reaching Resilience: Handbook Resilience 2.0 for Aid Practitioners and Policymakers in Disaster Risk Reduction, Climate Change Adaptation and Poverty Reduction* (The Hague: CARE Netherlands/Wageningen University).

Cassier, E. (2009) *The Philosophy of the Enlightenment* (Princeton, NJ: Princeton University Press).

Celikates, R. (2006) 'From Critical Social Theory to a Social Theory of Critique: On the Critique of Ideology after the Pragmatic Turn', *Constellations*, 13(1): 21–40.

Cesarini, P. and Hite, K. (2004) 'Introducing the Concept of Authoritarian Legacies', in Hite and Cesarini (eds) *Authoritarian Legacies and Democracy in Latin America and Southern Europe* (Notre Dame: University of Notre Dame Press).

Chandler, D. (1998) 'Democratization in Bosnia: The Limits of Civil Society Building Strategies', *Democratization*, 5(4): 78–102.

Chandler, D. (2009) *Hollow Hegemony: Rethinking Global Politics, Power and Resistance* (London: Pluto Press).

Chandler, D. (2010) *International Statebuilding: The Rise of Post-Liberal Governance* (London: Routledge).

Chandler, D. (2013a) *Freedom vs Necessity in International Relations: Human-Centred Approaches to Security and Development* (London: Zed Books).

Chandler, D. (2013b) 'Resilience and the Autotelic Subject: Towards a Critique of the Societalization of Security', *International Political Sociology*, 7(2): 210–26.

Chandler, D. (2013c) '"Human-Centred" Development? Rethinking "Freedom" and "Agency" in Discourses of International Development', *Millennium: Journal of International Studies*, 42(1): 3–23.

Chandler, D. (2013d) 'Promoting Democratic Norms? Social Constructivism and the "Subjective" Limits to Liberalism', *Democratization*, 20(2): 215–39.

Cheah, P. and Robbins, B. (eds) (1998) *Cosmopolitics – Thinking and Feeling Beyond the Nation* (Minneapolis: University of Minnesota Press).

Cheng, C.-Y. (2011) 'The *Yijing*: The Creative Origin of Chinese Philosophy', in J. L. Garfield and W. Edelglass (eds) *The Oxford Handbook of World Philosophy* (Oxford: Oxford University Press), 13–25.

Chesterman, S. (2001) *Just War or Just Peace? Humanitarian Intervention and International Law* (Oxford: Oxford University Press).

Cilliers, P. (1998) *Complexity and Postmodernism: Understanding Complex Systems* (Abingdon: Routledge).

Coaffee, J. and Wood, D. M. (2006) 'Security Is Coming Home: Rethinking Scale and Constructing Resilience in the Global Urban Response to Terrorist Risk', *International Relations*, 20(4): 503–17.

Coleman, P. T., Vallacher, R., Bartoli, B., Nowak, A. and Bui-Wrzosinska, L. (2011) 'Navigating the Landscape of Conflict: Applications of Dynamic Systems Theory to Addressing Protracted Conflict', in D. Körppen, N. Ropers and H. J. Giessmann (eds) *The Non-Linearity of Peace Processes – Theory and Practice of Systemic Conflict Transformation* (Opladen: Barbara Budrich Verlag), 39–56.

Collier, P. (2007) *The Bottom Billion: Why the Poorest Countries are Failing and What Can be Done about It* (Oxford: Oxford University Press).

Collier, P. (2010) *Wars, Guns and Votes: Democracy in Dangerous Places* (London: Vintage Books).

Collier, P. and Hoeffler, A. (2004) 'Greed and Grievance in Civil War', *Oxford Economic Papers*, 56: 563–95.

Collier, P., Hoeffler, A. and Rohner, D. (2006) 'Beyond Greed and Grievance: Feasibility and Civil War', *CSAE Working Paper Series 2006–10* (Oxford: Centre for the Study of African Economies, University of Oxford).

Conner, D. R. (1993) *Managing at the Speed of Change* (New York: Random House).

Connolly, W. E. (1991) 'Democracy and Territoriality', *Millennium: Journal of International Studies*, 20(3): 463–84.

Connolly, W. E. (2005) 'The Evangelical-Capitalist Resonance Machine', *Political Theory*, 33(6): 869–86.

Connolly, W. E. (2004) 'Method, Problem, Faith', in I. Shapiro, R. M. Smith and T. E. Masoud (eds) *Problems and Methods in the Study of Politics* (Cambridge: Cambridge University Press), 332–39.

Connolly, W. E. (2011) *A World of Becoming* (Durham, NC: Duke University Press).

Connolly, W. E. (2013a) *The Fragility of Things: Self-Organizing Processes, Neoliberal Fantasies, and Democratic Activism* (London: Duke University Press).

Connolly, W. E. (2013b) 'The 'New Materialism' and the Fragility of Things', *Millennium: Journal of International Studies*, 41(3), 399–412.

Cooke, G. and Muir, R. (2012) 'The Possibilities and Politics of the Relational State', in G. Cooke and R. Muir (eds) *The Relational State: How Recognising the Importance of Human Relationships Could Revolutionise the Role of the State* (London: IPPR), 3–19.

Coole, D. and Frost, S. (2010a) (eds), *New Materialisms: Ontology, Agency and Politics* (London: Duke University Press).

Coole, D. and Frost, S. (2010b) 'Introducing the New Materialisms', in D. Coole and S. Frost (eds) *New Materialisms: Ontology, Agency and Politics* (London: Duke University Press), 1–43.

Cortell, A. P. and Davis, J. W. (2000) 'Understanding the Domestic Impact of International Norms: A Research Agenda', *International Studies Review*, 2(1): 65–87.

Coutu, D. L. (2002) 'How Resilience Works', *Harvard Business Review*, May. Available at: http://nonprofitlearningpoint.org/wp-content/uploads/2010/03/Resilience-article.pdf.

Cudworth, E. and Hobden, S. (2011) *Posthuman International Relations: Complexity, Ecologism and Global Politics* (London: Zed Books).

Cummings, D. (2013) 'Some Thoughts on Education and Political Priorities', *Guardian*, 11 October. Available at: http://static.guim.co.uk/ni/1381763590219/-Some-thoughts-on-education.pdf.

Dallmayr, F. (1993) *The Other Heidegger* (New York: Cornell University Press).

Dallmayr, F. (2010) *The Promise of Democracy: Political Agency and Transformation* (Albany: State University of New York Press).

Dean, M. (2010) *Governmentality: Power and Rule in Modern Society* (London: Sage).

de Beistegui, M. (2007) 'Questioning Politics, or Beyond Power', *Political Theory*, 6(1): 87–103.

Debord, G. E. (1983) *The Society of the Spectacle* (Detroit: Black and Red).

de Certeau, M. (1998) *The Practice of Everyday Life* (Berkeley: University of California Press).

DEFRA (2013a) Department for Environment, Food and Rural Affairs, *The National Adaptation Programme: Making the Country Resilient to a Changing Climate* (London: HM Government/DEFRA).

DEFRA (2013b) Department for Environment, Food and Rural Affairs, *2013 Strategy for Exercising the Adaptation Reporting Power and List of Priority Reporting Authorities* (London: HM Government/DEFRA).

DEFRA (2013c) Department for Environment, Food and Rural Affairs, *The National Adaptation Programme Report Analytical Annex: Economics of the National Adaptation Programme* (London: HM Government/DEFRA).

De Herdt, T. and Abega, S. (2007) 'Capability Deprivations and Political Complexities: The Political Economy of Onions in the Mandara Mountains, Cameroon', *Journal of Human Development*, 8(2): 303–23.

DeLanda, M. (2006) *A New Philosophy of Society: Assemblage Theory and Social Complexity* (London: Continuum).

Deleuze, G. (1988) *Spinoza: Practical Philosophy* (San Francisco: City Lights).

Deleuze, G. and Guattari, F. (2004) *A Thousand Plateaus: Capitalism and Schizophrenia* (London: Continuum).

Demchak, C. C. (2011) *Wars of Disruption and Resilience: Cybered Conflict, Power, and National Security* (Athens: University of Georgia Press).

Dennett, D. C. (2005) 'Show Me the Science', *New York Times*, 28 August. Available at: http://www.nytimes.com/2005/08/28/opinion/28dennett.html?pagewanted=all.

Dewey, J. (1927) *The Public and Its Problems* (New York: Swallow Press).

Dewey, J. (2007) *Democracy and Education* (Teddington: Echo Library).

DfID (2011) *Building Stability Overseas Strategy* (London: Department for International Development, Foreign and Commonwealth Office and Ministry of Defence).

DfID (2013) Department for International Development, *Operational Plan 2011–2015 DFID Growth and Resilience Department* (London: Department for International Development).

Dillon, M. (2007) 'Governing Terror: The State of Emergency of Biopolitical Emergence', *International Political Sociology*, 1(1): 1–28.

Dillon, M. and Reid, J. (2009) *The Liberal Way of War: Killing to Make Life Live* (London: Routledge).

Disch, L. (1997) '"Please Sit Down, but Don't Make Yourself at Home": Arendtian "Visiting" and the Prefigurative Politics of Consciousness-Raising', in C. Calhoun and J. McGowan (ed.) *Hannah Arendt and the Meaning of Politics* (Minneapolis: University of Minnesota Press), 132–65.

Dobriansky, P. J. (2004) 'Promoting a Culture of Lawfulness', Remarks at Georgetown University, Washington, DC, 13 September. Available at: http://2001-2009.state.gov/g/rls/rm/2004/37196.htm.

Dobson, A. (2003) *Citizenship and the Environment* (Oxford: Oxford University Press).

Dryzek, J. (2012) *Foundations and Frontiers of Deliberative Governance* (Oxford: Oxford University Press).

Duffield, M. (2007) *Development, Security and Unending War: Governing the World or Peoples* (Cambridge: Polity).

Dyer, J. G. and McGuinness, T. M. (1996) 'Resilience: Analysis of the Concept', *Archives of Psychiatric Nursing*, 10(5): 276–82.

Edwards, C. (2009) *Resilient Nation* (London: Demos).

Ekici, S., Ekici, A., McEntire, D. A., Ward, R. H. and Arlikatti, S. S. (eds) *Proceedings of the NATO Advanced Workshop on Together Against Terrorism: Building Terrorism Resistant Communities* (Amsterdam: IOS Press).

Elster, J. (ed.) (1998) *Deliberative Democracy* (Cambridge: Cambridge University Press).

Engels, F. (1947) *Anti-Dühring: Herr Eugen Dühring's Revolution in Science* (Moscow: Progress Publishers). Available at: http://www.marxists.org/archive/marx/works/1877/anti-duhring/.

Eschler, C. and Maiguashca, B. (eds) (2005) *Critical Theories, International Relations and 'the Anti-Globalisation Movement': The Politics of Global Resistance* (London: Routledge).

Evans, B. and Reid, J. (2013) 'Dangerously Exposed: the Life and Death of the Resilient Subject', *Resilience: International Policies, Practices and Discourses*, 1(2): 83–98.

Falk, R. A. (1995) *On Humane Governance: Toward a New Global Politics* (Cambridge: Polity).

Fine, K. (1996) 'Fragile Stability and Change: Understanding Conflict during the Transitions in East Central Europe', in A. Chayes and A. H. Chayes (eds) *Preventing Conflict in the Post-Communist World* (Washington, DC: Brookings Institution), 541–81.

Fishkin, J. (2011) *When the People Speak: Deliberative Democracy and Public Consultation* (Oxford: Oxford University Press).

Fleming, T. (2012) 'The Insane Rationality of Anders Breivik', *Daily Mail*, 19 April.

Forest, J. and Mehier, C. (2001) 'John R. Commons and Herbert A. Simon on the Concept of Rationality', *Journal of Economic Issues*, 35(3): 591–605.

Foucault, M. (1981) *The History of Sexuality, Volume 1: An Introduction* (London: Penguin).

Foucault, M. (2002) *The Order of Things: An Archaeology of the Human Sciences* (Abingdon: Routledge).

Foucault, M. (2003) *"Society Must Be Defended": Lectures at the Collège de France 1978–1979* (London: Allen Lane).

Foucault, M. (2007) *Security, Territory, Population: Lectures at the Collège de France 1977–1978* (Basingstoke: Palgrave Macmillan).

Foucault, M. (2008) *The Birth of Biopolitics: Lectures at the Collège de France 1978–1979* (Basingstoke: Palgrave Macmillan).

Foucault, M. (2010) *The Government of the Self and Others: Lectures at the Collège de France 1982–1983* (Basingstoke: Palgrave Macmillan).

Foucault, M. (2011) *The Courage of Truth: Lectures at the Collège de France 1983–1984* (Basingstoke: Palgrave Macmillan).

Fritz, V., Kaiser, K. and Levy, B. (2009) *Problem-Driven Governance and Political Economy Analysis: Good Practice Framework* (Washington, DC: International Bank for Reconstruction and Development/World Bank).

Frost, S. (2010) 'Fear and the Illusion of Autonomy', in D. Coole and S. Frost (eds) *New Materialisms: Ontology, Agency and Politics* (London: Duke University Press), 158–77.

Fukuyama, F. (1995) 'The Primacy of Culture', *Journal of Democracy*, 6(1): 7–14.

Fung, A. and Wright, E. O. (2003) 'Thinking about Empowered Participatory Governance', in A. Fung and E. O. Wright (eds) *Deepening Democracy: Institutional Innovations in Empowered Participatory Governance* (London: Verso), 3–42.

Furedi, F. (2011) *On Tolerance: A Defence of Moral Independence* (London: Continuum).

Gamble, A. (1996) 'Hayek and the Left', *Political Quarterly*, 67(1): 46–53.

Ganson, B. and Wennmann, A. (2012) 'Operationalising Conflict Prevention as Strong, Resilient Systems: Approaches, Evidence, Action Points', *Geneva Peacebuilding Platform Paper*, 3. Available at: http://issat.dcaf.ch/content/download/7875/72500/file/PP%2003%20-%20Operationalising%20Conflict%20Prevention%20as%20Strong%20Resilient%20Systems%20-%20January%202012.pdf.

Garside, J. (2013) 'Nasdaq Crash Triggers Fear of Data Meltdown', *Guardian*, 23 August. Available at: http://www.theguardian.com/technology/2013/aug/23/nasdaq-crash-data.

Gay, P. (1996) *The Enlightenment, Vol. 2: The Science of Freedom* (New York: Knopf).

Gephart, W. (2010) *Law as Culture: For a Study of Law in the Process of Globalization from the Perspective of the Humanities* (Frankfurt am Main: Vittorio Klostermann).

Giddens, A. (1984) *The Constitution of Society: Outline of the Theory of Structuration* (Cambridge: Polity).

Giddens, A. (1994) *Beyond Left and Right: The Future of Radical Politics* (Cambridge: Polity).

Giddens, A. (1998) *The Third Way: The Renewal of Social Democracy* (Cambridge: Polity).

Giddens, A. (2002) *Runaway World: How Globalisation is Reshaping our Lives* (London: Profile Books).

Giessman, H. J. (2011) 'Foreword', in D. Körppen, N. Ropers and H. J. Giessmann (eds) *The Non-Linearity of Peace Processes – Theory and Practice of Systemic Conflict Transformation* (Opladen: Barbara Budrich Verlag), 7–9.

Gleick, J. (1998) *Chaos: Making a New Science* (London: Vintage).

Gould, S. J. (2007) *The Richness of Life* (London: Vintage).

Grindle, M. S. (2004) 'Good Enough Governance: Poverty Reduction and Reform in Developing Countries', *Governance: An International Journal of Policy, Administration and Institutions*, 17(4): 525–48.

Grindle, M. S. (2007) 'Good Enough Governance Revisited', *Development Policy Review*, 25(5): 553–74.

Grist, M. (2009) *Changing the Subject: How New Ways of Thinking About Human Behaviour Might Change Politics, Policy and Practice* (London: RSA).

Grove, K. (2013) 'Hidden Transcripts of Resilience: Power and Politics in Jamaican Disaster Management', *Resilience: International Policies, Practices and Discourses*, 1(3): 193–209.

Gunderson, L. H. and Holling C. S. (eds) (2002) *Panarchy: Understanding Transformations in Human and Natural Systems* (Washington, DC: Island Press).

Gutmann, A. (ed.) (1994) *Multiculturalism: Examining the Politics of Recognition* (Princeton, NJ: Princeton University Press).

Gutmann, A. and Thompson, D. (2004) *Why Deliberative Democracy?* (Princeton, NJ: Princeton University Press).

Guy Peters, B. (2005) *Institutional Theory in Political Science: The 'New Institutionalism'* (London: Continuum).

Habermas, J. (1986) *The Theory of Communicative Action: Vol. 1, Reason and the Rationalization of Society* (Cambridge: Polity).

Hameiri, S. (2010) *Regulating Statehood: State Building and the Transformation of the Global Order* (Basingstoke: Palgrave Macmillan).

Hanisch, C. (1969) 'The Personal Is Political'. Available at: http://www.carolhanisch.org/CHwritings/PIP.html.

Hardt, M. and Negri, A. (2000) *Empire* (Cambridge, MA: Harvard University Press).

Hardt, M. and Negri, A. (2005) *Multitude: War and Democracy in the Age of Empire* (London: Penguin).

Harford, T. (2012) *Adapt: Why Success Always Starts with Failure* (London: Abacus).

Hayek, F. A. (1945) 'The Use of Knowledge in Society', *American Economic Review*, 35(4): 519–30.

Hayek, F. A. (1952) *The Sensory Order: An Enquiry into the Foundations of Theoretical Psychology* (Chicago: University of Chicago Press).

Hayek, F. A. (1960) *The Constitution of Liberty* (London: Routledge).

Hayek, F. A. (1978a) 'Lecture on a Master Mind: Dr. Bernard Mandeville', in F. A. Hayek, *New Studies in Philosophy, Politics, Economics and the History of Ideas* (London: Routledge & Kegan Paul), 125–41.

Hayek, F. A. (1978b) *The Three Sources of Values* (London: London School of Economics and Political Science).

Hayek, F. A. (1982) *Law, Legislation and Liberty: A New Statement of the Liberal Principles of Justice and Political Economy* (London: Routledge).

Hayek, F. A. (1991) *The Fatal Conceit: The Errors of Socialism* (Chicago: University of Chicago Press).

Heartfield, J. (2002) *The 'Death of the Subject' Explained* (Sheffield: Sheffield Hallam University Press).

Heidegger, M. (1978) *Being and Time* (London: Wiley-Blackwell).

Held, D. (1995) *Democracy and the Global Order* (Cambridge: Polity).

Hodgson, G. M. (2006) 'Instinct and Habit before Reason: Comparing the Views of John Dewey, Friedrich Hayek and Thorstein Veblen', *Advances in Austrian Economics*, 9: 109–43.

Hollander, J. A. and Einwohner, R. L. (2004) 'Conceptualizing Resistance', *Sociological Forum*, 19(4): 533–54.

Holling, C. S. (1973) 'Resilience and Stability of Ecological Systems', *Annual Review of Ecology and Systematics*, 4: 1–23.

Holloway, J. (2002) *Change the World Without Taking Power: The Meaning of Revolution Today* (London: Pluto).

Holsti, K. (1996) *The State, War, and the State of War* (Cambridge: Cambridge University Press).

Hussain, M. (2013) 'Resilience: Meaningless Jargon or Development Solution?', *Guardian*, 5 March. Available at: http://www.theguardian.com/global-development-professionals-network/2013/mar/05/resilience-development-buzzwords.

Husserl, E. (1970) *The Crisis of European Sciences and Transcendental Phenomenology* (Evanston, IL: Northwestern University Press).

Ilyenkov, E.V. (1982) *Leninist Dialectics and the Metaphysics of Positivism: Reflections on V. I. Lenin's Book, 'Materialism and Empirio-Criticism'* (London: New Park Publications).

IMF (2005) International Monetary Fund, *World Economic Outlook, September 2005: Building Institutions* (Washington, DC: IMF).

IPCC (2012) Intergovernmental Panel on Climate Change, *Managing the Risks of Extreme Events and Disasters to Advance Climate Change Adaptation: Summary for Policymakers* (Cambridge: Cambridge University Press).

Israel, J. I. (2008) *Enlightenment Contested: Philosophy, Modernity, and the Emancipation of Man 1670–1752* (Oxford: Oxford University Press).

Jabri, V. (2007) *War and the Transformation of Global Politics* (Basingstoke: Palgrave Macmillan).

Jackson, R. H. (1990) *Quasi-States: Sovereignty, International Relations and the Third World* (Cambridge: Cambridge University Press).

James, W. (1957) *The Principles of Psychology* (New York: Dover Publications).

Jameson, F. (2003) 'Future City', *New Left Review*, 21: 65–79.

Jervis, R. (1998) *System Effects: Complexity in Political and Social Life* (Princeton, NJ: Princeton University Press).

John, P. et al. (2011) *Nudge, Nudge, Think, Think: Experimenting with Ways to Change Civic Behaviour* (London: Bloomsbury).

Johnson, S. (2001) *Emergence: The Connected Lives of Ants, Brains, Cities and Software* (London: Penguin).

Joseph, J. (2012) *The Social in the Global: Social Theory, Governmentality and Global Politics* (Cambridge: Cambridge University Press).

Joseph, J. (2013) 'Resilience as Embedded Neoliberalism: A Governmentality Approach', *Resilience: International Policies, Practices and Discourses*, 1(1): 38–52.

Kaldor, M. (1999) *New and Old Wars: Organized Violence in a Global Era* (Cambridge: Polity).

Kaldor, M. and Selchow, S. (2012) *The 'Bubbling Up' of Subterranean Politics in Europe* (London: Civil Society and Human Security Research Unit, London School of Economics and Political Science), June. Available at: http://rio20.net/wp-content/uploads/2012/07/subterraneanpolitics_report_21-06-12.pdf.

Kant, I. (1991) 'An Answer to the Question: "What Is Enlightenment"', in *Kant: Political Writings* (Cambridge: Cambridge University Press), 54–60.

Kauffman, S. (1993) *The Origins of Order: Self-Organization and Selection in Evolution* (Oxford: Open University Press).

Kauffman, S. (2008) *Reinventing the Sacred: A New View of Science, Reason, and Religion* (New York: Basic Books).

Keane, J. (2009) *The Life and Death of Democracy* (London: Simon and Schuster).

Keane, J. (2011) 'Monitory Democracy', in S. Alonso, J. Keane and W. Merkel (eds) *The Future of Representative Democracy* (Cambridge: Cambridge University Press), 212–35.

Keck, M. E. and Sikkink, K. (1998) *Activists Beyond Borders: Advocacy Networks in International Politics* (Ithaca, NY: Cornell University Press).

Khalil, E. L. (1996) 'Social Theory and Naturalism', in E. L. Khalil and K. E. Boulding (eds) *Evolution, Order and Complexity* (London: Routledge), 1–39.

Knott, P. (2012) 'Anders Breivik: Lessons Learned from the Norway Massacre', *Sabotage Times*, 19 April. Available at: http://www.sabotagetimes.com/life/anders-breivik-lessons-learned-from-the-norway-massacre/.

Koopman, C. (2009) 'Morals and Markets: Liberal Democracy Through Dewey and Hayek', *Journal of Speculative Philosophy*, 23(3): 151–79.

Körppen, D. and Ropers, N. (2011) 'Introduction: Addressing the Complex Dynamics of Conflict Transformation', in D. Körppen, N. Ropers and H. J. Giessmann (eds) *The Non-Linearity of Peace Processes – Theory and Practice of Systemic Conflict Transformation* (Opladen: Barbara Budrich Verlag, 2011), 11–20.

Kymlicka, W. (1995) *Multicultural Citizenship* (New York: Oxford University Press).

Laclau, E. (1996) 'Deconstruction, Pragmatism and Hegemony', in C. Mouffe (ed.) *Deconstruction and Pragmatism* (Abingdon: Routledge), 47–67.

Laclau, E. and Mouffe, C. (2001) *Hegemony and Socialist Strategy: Towards a Radical Democratic Politics* (London: Verso).

Lash, S. (2002) 'Forward: Individualization in a Non-Linear Mode', in U. Beck and E. Beck-Gernsheim, *Individualization: Institutionalized Individualism and Its Social and Political Consequences* (London: Sage), vii–xiii.

Latour, B. (1993) *We Have Never Been Modern* (Cambridge, MA: Harvard University Press).

Latour, B. (2003) 'Is Re-modernization Occurring – And If So, How to Prove It? A Commentary on Ulrich Beck', *Theory, Culture and Society*, 20(2): 35–48.

Latour, B. (2004a) *Politics of Nature: How to Bring the Sciences into Democracy* (Cambridge, MA: Harvard University Press).

Latour, B. (2004b) 'Why Has Critique Run out of Steam?' *Critical Inquiry*, 30: 225–48.

Latour, B. (2007) *Reassembling the Social: An Introduction to Actor-Network-Theory* (Oxford: Oxford University Press).

Law, J. (2004) *After Method: Mess in Social Science Research* (Abingdon: Routledge).

Lederach, J. P. (1997) *Building Peace: Sustainable Reconciliation in Divided Societies* (Washington, DC: United States Institute of Peace).

Lee, A. (2011) 'CEO's Foreword', in Sustainable Development Commission, *Governing for the Future – The Opportunities for Mainstreaming Sustainable Development* (London: Sustainable Development Commission), 5.

Lefebvre, H. (1987) 'The Everyday and Everydayness', *Yale French Studies*, 73: 7–11.

Leipold, B. and Greve, W. (2009) 'Resilience: A Conceptual Bridge between Coping and Development', *European Psychologist*, 14(1): 40–50.

Lemay-Hébert, N. (2009) 'Statebuilding without Nation-building? Legitimacy, State Failure and the Limits of the Institutionalist Approach', *Journal of Intervention and Statebuilding*, 3(1): 21–45.

Lenin, V. I. (1956) *Materialism and Empirio-Criticism: Critical Comments on a Reactionary Philosophy* (London: Lawrence and Wishart).

Levine, S., Pain, A., Bailey, S. and Fan, L. (2012) 'The Relevance of "Resilience"?' *Humanitarian Policy Group Policy Brief*, 49 (London: Overseas Development Institute).

Lifton, R. J. (1999) *The Protean Self: Human Resilience in an Age of Fragmentation* (Chicago: University of Chicago Press).

Linklater, A. (1998) *The Transformation of Political Community* (Cambridge: Polity).

Lippmann, W. (1993) *The Phantom Public* (New Brunswick, NJ: Transaction Publishers).

Little, A. (2012) 'Political Action, Error and Failure: The Epistemological Limits of Complexity', *Political Studies*, 60(1): 3–19.

Luhmann, N. (1995) *Social Systems* (Stanford, CA: Stanford University Press).

Lundborg, T. and Vaughan-Williams, N. (2011) 'Resilience, Critical Infrastructure, and Molecular Security: The Excess of "Life" in Biopolitics', *International Political Sociology*, 5(4): 367–83.

Lyotard, J-F. (1984) *The Postmodern Condition: A Report on Knowledge* (Manchester: Manchester University Press).

Mac Ginty, R. (2008) 'Indigenous Peace-Making versus the Liberal Peace', *Cooperation and Conflict*, 43(2): 139–63.

Mac Ginty, R. (2011) *International Peacebuilding and Local Resistance: Hybrid Forms of Peace* (Basingstoke: Palgrave Macmillan).

Mahoney, J. and Thelen, K. (eds) (2010) *Explaining Institutional Change: Ambiguity, Agency, and Power* (Cambridge: Cambridge University Press).

Mamdani, M. (2009) *Saviours and Survivors: Darfur, Politics and the War on Terror* (London: Verso).

Marchart, O. (2007) *Post-Foundational Political Thought: Political Difference in Nancy, Lefort, Badiou and Laclau* (Edinburgh: Edinburgh University Press).

Marres, N. (2012) *Material Participation: Technology, the Environment and Everyday Politics* (Basingstoke: Palgrave Macmillan).

Marx, K. (1954) *Capital: A Critique of Political Economy, Volume 1* (London: Lawrence and Wishart).

Marx, K. (1974) *Grundrisse: Foundations of the Critique of Political Economy* (Harmondsworth: Penguin).

Marx, K. (1975) 'Critique of Hegel's Philosophy of Right: Introduction', in L. Colletti (ed.) *Marx: Early Writings* (Harmondsworth: Penguin Books), 243–57.

Marx, K and Engels, F. (1970) *The German Ideology* (London: Lawrence and Wishart).

Massumi, B. (2002) *Parables for the Virtual: Movement, Affect, Sensation* (London: Duke University Press).

Menon, K. U. (2005) 'National Resilience: From Bouncing Back to Prevention', *Ethos*, Jan-Mar. Available at: http://www.cscollege.gov.sg/Knowledge/Ethos/Issue%201%20Jan%202005/Pages/06National.pdf.

Miller, P. and Rose, N. (2008) *Governing the Present: Administering Economic, Social and Personal Life* (Cambridge: Polity).

Miraglia, P., Ochoa, R. and Briscoe, I. (2012) 'Transnational Organised Crime and Fragile States', *OECD Development Cooperation Working Paper*, 3.

Mirowski, P. (2002) *Machine Dreams: Economics Becomes a Cyborg Science* (Cambridge: Cambridge University Press).

Mirowski, P. and Nik-Khah, E. (2007) 'Markets Made Flesh: Performativity, and a Problem in Science Studies, Augmented with Consideration of the FCC Auctions', in D. MacKenzie, F. Muniesa and L. Siu (eds) *Do Economists Make Markets? On the Performativity of Economics* (Princeton, NJ: Princeton University Press), 190–224.

Mitchell, A. (2011) 'Quality/Control: International Peace Interventions and 'The Everyday', *Review of International Studies*, 37(4): 1623–45.

Mitchell, M. (2009) *Complexity: A Guided Tour* (Oxford: Oxford University Press).

Moe, L. W. and Simojoki, M. V. (2013) 'Custom, Contestation and Cooperation: Peace and Justice in Somaliland', *Conflict, Security and Development*, 13(4): 393–416.

Mol, A. (2008) *The Logic of Care: Health and the Problem of Patient Choice* (London: Routledge).

Moore, S. (2012) 'Breivik's Ideology Is All Too Familiar: That's Our Big Problem', *Guardian*, 18 April.

Morton, A. D. (2011) 'Failed-State Status and the War on Drugs in Mexico', *Global Dialogue*, 13(1).

Mouffe, C. (2005) *On the Political* (London: Verso).

Mulligan, R. (2006) 'John Dewey's Ways of Knowing and the Radical Subjectivism of the Austrian School', *Education and Culture*, 22(2): 61–82.

Naím, M. (2013) *The End of Power* (New York: Basic Books).

Nanyang Technological University (2009) *Climate Insecurities, Human Security and Social Resilience* (Singapore: Nanyang Technological University).

Negri, M. (1999) *The Savage Anomaly: The Power of Spinoza's Metaphysics and Politics* (Minneapolis: University of Minnesota Press).

Negri, M. (2004) *Subversive Spinoza: (Un)contemporary Variations* (Manchester: Manchester University Press).

Neocleous, M. (2013) 'Resisting Resilience', *Radical Philosophy*, 178: 2–7.

Newman, E., Paris, R. and Richmond, O. P. (eds) (2009) *New Perspectives on Liberal Peacebuilding* (New York: United Nations University).

Nietzsche, F. W. (2003) *Genealogy of Morals* (New York: Dover Publications).

Nietzsche, F. W. (2007) 'The Antichrist', in F. W. Nietzsche, *The Twilight of the Idols* (Ware, Hertfordshire: Wordsworth Classics of World Literature), 91–163.

Norris, F. H., Stevens, S. P., Pfefferbaum, B., Wyche, K. F. and Pfefferbaum, R. L. (2008) 'Community Resilience as a Metaphor, Theory, Set of Capacities, and Strategy for Disaster Readiness', *American Journal of Community Psychology*, 41 (1–2): 127–50.

North, D. C. (1990) *Institutions, Institutional Change and Economic Performance* (Cambridge: Cambridge University Press).

North, D. C. (1999) 'Dealing with a Non-Ergodic World: Institutional Economics, Property Rights, and the Global Environment', *Duke Environmental Law and Policy Forum*, 10(1): 1–12.

North, D. C. (2005) *Understanding the Process of Economic Change* (Princeton, NJ: Princeton University Press).

North, D. C., Wallis, J. J. and Weingast, B. R. (2009) *Violence and Social Orders: A Conceptual Framework for Interpreting Recorded Human History* (Cambridge: Cambridge University Press).

NSIC (2011) National Strategy Information Centre, *Fostering a Culture of Lawfulness: Multi-Sector Success in Pereira, Columbia 2008–2010* (April). Available at: http://pdf.usaid.gov/pdf_docs/PDACT131.pdf.

OAS (2013a) Organization of African States, *The Drug Problem in the Americas* (Washington, DC: OAS).

OAS (2013b) Organization of African States, *Scenarios for the Drug Problem in the Americas 2013–2025* (Washington, DC: OAS).

OECD (2011) Organisation for Economic Co-operation and Development, *Busan Partnership for Effective Development Cooperation, Fourth High Level Forum on Aid Effectiveness, Busan, Republic of Korea*. Available at: http://www.oecd.org/dac/effectiveness/49650173.pdf.

OECD (2013) Organisation for Economic Co-operation and Development, 'What Does "Resilience" Mean for Donors?: An OECD Factsheet'. Available at: http://www.oecd.org/dac/governance-development/May%2010%202013%20FINAL%20resilience%20PDF.pdf.

O'Malley, P. (2004) *Risk, Uncertainty and Government* (London: Routledge).

O'Malley, P. (2010) 'Resilient Subjects: Uncertainty, Warfare and Liberalism', *Economy and Society*, 29(4): 488–509.

Orange, R. (2012) '"Answer Hatred with Love": How Norway Tried to Cope with the Horror of Anders Breivik', *Guardian*, 15 April. Available at: http://www.theguardian.com/world/2012/apr/15/anders-breivik-norway-copes-horror.

Orford, A. (2003) *Reading Humanitarian Intervention: Human Rights and the Use of Force in International Law* (Cambridge: Cambridge University Press).

Ostrom, E. (1990) *Governing the Commons: The Evolution of Institutions for Collective Action* (Cambridge: Cambridge University Press).

Owens, P. (2012) 'Human Security and the Rise of the Social', *Review of International Studies*, 38(3): 547–67.

Paffenholz, T. (2009) *Civil Society and Peacebuilding: A Critical Assessment* (Boulder, CO: Lynne Rienner).

Paffenholz, T. (2012) 'Conflict Transformation Theory: A Reality Check', Paper presented at the International Studies Association Annual Convention, San Diego, California, 1–4 April.

Paris, R. (2004) *At War's End: Building Peace after Civil Conflict* (Cambridge: Cambridge University Press).

Paris, R. and Sisk, T. D. (eds) (2009) *The Dilemmas of Statebuilding: Confronting the Contradictions of Postwar Peace Operations* (London: Routledge).

Paton, D. and Johnston, D. (2001) 'Disasters and Communities: Vulnerability, Resilience and Preparedness', *Disaster Prevention and Management*, 10(4): 270–77.

Pierce, A. (2012) 'What Is Red Ed's New Guru Talking About?' *Daily Mail*, 2 December. Available at: http://www.dailymail.co.uk/debate/article-2241939/What-Ed-Milibands-new-guru-Professor-Marc-Stears-talking-about.html.

Plato (2007) *The Republic* (London: Penguin).

Plehwe, D. (2009) 'The Origins of the Neoliberal Economic Development Discourse', in P. Mirowski and D. Plehwe (eds) *The Road from Mont Pelerin: The Making of the Neoliberal Thought Collective* (Cambridge, MA: Harvard University Press), 238–79.

Pogge, T. (2002) *World Poverty and Human Rights: Cosmopolitan Responsibilities and Reforms* (Cambridge: Polity).

Pogge, T. (2007) 'Achieving Democracy', *Ethics and International Affairs*, 21(1): 249–73.

Pogge, T. (2008) *World Poverty and Human Rights*, 2nd ed. (Cambridge: Polity).

Pogge, T. (2010) 'Responses to the Critics', in A. M. Jaggar (ed.) *Thomas Pogge and His Critics* (Cambridge: Polity), 175–250.

Pogge, T. (2011a) 'Are We Violating the Human Rights of the World's Poor', *Yale Human Rights and Development Law Journal*, 14(2): 1–33.

Pogge, T. (2011b) 'We Must Be Opportunistic in the Pursuit of Justice', *The European*, 14 December. Available at: http://theeuropean-magazine.com/315-pogge-thomas/374-global-justice.

Popolo, D. (2011) *A New Science of International Relations: Modernity, Complexity and the Kosovo Conflict* (Farnham: Ashgate).

Prigogine, I. (2003) *Is Future Given?* (New York: Bantam).

Prigogine, I. and Stengers, I. (1984) *Order Out of Chaos: Man's New Dialogue with Nature* (New York: Bantam).

Prigogine, I. and Stengers, I. (1997) *The End of Certainty: Time, Chaos and the New Laws of Nature* (New York: Free Press).

Pupavac, V. (2005) 'Human Security and the Rise of Global Therapeutic Governance', *Conflict, Security and Development*, 5(2): 161–81.

Ralston, S. J. (2012) 'Dewey and Hayek on Democratic Experimentalism', 5 April, working paper, Social Science Research Network.

Rancière, J. (1999) *Disagreement: Politics and Philosophy* (Minneapolis: University of Minnesota Press).

Rancière, J. (2011) *Althusser's Lesson* (London: Continuum).

Rawls, J. (1955) 'Two Concepts of Rules', *Philosophical Review*, 64(1): 3–32.

Reghezza-Zitt, M., Rufat, S., Djament-Tran, G., Le Blanc, A. and Lhomme, S. (2012) 'What Resilience Is Not: Uses and Abuses', *Cybergeo: European Journal of Geography*, 621. Available at: http://cybergeo.revues.org/25554.

Reginster, B. (2008) *The Affirmation of Life: Nietzsche on Overcoming Nihilism* (Harvard: Harvard University Press).

Resnick, M. (1999) *Turtles, Termites, and Traffic Jams: Explorations in Massively Parallel Microworlds* (Cambridge, MA: MIT Press).

Richards, D. (ed.) (2000) *Political Complexity: Non-linear Models of Politics* (Ann Arbor, MI: University of Michigan Press).

Richardson, G. E. (2002) 'The Metatheory of Resilience and Resiliency', *Journal of Clinical Psychology*, 58(3): 307–21.

Richardson, J. (2012) *Heidegger* (London: Routledge).

Richmond, O. P. (2009) 'A Post-Liberal Peace: Eirenism and the Everyday', *Review of International Studies*, 35(3): 557–80.

Richmond, O. P. (2010) 'Resistance and the Post-liberal Peace', *Millennium: Journal of International Studies*, 38(3): 665–92.

Richmond, O. P. (2011a) *A Post-Liberal Peace* (London: Routledge).

Richmond, O. P. (2011b) 'Critical Agency, Resistance and a Post-Colonial Civil Society', *Cooperation and Conflict*, 46(4): 419–40.

Richmond, O. P. and Kappler, S. (2011) 'Peacebuilding and Culture in Bosnia and Herzegovina: Resistance or Emancipation?', *Security Dialogue*, 42(3): 261–78.

Richmond, O. P. and Mitchell, A. (eds) (2012) *Hybrid Forms of Peace: From Everyday Agency to Post-Liberalism* (Basingstoke: Palgrave Macmillan).

Ricoeur, P. (1970) *Freud and Philosophy: An Essay on Interpretation* (New Haven, CT: Yale University Press).

Risse, T., Ropp, S. C. and Sikkink, K. (eds) (1999) *The Power of Human Rights: International Norms and Domestic Change* (Cambridge: Cambridge University Press).

Roberts, D. (2008) 'Hybrid Polities and Indigenous Pluralities: Advanced Lessons in Statebuilding from Cambodia', *Journal of Intervention and Statebuilding*, 2(1): 63–86.

Room, G. (2011) *Complexity, Institutions and Public Policy: Agile Decision-Making in a Turbulent World* (Cheltenham: Edward Elgar).

Rose, M. (2013) 'Negative Governance: Vulnerability, Biopolitics and the Origins of Government', *Transactions of the Institute of British Geographers* (forthcoming, Early View first published online: 26 July 2013).

Rose, N. (1989) *Governing the Soul: Shaping of the Private Self* (London: Free Association).

Rose, N. (1999) *Powers of Freedom: Reframing Political Thought* (Cambridge: Cambridge University Press).

Rosenau, J. N. and Czempiel, E.-O. (1992) (eds) *Governance without Government: Order and Change in World Politics* (Cambridge: Cambridge University Press).

Rousseau, J. J. (1998) *The Social Contract* (Ware: Wordsworth).

Sabaratnam, M. (2013) 'Avatars of Eurocentrism in the Critique of the Liberal Peace', *Security Dialogue*, 44(3): 259–78.

Salter, M. (2013) 'Introduction', in M. Salter and C. E. Mutlu (eds) *Research Methods in Critical Security Studies: An Introduction* (Abingdon: Routledge).

Samons, L. J. (2004) *What's Wrong with Democracy? From Athenian Practice to American Worship* (Los Angeles: University of California Press).

Schmidt, J. (2013) 'The Empirical Falsity of the Human Subject: New Materialism, Climate Change and the Shared Critique of Artifice', *Resilience: International Policies, Practices and Discourses*, 1(3): 174–92.

Schmitt, C. (1996) *The Concept of the Political* (Chicago: University of Chicago Press).

Scott, D. (2003) 'Culture in Political Theory', *Political Theory*, 31(1): 92–115.

Scott, J. C. (1990) *Domination and the Arts of Resistance: Hidden Transcripts* (New Haven, CT: Yale University Press).

Scott, J. C. (1998) *Seeing Like a State: How Certain Schemes to Improve the Human Condition Have Failed* (New Haven, CT: Yale University Press).

Scott, R. W. (2008) *Institutions and Organizations: Ideas and Interests* (London: Sage).

Searle, J. R. (1969) *Speech Acts* (Cambridge: Cambridge University Press).

Segal, P. (2008) 'Review of Paul Collier's The Bottom Billion', *Renewal*, 16(2). Available at: http://paulsegal.org/documents/Segal_Review_of_Collier.pdf.

Semenova, E. (2012) 'Representative Elites in Central and Eastern Europe: Recruitment and Development, 1990 to 2010', Paper presented at the international conference 'Domestic Elites and Public Opinion – The Neglected Dimension of Externally Induced Democratization', University of Konstanz, 5–7 September.

Sending, O. J. (2009) 'Why Peacebuilders Fail to Secure Ownership and Be Sensitive to Context', *NUPI Working Paper* 755 (Oslo: Norwegian Institute of International Affairs).

Sewell, W. H. Jr. (1999) 'The Concept(s) of Culture', in Victoria Bonnell and Lynn Hunt (eds) *Beyond the Cultural Turn: New Directions in the Study of Society and Culture* (Berkeley: University of California Press), 35–61.

Shannon, C. (1995) 'A World Made Safe for Differences: Ruth Benedict's "Chrysanthemum and the Sword"', *American Quarterly*, 47(4): 659–80.

Smith, B. W., Dalen, J., Wiggins, K., Tooley, E., Christopher, P. and Bernard, J. (2008) 'The Brief Resilience Scale: Assessing the Ability to Bounce Back', *International Journal of Behavioral Medicine*, 15(3): 194–200.

Sogge, D. (2009) *Repairing the Weakest Links: A New Agenda for Fragile States* (Madrid: FRIDE).

Solana, J. (2009) 'Five Lessons in Global Diplomacy', *Financial Times*, 21 January, 13.

Srnicek, N. (2012) *Assemblage Theory, Complexity and Contentious Politics: The Political Ontology of Gilles Deleuze*. Available at: http://www.academia.edu/178031/Assemblage_Theory_Complexity_and_Contentious_Politics_The_Political_Ontology_of_Gilles_Deleuze.

Stears, M. (2011) *Everyday Democracy: Taking Centre-Left Politics Beyond State and Market* (London: IPPR).

Stears, M. (2012) 'The Case for a State that Supports Relationships, Not a Relational State', in G. Cooke and R. Muir (eds) *The Relational State: How Recognising the Importance of Human Relationships Could Revolutionise the Role of the State* (London: IPPR), 35–44.

Steinmo, S., Thelen, K. and Longstreth, F. (1992) *Structuring Politics: Historical Institutionalism in Comparative Analysis* (Cambridge: Cambridge University Press).

Stengers, I. (2010) *Cosmopolitics I* (Minneapolis: University of Minnesota Press).

Stengers, I. (2011) *Cosmopolitics II* (Minneapolis: University of Minnesota Press).

Swindler, A. (1986) 'Culture in Action: Symbols and Strategies', *American Sociological Review*, 51(2): 273–86.

Tadjbakhsh, S. (ed.) (2011) *Rethinking the Liberal Peace: External Models and Local Alternatives* (London: Routledge).

Tamanaha, B. Z. (2004) *On the Rule of Law: History, Politics, Theory* (Cambridge: Cambridge University Press).

Tambakaki, P. (2009) 'When Does Politics Happen?' *Parallax*, 15(3): 102–13.

Thaler, R. and Sunstein, C. (2008) *Nudge: Improving Decisions about Health, Wealth and Happiness* (London: Penguin).

Thrift, N. (2008) *Non-Representational Theory: Space, Politics, Affect* (Abingdon: Routledge).

Toffler, A. (1984) 'Foreword: Science and Change', in I. Prigogine and I. Stengers, *Order Out of Chaos: Man's New Dialogue with Nature* (New York: Bantam), xi–xxvi.

Tokatliaán, J. G. (2011) *Organised Crime, Illicit Drugs and State Vulnerability* (Oslo: Norwegian Peacebuilding Centre).

Toulmin, S. (1990) *Cosmopolis* (Chicago: University of Chicago Press).

Traufetter, G. (2012a) 'Court Orders New Psychiatric Review for Breivik', *Speigel*, 13 January.

Traufetter, G. (2012b) 'New Report Finds Breivik Sane Ahead of Trial', *Speigel*, 10 April.

Tully, J. (1995) *Strange Multiplicity: Constitutionalism in an Age of Diversity* (Cambridge, UK: Cambridge University Press).

UN (2004) United Nations, *Living with Risk: A Global Review of Disaster Reduction Initiatives*, Vol. 1 (New York: United Nations).

Virno, P. (2004) *A Grammar of the Multitude: For an Analysis of Contemporary Forms of Life* (New York: Semiotext(e)).

Vulliamy, E. and Ray, S. (2013) 'David Simon, Creator of *The Wire*, Says New US Drug Laws Help Only "White, Middle-Class Kids"', *The Observer*, 25 May. Available at: http://www.guardian.co.uk/world/2013/may/25/the-wire-creator-us-drug-laws.

Wagner, K. (2012) 'Resilience: A New Buzzword or a New Understanding?', The Club of Rome. Available at: http://www.clubofrome.org/?p=5499.

Wales College (2006) 'Resilience: Research in Practice' (Wales College. Research in Practice Development Group).

Walker, B., Holling, C. S., Carpenter, S. R. and Kinzig, A. (2004) 'Resilience, Adaptability and Transformability in Social–ecological Systems', *Ecology and Society*, 9(2), 5.

Walker, B. and Salt, D. (2006) *Resilience Thinking: Sustaining Ecosystems and People in a Changing World* (Washington, DC: Island Press).

Walker, J. and Cooper, M. (2011) 'Genealogies of Resilience: From Systems Ecology to the Political Economy of Crisis Adaptation', *Security Dialogue*, 42(2): 143–60.

Walker, P. (2013) 'School of Hard Knocks: MPs Seek to Boost Young People's "Resilience"', *Guardian*, 6 February. Available at: http://www.theguardian.com/education/2013/feb/06/school-young-people-resilience-failure.

Walzer, M. (1983) *Spheres of Justice* (New York: Basic Books).

Warner, J. and Grünewald, F. (2012) 'Resilience: Buzz Word or Useful Concept?', *Humanitarian Aid on the Move*, Groupe Urgence Réhabilitation Développement, 10: 14–19.

Weber, M. (1951) *The Religion of China: Confucianism and Taoism* (Glencoe, IL: Free Press).

Weber, M. (2004) 'Politics as a Vocation', in *The Vocation Lectures* (Indianapolis, IN: Hackett Publishing), 32–94.

Welsh, J. M. (ed.) (2004) *Humanitarian Intervention and International Relations* (Oxford: Oxford University Press).

Whitehead, A. N. (1978) *Process and Reality: An Essay in Cosmology* (New York: Free Press).

Wintour, P. (2012) 'Marc Stears: The University Friend Who Helped to Shape Ed Miliband's Speech', *Guardian*, 2 October. Available at: http://www.theguardian.com/politics/2012/oct/02/ed-miliband-speech-marc-stears.

Woodward, S. (2007) 'Do the Root Causes of Civil War Matter? On Using Knowledge to Improve Peacebuilding Interventions', *Journal of Intervention and Statebuilding*, 1(2): 143–70.

World Bank (2002) *World Development Report 2002: Building Institutions for Markets* (Washington, DC: Oxford University Press).

World Bank (2008) *The Political Economy of Policy Reform: Issues and Implications for Policy Dialogue and Development Operations*, Report No. 44288-GLB (Washington, DC: International Bank for Reconstruction and Development/World Bank).

Wright, S. (2002) *Storming Heaven: Class Composition and Struggle in Italian Autonomist Marxism* (London: Pluto Press).

Zautraa, A. J., Arewasikporna, A. and Davisa, M. C. (2010) 'Resilience: Promoting Well-Being Through Recovery, Sustainability, and Growth', *Research in Human Development*, 7(3): 221–38.

Zimmermann, A. (2007) 'The Rule of Law as a Culture of Legality: Legal and Extra-legal Elements for the Realisation of the Rule of Law in Society', 10–31. Available at: http://elaw.murdoch.edu.au/archives/issues/2007/1/eLaw_rule_law_culture_legality.pdf.

Zizek, S. (2011) 'Slavoj Zizek speaks at Occupy Wall Street: Transcript', *Impose Magazine*, posted 10 October. Available at: http://www.imposemagazine.com/bytes/slavoj-zizek-at-occupy-wall-street-transcript.

Zizek, S. (2012) 'Occupy Wall Street: What Is to Be Done Next?', *Guardian*, 24 April. Available at: http://www.guardian.co.uk/commentisfree/cifamerica/2012/apr/24/occupy-wall-street-what-is-to-be-done-next.

Zürcher, C. (2012) 'Costly Democracy: Peacebuilding and Democratic Transition', Paper presented at the international conference 'Domestic Elites and Public Opinion – The Neglected Dimension of Externally Induced Democratization', University of Konstanz, 5–7 September.

Zürcher, C., Manning, C., Evenson, K., Hayman, R., Riese, S. and Roehner, N. (2013) *Costly Democracy: Peacebuilding and Democratization after War* (Stanford, CA: Stanford University Press).

INDEX